Marxism and the Movies

Marxism and the Movies

Critical Essays on Class Struggle in the Cinema

Edited by MARY K. LEIGH *and* KEVIN K. DURAND

McFarland & Company, Inc., Publishers
Jefferson, North Carolina, and London

LIBRARY OF CONGRESS CATALOGUING-IN-PUBLICATION DATA

Marxism and the movies : critical essays on class struggle in the cinema / edited by Mary K. Leigh and Kevin K. Durand.
    p.   cm.
Includes bibliographical references and index.

    ISBN 978-0-7864-7123-2
    softcover : acid free paper ∞

    1. Motion pictures—History. 2. Marxist criticism. I. Leigh, Mary K., editor of compilation. II. Durand, Kevin K. J. (Kevin Karl Jones), 1967– editor of compilation.
PN1993.5.A1M37 2013
791.4309—dc23   2013030976

BRITISH LIBRARY CATALOGUING DATA ARE AVAILABLE

© 2013 Mary K. Leigh and Kevin K. Durand. All rights reserved

No part of this book may be reproduced or transmitted in any form or by any means, electronic or mechanical, including photocopying or recording, or by any information storage and retrieval system, without permission in writing from the publisher.

On the cover: scene from *Metropolis*, 1927 (UFA/Photofest); background © 2013 Shutterstock

Manufactured in the United States of America

McFarland & Company, Inc., Publishers
   Box 611, Jefferson, North Carolina 28640
   www.mcfarlandpub.com

Table of Contents

Preface (KEVIN K. DURAND)   1

Introduction: Marx, Critical Theory and the Cinema
   (KEVIN K. DURAND)   3

Part I: The Pre-War/Silent Era

Marx and *Metropolis*: The Farce of Religion in the Face
   of Dystopia (MARY K. LEIGH)   17

Metropolis: Proletarian Triumph or Opiate of the Masses?
   (ALAN WILLIAMS)   29

Love in the Time of Capitalism: A Marxist Feminist Reading
   of *Modern Times* (BROOKE BELOSO)   40

Part II: The Post–War Era

"She look like a wrong one to you?" BloodyMoneyBody —
Marxist Subversion in Hitchcock's *Psycho* and Frear's
The Grifters (GREGORY BORSE)   53

Replicants and the Commodity Form: A Marxian Reading
   of *Blade Runner* (J. ERIC LAMBERT)   77

"Somewhere That's Green": The Dream of the Middle Class
   in Frank Oz's *Little Shop of Horrors* (TRACI J. COHEN)   97

Apocalyptic Redux: (Re)Vision and Recognition
   in Terry Gilliam's *Twelve Monkeys* (JEREMY BURNS)   104

Table of Contents

Part III: The New Millennium

Tech-Noir and the Critical Dystopia in the 21st Century:
  Wimmer's *Equilibrium* (ALEXANDER CHARLES OLIVER HALL)   121

Who's Coming for Dinner? An Examination of *A History
  of Violence* (LESLIE SEAWRIGHT)   133

A Marxist Look at *Avatar* (TIM DELANEY AND ELLEN REED)   145

A Myth (Not So) Betrayed: Ridley Scott's *Robin Hood*
  and the Political Evolution of the Greenwood (JACOB LEWIS)   164

About the Contributors   185

Index   187

Preface
Kevin K. Durand

This volume considers a wide cross-section of cinematic history and provides analysis of blockbusters, cult hits, comedies, suspenseful dramas, and history-making films within a framework of power, power relations, and class struggle. For this text, we employ a Critical Engagement approach to critical theory and popular culture that explores the statements and worldviews that the films themselves are making. Following an introduction, the collection is divided into three parts—I: The Pre-War/Silent Era, II: The Post–War Era, and III: The New Millennium. Readers and scholars can thus see a fairly comprehensive cross-section of cinematic history within the 11 essays.

The first two essays of Part I examine one of the most ground-breaking films in the era. *Metropolis* is often cited as a paradigmatic example of dystopian film and the influences of the film and its director, Fritz Lang, are widely credited by modern directors as seminal in their influence. Mary K. Leigh explores the futility of religious structures in the face of dystopia, pointing out that the subversion of religious language and symbols by an oppressive bourgeois system actually facilitates the perpetuation of that system. Her essay is a striking counterpoint to Alan Williams's essay in which he suggests that, as Marx would have held, religion is the opiate of the masses, although there is the hint of a proletarian triumph as well. Brooke Beloso rounds out Part I with an examination of *Modern Times*, illustrating that within critical theory, there is a strong affinity for feminist theorists, resulting in a Marxist feminist analysis of the Charlie Chaplin classic.

Part II sees a continuation of a dystopian theme, although the variety of film is striking—from *Psycho* and *Blade Runner* to *Little Shop of Horrors*. Gregory Borse opens the section by exploring the subtlety with which Hitchcock and Frear weave themes of capital and suspense/horror in movies that redefined the genre. J. Eric Lambert's examination of *Blade Runner* explores the notion of what it means to be truly human, particularly from the perspective of the replicants who are considered nothing more than commodities.

Traci J. Cohen's essay on the cult hit *Little Shop of Horrors* examines the notion of a "middle class," suggesting that the movie portrays it as little more than a dream of those on Skid Row, and, by extension, of all of those not part of the bourgeoisie. Jeremy Burns ends Part II with a thorough development of the notion of alienation and estrangement in the ironic *Twelve Monkeys*.

As the millennium changed, the scope of the dystopian films whose worldviews were particularly susceptible to critical theory interpretation widened as well, and this is the focus of Part III. From the futuristic/fantasy *Avatar* to the look back into the Middle Ages with *Robin Hood*, the films become the vehicles for exposition of particular views that serve as criticisms of prevailing political and economic norms and powers. Alexander Charles Oliver Hall's treatment of the tech-noir/science fiction fusion *Equilibrium* explores an "alternative future" in which emotion is the identified cause of all violence, and thus has been nearly eradicated. In Leslie Seawright's essay, a thread of the earlier futility of the American Dream resurfaces as she argues that *A History of Violence* is a call to the audience to examine the patriarchy and capitalistic government that created the lie of the American Dream. Tim Delaney and Ellen Reed team up to propose an interpretation of the blockbuster *Avatar* that explores notions of overpopulation, debt, and the colonialistic oppression of an idyllic world. And, finally, Jacob Lewis closes Part III and the book with a thorough examination of the Robin Hood legend, illustrating Ridley Scott's use of the various medieval tales to argue that the politics of the Greenwood have shifted; arguing that ultimately, Scott's message of rebellion is attenuated by the "muddled politics and impractical solutions" that he proposes. In using a critical engagement approach to critical theory and popular culture, it is the hope of the editors that this collection will inspire further critical analysis of Marxism in film and thereby encourage a view of popular culture as academic as well as entertaining.

Introduction: Marx, Critical Theory and the Cinema
KEVIN K. DURAND

The history of all hitherto existing society is the history of class struggles.—*Karl Marx and Friedrich Engels*, The Communist Manifesto *(1848)*

DENNIS: What I object to is you automatically treat me like an inferior!
ARTHUR: Well, I AM king...
DENNIS: Oh king, eh, very nice. An' how'd you get that, eh? By exploitin' the workers—by 'angin' on to outdated imperialist dogma which perpetuates the economic an' social differences in our society! If there's ever going to be any progress—
WOMAN: Dennis, there's some lovely filth down here. Oh—how d'you do?
ARTHUR: How do you do, good lady. I am Arthur, King of the Britons. Who's castle is that?
WOMAN: King of the who?
ARTHUR: The Britons.
WOMAN: Who are the Britons?
ARTHUR: Well, we all are. We're all Britons and I am your king.
WOMAN: I didn't know we had a king. I thought we were an autonomous collective.
DENNIS: You're fooling yourself. We're living in a dictatorship. A self-perpetuating autocracy in which the working classes—
WOMAN: Oh there you go, bringing class into it again.
DENNIS: That's what it's all about if only people would—
Monty Python and the Holy Grail *(1975)*

It might come as a surprise to casual cinema-goers, particularly in the United States, that a great many of Karl Marx's perspectives on life, economics, power, and privilege are profitable lenses through which to critically interpret movies. Sometimes this is obvious—take, for example, the pair of epigraphs for this introduction; one from Marx and one from Python. Indeed, one could very nearly merge the two without losing anything from either:

MARX: The history of all hitherto existing society is the history of class struggles.
WOMAN: Oh there you go, bringing class into it again.
DENNIS: That's what it's all about if only people would —

And, indeed, at the heart of the Marxist critique of capital and economics is the notion of class struggle. As struggle — against self, against oppression, against imperialism, against a rowdy fraternity — is the most common theme of cinematic expression, it is not at all surprising that philosophers, literary scholars, movie critics, and others would notice a common and abiding thread of Marxist thought. Although Communism was the spectre haunting Europe, rampant and unchecked capitalism was the tyrant that had Europe in its iron fist. Marx's criticism of the capitalism emerging from the Industrial Revolution echoes Charles Dickens' themes in *Oliver Twist*, and in turn is echoed by Upton Sinclair's *The Jungle*, and by Tennessee Ernie Ford's "Sixteen Tons."

This introduction presents a discussion of the groundings of Marxist Critical Theory, along with examples drawn from cinema as illustrations of the close connection. The intention is to both present an overview of basic Marxist theory along with a discussion of its use in both developing motion pictures and critically analyzing them. This is a useful segue into the cinematic arts, as Ford's "Sixteen Tons" plays an integral role in setting the dramatic scene of the 20th century cult hit, *Joe Versus the Volcano*.

The early Tom Hanks and Meg Ryan vehicle was not particularly well-reviewed upon its debut, but in many ways presaged the two stars' later successful pairings in romantic comedies like *Sleepless in Seattle* and *You've Got Mail*. *Joe* is a far quirkier movie — with Joe Banks being a failed drudge in a dreary job diagnosed with a terminal "brain cloud" by a doctor in the employ of a sinister multimillionaire with designs on the mineral wealth of a tiny south Pacific island in need of a human sacrifice to appease their volcano god. Meg Ryan playing multiple roles (twins) is both instrument of Joe's recruitment to sacrifice his life for remuneration as the materialistic twin and love-interest as the golden-hearted twin.

Joe's plight at the outset of the movie is keenly felt as the gray scene is accented by "16 Tons." It's clear that Joe seems to owe his soul to the company store, and this company store is American Panascope Corp., or, quite literally, the American All-Seeing Corporation. With its lightning bolt logo, there is further connection to Zeus, god of lightning whose displeasure often resulted in a bolt from the blue smiting the poor soul who was the source of the displeasure. The trail of workers moving glumly toward the entrance of the factory are carrying gray and black umbrellas, dressed in gray or black outfits, entering a gray building on a gray rainy day. They have been completely assimilated to the company as their line takes the same shape as the lightning bolt logo. Among this group of depressed and beaten workers is Joe Banks, a beaten and depressed man who, upon stepping into a puddle and discovering that his shoe is coming apart, continues trudging along, squishing all the way.

The opening scene is deeply powerful precisely because it echoes a profound and common experience of the American labor force. From Ford's protagonist gaining only more debt and age in "16 Tons" to Johnny Paycheck's protagonist in the often misunderstood "Take This Job and Shove It" singing that he *wishes* he could tell his boss to shove it, to the contemporary dismantling of organized labor, this scene is either familiar or a psychical representation of the deep-seated ambivalence the worker sees in his or her labor experience. A simple cursory reading of this opening scene reveals the scope of the American capitalist scene — absentee bourgeoisie owner disconnected from the plight of the workers on whose labor his profit is obtained, a systematic dehumanization of the worker to enhance productivity and suppress any spirit that would object to the unfairness of the abject treatment, a training of the worker, shaping him into the image of the company, and a reduction of humanity to human resource — a resource like any other, to be manipulated and exploited at the whim of the bourgeoisie with no need to consider the human dignity of the worker because it has been snuffed out. Marx, writing in the 19th century, would have quickly recognized this image and its consistency with the workhouses and industrialized London of his own era. In a sense, this prefigures the famous quote of Warren Buffet — "If this is class warfare, then my class won." Indeed, there is little struggle left in these workers.

Marx's *Communist Manifesto* is a portrait of economic power destroying societal structures and replacing them with a state of conflict between two antithetical groups — the Bourgeoisie and the Proletariat. Although this is but the latest conflict between differing economic classes, it is but another — the most recent — in a long line of class warfare. Indeed, in Marx's view, the history of society is a history of class struggle and conflict.

In this interpretation of the sweep of history, Marx appropriates the Hegelian philosophy of history and reinterprets it through the lens of economic antagonisms. A contemporary Marxist critic might well see these antagonisms in the cinematic representation of Victorian London reflected in Stephen Sondheim's musical and Tim Burton's adaptation of that musical to the big screen, *Sweeney Todd*. Here, the plight of the Victorian proletariat is not so different from the worker drones of *Joe Versus the Volcano*, although it is stripped of the comedic rendering and hopeful denouement. *Todd* quite clearly presents the economic antagonisms identified by Marx.

Much like the absent (cinematically) bourgeoisie owner of the "Home of the Rectal Probe," American Panascope Corp., Judge Turpin in *Todd* cynically and effectively manipulates the lives of those whom he controls to meet his own wishes. Unlike the owner of American Panascope, however, Turpin is quite successful in disposing of Benjamin Barker, although ultimately not as successful as he had thought or hoped, to his own disappointment and demise. Powerful as these images and situations seem, for Marx the analogous situations in the real world are simply inevitable. They are merely the necessary consequents of the materialist sweep of history.

Marx takes investigations of the sweep and progression of history to be a science in the same way that physics is. In that picture, the universe is comprised of uncountably many extraordinarily tiny bits of matter. Pieces of matter mindlessly bang into each other at the atomic level and thus drive the life of the planet and all those things comprised of these tiny bits of matter. Thus, physics is a matter of understanding collisions of atoms and forces like gravity and momentum and friction. From these unthinking building blocks, the entirety of the universe is constructed. Because there is a regular and determinable order to these forces and collisions that can be understood with a sophisticated and careful theory of cause and effect, science progresses because those regularities can be approximated, tested, and evaluated. The understanding of the universe is that of a predictably regular and understandable place. It is this notion of materialism that Marx imports to his philosophy of history. Just as humans are caught in the causal nexus of physical laws and mechanistic physics, so, too, are humans caught in the causal nexus of the laws of history and its progression.

Just as atoms collide and drive the universe, Marx takes the progression of history to be driven by conflict. The way in which he conceptualizes the violent nature of history's development is one of the places in which he appropriates notions from Hegel. In this case, it is Hegel's dialectic marked by the conflict of ideas, thesis, antithesis and the conflict between them that gives rise to a synthesis which in turn becomes the new thesis and so on. Marx uses this notion of the thesis, antithesis, synthesis, coupling it with an economic interpretation of societal interactions to develop the dialectical quality of his philosophy of history.

For Marx, each epoch in human history is marked by a sort of thesis. Let us return briefly to the year 787. (Note that the year is not given in *Holy Grail*; it is only offered as part of the opening to the King Arthur skit in the Python's live concert show.) Arthur having proclaimed that he is king—"Well, I am King!"—does not receive a kingly reception.

> WOMAN: I didn't know we had a king. I thought we were an autonomous collective.
> DENNIS: You're fooling yourself. We're living in a dictatorship: a self-perpetuating autocracy in which the working classes...
> WOMAN: Oh, there you go bringing class into it again.

> ...
> ARTHUR: Who is your lord?
> WOMAN: We don't have a lord.
> DENNIS: I told you. We're an anarcho-syndicalist commune. We take it in turns to be a sort of executive officer for the week...
> ...
> ARTHUR: Be quiet! I order you to be quiet!
> WOMAN: Order, eh? Who does he think he is? Heh.
> ARTHUR: I am your king!
> WOMAN: Well, I didn't vote for you.
> ARTHUR: You don't vote for kings.
> WOMAN: Well, how'd you get to become king, then?
> ARTHUR: The Lady of the Lake, her arm clad in the purest shimmering samite, held aloft Excalibur from the bosom of the water signifying by Divine Providence that I, Arthur, was to carry Excalibur. That is why I'm your king.

Dennis, in a fine bit of Marxist pique, dismisses such a fantastical claim (one that was not so far different from some of the machinations that have historically gone into the defense of a Divine Right of authoritarian kings).

> DENNIS: Listen. Strange women lying in ponds distributing swords is no basis for a system of government. Supreme executive power derives from a mandate from the masses, not from some farcical aquatic ceremony.
> ARTHUR: Be quiet!
> DENNIS: Well, you can't expect to wield supreme executive power just 'cause some watery tart threw a sword at you!
> ARTHUR: Shut up!
> DENNIS: I mean, if I went 'round sayin' I was an emperor just because some moistened bint had lobbed a scimitar at me, they'd put me away!
> ARTHUR: Shut up! Will you shut up!
> DENNIS: Ah, now we see the violence inherent in the system.
> ARTHUR: Shut up!
> DENNIS: Oh! Come and see the violence inherent in the system! Help! Help! I'm being repressed!

Repressed, indeed. As Marx begins the *Manifesto* with the claim that all history heretofore has been one of class struggle, so the Pythons intimate as Dennis is repressed. Indeed, for Marx, every political, economic, and societal epoch up until the Revolution is one marked by violence — the violence of the overclass against the underclass(es), resulting ultimately in the violence of a revolution. In Marx's view, there can be no gentle changeover in the system — one system ultimately and totally overthrows the previous. Thus, in Medieval feudalism, there were the feudal lords who reigned as the dominant power, anarcho-syndicalist communes notwithstanding. Their power was not merely a matter of heredity or "royalty" but of economics, of wealth, of property.

However, each thesis gives rise necessarily to its antithesis. Thus, out of the serfs grew the burghers and from these developed the first strands of the bourgeoisie. For Marx, the seeds of the destruction of an epoch are planted by the dominant force within it; thus each economical dominant class sows its own destruction by giving rise to a class in opposition. Thus, the merchant becomes the opponent of the feudal lord. As the markets demand greater choice and more variety, and as kings and countries spend themselves in war against each other, those twin forces cause the merchant class to become more and more wealthy. As the industrial revolution begins to dawn, only the merchant class has the capital to take advantage of the advances, creating factories, consolidating labor into single shops. The guilds that had fostered the development of individual trades and widely diversified the labor force are overthrown and labor is consolidated into a single, efficient body. The rise of the machine made the *modern industry* possible. So, the feudal thesis and its antithesis give rise to a new synthesis, and as the march of history proceeds, the modern capitalist becomes the dominant thesis of the modern era.

That industrial revolution entrenches a class struggle exemplified in the award-winning *Sweeney Todd*. The conflict there is not the comedic fare of Python; it is the brutal, crushing violence of Victorian England. Sweeney sings to Mrs. Lovett of their being but two kinds of men in all the world — those who stay in their place, which is always a place beneath the halls of power — like Benjamin Barker (Todd's earlier existence), his wife, and Mrs. Lovett — and those whose boot is constantly in the face of those weaker. Judge Turpin clearly personifies this sort of unchecked, indeed, self-privileged evil of oppression. He can do as he pleases because none dare stand up to him. He, and his capitalist captains of industry friends, brutally rape Barker's wife, Lucy, after having him committed to a penal colony on trumped up charges. Turpin and his lackey, Beadle Bamford, are embodiments not only of the privileged capitalist class that has supplanted the feudal lords of the prior epoch, they are the embodiment of the excesses of entitlement and power centralized in the hands of the view. Todd and Lovett, on the other hand, clearly encapsulate the struggle, pain, and hopelessness that stifles and nearly smothers the proletariat. And, in a distinctly Marxist twist, Todd and Lovett begin a revolutionary uprising (ultimately thwarted) by literally and figuratively eating the rich.

The culmination of the history of class struggle, the revolution, is controversial, but consistent with the underlying philosophical foundation of Marxist analysis. The struggle between the thesis and antithesis could be imagined as a minor tension that is played out within a moment and gives birth to a synthesis that is a compromise between the two initial propositions. However, the sweep of history is not gentle or compromising. It is marked by warfare and overthrow. While one might theoretically imagine one epoch gliding gently into the next, the reality of observation is that cultural systems do not go gently into that good night. They grip power with an ever-tightening grip until it is wrested from them, most often with bloodshed and carnage. The oppressed, when they rise up in revolution, have almost never been merciful and accommodating to their previous overlords. This experience, replayed again and again in the course of history, is taken by Marx to be an inevitable feature of the struggle of class against class, and indicative of human nature that that which is oppressed, upon overthrow of its oppressor, becomes oppressive itself. In every era, then, the cry, "The revolution is coming!" is an accurate one; the spiral of human history is one of progress, perhaps, but also of one revolution following upon another. Let us return to *Sweeney Todd* for a rendition of what this brutal experience of the proletariat looks like.

Marx writes, "These labourers, who must sell themselves piecemeal, are a commodity." The proletariat has become nothing more than a part of the system that the bourgeoisie has created. While one might suppose that the only oppression that the proletarian suffers is through his employment, this view is incorrect and limited for, as Marx points out, "no sooner is the exploitation of the labourer by the manufacturer, so far, at an end, that he receives his wages in cash, than he is set upon by the other portions of the bourgeoisie, the landlord, the shopkeeper, the pawnbroker, etc." This leaves the proletarian as nothing but another pawn in the social construct as he is needed only as long as he is useful. When his usefulness is not longer sufficient or another can be more efficient or less problematic, he is cast out and abandoned by bourgeois society.

Tim Burton enhances the world of *Sweeney Todd* to emphasize the class distinction is his film adaptation of Steven Sondheim's classic horror musical. The film opens with Todd and Anthony, a young sailor who saved Todd from drowning, standing on board a ship as it comes into port in London. Todd has escaped from prison after Turpin sentenced him to life as part of a plot to gain and ravage Lucy; a plot that was successful, insofar as it afforded Turpin and his capitalist, bourgeoisie cronies access to Lucy, but not insofar as it was supposed to eliminate Barker forever. Barker, now Todd, returns to his former neighborhood where he encounters Mrs. Lovett. Lovett has the role of explaining the situation to both Todd and the audience. When Todd enters her pie shop, she explains the situation that is all to common in this society while referring to her pies—the price of meat being what it is, people have begun to think it a treat even to find dying animals. This is a stark contrast to the vision of Bamford and Turpin. Turpin's house is as magnificent as Lovett's shop (and tiny, dingy rooms attached to it) are squalid—it is large, almost palatial, and appointed in only the finest, from furniture to window treatments. Turpin's manse appears to encompass the entirety of a city block, and it stands two stories tall within which luxuries abound. The plight of the proletariat and the luxury of the bourgeoisie could hardly be better portrayed.

While Turpin ruins lives at a whim, Todd slowly begins to take revenge, moving inexorably closer to his goal of destroying Turpin. One by one, Turpin's friends (or simply those that move in the rarefied air of the bourgeoisie) are dispatched by the Demon Barber of Fleet Street. One by one, they find themselves turned into pies and served to the very proletariat they oppress. Ironically, so good are the pies that even the proletarians find themselves muscled out of the key places in the shop so that the bourgeoisie can dine there.

Let us look next at another application of Marxist analysis to the economic situation of the 19th century. The era of modern industry was unique in its particulars. Clearly, all eras are unique, but a bit of novelty was introduced by the class struggle that gave rise to the modern capitalist moment. In this moment, the class struggle itself was refined, and sharply so. While in preceding eras there were a variety of classes, within the industrial capitalist era, Marx sees the gradual development of but two—the bourgeoisie and the proletariat—squaring off against one another in a truly epic struggle. This breaking down of class and consolidation of ancient arguments into two camps makes the struggle all the more revolutionary in its scope. An analysis of the modern capitalist industry will serve to make the intensity of this conflict clear.

As modern factories began to dawn and the agrarian model of the prior feudal system faded as the dominant model, more and more people began to flock to cities in search of work. The rural system had been broken and could no longer support the increasing demands of the market. As the immigration to the cities became exponential in scope, the major cities, like London, were fundamentally incapable of providing services for all of the new arrivals. There simply was insufficient infrastructure to support the vast numbers of people. The resulting city life was one of grinding poverty, horrific pollution, crime, and disease. One need spend only a bit of time in the back alleys and orphanages of Charles Dickens or the opium dens of Sir Arthur Conan Doyle to get a glimpse of the overwhelming sense of hopelessness and despair that festered in the hearts of the new major population centers.

Fast-forward to the late 20th century. Joe arrives at his job at American Panascope, "Home of the Rectal Probe." Oddly enough, Joe is strangely similar to Beadle Bamford — not in the homicidal sycophant way, however. Joe works in the Advertising Department. As Beadle, a member of the proletariat by station and by wealth, works for Turpin, thus betraying his class and his people, Joe works to promote the very culture that is oppressing him and his peers. Closer to Bamford, though, is Joe's immediate supervisor, Mr. Waturi. He almost delights in forcing his colleagues to harder work. He is no member of the bourgeoisie, privy to its pleasures and luxuries. He works in the same cinderblock cesspool with Joe — in fact, only feet away from him. But he is dedicated to pushing his workers ever harder for the corporation. Ironically, Dede asks Joe about his shoe (that was the focus of the earlier scene). He replies, with only a slight sense of irony, but in a way that the audience is invited to imagine is of great importance, "I'm losing my sole."

Marx anticipates this. The development of the class consciousness is not universal among the repressed and oppressed proletariat. Many will, at least for a very long time, continue to work for the bourgeoisie masters simply because it is safer than rebelling. After all, a failed revolution presents the worker with an even starker set of choices than the world in which they live. Consider the rebels of *Les Misérables*. They are confident that the underclass will rally to their banner; all it will take is their own fuse to light the tinderbox of revolution. And, yet, no one comes to their aid. Only the help of Jean Valjean saves any of them. They are slaughtered like sheep, and while perhaps remembered in death, the *status quo ante* remains.

Joe, however, is given some aid in learning that his "brain cloud" gives him only a short while to live. Only then is he capable of telling Mr. Waturi to, in the words of Johnny Paycheck, "shove it." He quits. He quits the job with insufficient light, with a world so devoid of color that it almost imprints itself on the mind of the viewer as being in black and white. Only then can he defiantly plug in the lamp that Waturi had ordered him to remove in an earlier scene and pronounce that he quits. No one follows him. Like the rebels at the barricade, he revolts alone. The bourgeoisie manage the system in such a way that though confronted with sole devastating and soul destroying circumstances, the proletariat are given no hope that even a revolution will ease their plight.

Joe Versus the Volcano is a cult classic, and though both critically praised and panned, it has resonated in ways unnoticed by those who have not seen it. For example, the opening musical credits for the hit British television show *The Office* almost surreally borrow from the opening of *Joe*. The gray, soulless buildings; the seemingly endless and inescapable traffic circle in front of the building; the tone and tenor of the cinematography are all reminiscent of *Joe*. And they are all illustrative of the Marxist class struggle between those with capital, who can ruin the lives of those in Swindon or those in Slough, of those in middle America at deadening and dead-end factory jobs, of those in London who have been manipulated into prison while all they have is confiscated. From *Sweeney Todd* to *Joe Versus the Volcano* to *The Office*, the sharp contrast between the hopeless plight of the workaday proletarian and their bourgeoisie capitalist overlords is made.

In the midst of this contrast and sharp divisions, it is still the case that in the industrial revolution, the factories need workers. In the 19th century, since the cities could not provide the necessary infrastructure for the human resources necessary for business, business took this role on itself. Mill houses were constructed, generally all of the same floor plan, cheaply and reasonably efficient. Since the people who would be working in the factories were incapable of making a down payment, much less purchasing a house, even a cheap one, outright, industry rented to them. However, since they could not generally make the first month's rent, that money was fronted to them as an advance on their first paychecks. Thus, the family moved into a mill house on the company property. For "protection" from the crime-riddled streets, these mill house villages were often fenced in so that the entire community was an island in the metropolitan sea.

The newly hired (and newly indebted) worker not only had to furnish the house and provide food and the like, he was also required to provide his uniforms for work. To provide for these needs, industries generally created company stores which doubled as company banks. Since the worker was newly hired, he was unlikely to have money to make these purchases and so again would find himself receiving a loan against his wages. So, prior to his first day on the job, the new worker would actually owe his new employer quite a substantial sum of money, at least relative to the money he would receive for his work. Indeed, it is not unlikely that he would owe more money to the company than he would receive in his first pay period. To make the ends meet from one pay period to another, given that he starts in debt, he would often have to take out greater loans. Even in those cases where he could begin to make some headway, he could not shop for better deals outside the industry compound. This is because rather than paying wages in the coin of the realm, each industrial complex tended to print its own company "scrip" which could only be used within the company store. Thus, the worker becomes a sort of indentured servant to the company. He lives in the company house, owes payment for credited items to the company store, and receives his wages from the company. He is a human resource and simply part of the set of resources that the company uses in order to produce its products. It does not take great imagination to hear the soulful strains of Tennessee Ernie Ford's "Sixteen Tons" or the plaintive cry of Johnny Paycheck's "Take This Job and Shove It."

On the Marxist analysis of this vignette of the class struggle, people and raw materials are treated alike — both resources, one a human resource and one a natural resource. On his view, this is one of the dehumanizing of the capitalist industrial system. It reduces humans to only that which is produced and then, through application of Market Theory of Value, alienates the worker even from that. That is, the worker becomes identified not with the product he produces but with merely his ability to do work. His contribution to the productive process is commodified, and he is reduced to the status of wage-earner instead of creative and productive member of society. Marx would argue that the systematic devaluation of the worker's labor coupled with the disconnection that he will eventually and necessarily feel from that which he produces will result not only in dissatisfaction with his lot in life, but with a deep feeling of alienation.

Let us recall poor Joe. Before the brain cloud diagnosis, he is clearly deeply alienated, exemplified in a crushing sort of depression that even the symbolic attempt at bringing light (in the form of a new lamp) is crushed. The long line of workers coming in to build the rectal probes cannot but be deeply alienated from the fruits of their labor. What product would the worker be less likely to want to acquire for their very own or to experience at the hands of a newly-minted resident intern than the rectal probe. Here, unlike in some factories, the workers are constructing something they want nothing to do with. Not only that, Joe is tasked with marketing the device widely enough that it might well find more extensive use. One might find it quite difficult to find another product of labor that is more alienated from the laborers whose work made it possible.

Comedic though this is, it illustrates the deadly serious Marxist analysis of the separation between the worker and his or her work. In Marx's view, any person's notion of self and self-worth is directly tied to that which he does. So, when a worker says that he is a miller, it is a statement of identity. His place in society is related to that which he produces and given that it is a valuable part of the community's life; his image of himself is that of a valuable contributor to the life of the community. With the rise of the modern capitalist industry, the work is no longer differentiated into valued labors (e.g., miller, carpenter, cobbler) but unified into assembly line style work. This work is often tedious and repetitive, and the worker is never truly identified with it because he is only a cog in the wheel that can be easily replaced. Indeed, workers who became injured or unable to work were quickly replaced. Thus, workers begin to see themselves as a faceless and identity-less resource that is employed in the work of the factory without true recognition of their contribution. Since any persons self-identity and self-worth is related, the worker comes to feel a sense of alienation from himself.

Whether or not Marx is right in the broadest scope of his analysis, he is at least in the right ballpark. While a person may well not be completely determined by what he does, it is also true that, at the very least, there is a sense of productivity and meaningfulness that derives from the sense of accomplishment and value that attends work. The cliché of the worker who merely does a job to get a paycheck and lives for his vacation and time off, seeing that which he does to acquire money as fundamentally separate from him is a cliché for a reason. Marx would say that it is a defense mechanism to prevent the grind of the experience of work as an easily replaceable part of a machine. The common feeling that one is not really oneself at work, but only truly alive away from the workplace is a symptom that Marx would argue supports his overall thesis.

Recall our protagonist from *Joe Versus the Volcano*, Joe Banks. Brain shadow or not, Joe is easily convinced to surrender the factory part of his life, indeed to surrender his life entirely for a quite short time of color and freedom and *selfness* apart from the machine.

In Marx's view, humans are distinguished from other animals in that we produce our means of subsistence. That is, we are what we are because of what we do. We create ourselves in the process of intentionally, or consciously, transforming and manipulating nature. In this, Marx enters the debate about the composition of human nature. While Aristotle argues that human nature is a matter of the human function, reason, and that humans are essentially rational animals, Marx concludes that human nature is really a function of the productive creativity that drives us to innovate. If Marx over-reads human creativity in his conclusion that we are what we do, it seems at true that what a person does is at least partially constitutive of his character.

One of the products of the alienation that marks the character of the modern capitalist industry is that the workers, over time, come to realize that they are all alike. Whatever differences mark them from each other, the fact that they are viewed by the corporation as identical parts of the large machinery of the company comes to cause them to view themselves as a single sort of object. While the corporation views them as a corporate whole, human resources to be exploited to the profits of the company, the workers come to have what Marx calls a *class consciousness*. Class consciousness is a recognition that whatever difference distinguish the workers from each other — ethnicity, religion, family of origin, nationality, etc. — they are all "in this together."

The third of the *Oceans* trilogy explores (or exploits) this notion of class consciousness in the service of its plot. While Danny Ocean and the majority of the gang plot to overthrow Willy Bank, two (Turk and Virgil Malloy) of their number have been dispatched to the dice factory in Mexico to rig the dice for part of their gambit. While there, Scott Caan's Turk and Casey Affleck's Virgil fosters a revolution among the workers that ends in a Molotov-cocktail throwing strike against the plant that could upset the entire run on Bank. The walkout is inspired, ultimately, by a fiery speech by Virgil, invoking the claims of concern for one another, being in it together, striking for their rights and the betterment of their families. The gathered members of the pack in Vegas are reviewing plans when the conversation turns to the "situation in Mexico." Brad Pitt's Rusty Ryan tells the group what he has heard from a female journalist friend of his:

> RUSTY RYAN: The strike hinges on labor conditions and the fact that the workers feel they are underpaid by, um, fifty percent. I'm sure you'll agree, Terry, it's always about the money.
> DANNY OCEAN: How much are we talking about?
> RUSTY RYAN: $36,000.
> DANNY OCEAN: How many workers?
> RUSTY RYAN: 200, give or take.
> DANNY OCEAN: Okay, that's...
> LIVINGSTON DELL: Just over seven million dollars.
> RUSTY RYAN: No, no, no. Not 36k per person. 36 total.
> FRANK CATTON: Turk and Virgil have them holding out for three dollars and fifty cents a week?!?
> RUSTY RYAN: It is a five percent increase.
> DANNY OCEAN: Write 'em a check. (Looks at Terry Benedict and shrugs) We'll postdate it.

The next scene is the unlocking of the gate to the factory. The viewer could not be blamed for wondering about the message communicated here. Terry Benedict, the most sophisticated and refined of the bourgeoisie and the Ocean's gang, have fomented a violent revolution in a third-world factory for the purpose of overthrowing another of the high-rolling bourgeoisie, Willy Bank. Simply put, the Marxist rhetoric and the revolution have been co-opted by the very bourgeoisie against whom it should have been directed. The bourgeoisie have co-opted and now control even the proletarian sentiments toward revolution. It is a powerful image, and not a hopeful one from a Marxist perspective, that the capitalists have swallowed even the proletarians' revolution. This runs counter to Marx's greater point, but in microcosm, does, at least, clearly illustrate the players in the drama of class struggle, and two distinct developments necessary for the ultimate revolution—the bourgeoisie and the development of a class consciousness within the proletariat.

In these two things—the development of a refined class conflict and the production of the class consciousness within the proletariat—are jointly the seeds of the destruction of the capitalist hold on the economy. Because labor and ownership are divided by their conceptions of one another—ownership views labor as "resource," labor views ownership as "oppressive"—there is little possibility, in Marx's view, that the coming revolution can be forestalled or that it will be anything less than a complete overturning of the capitalist system. The result of that upheaval will be, per Marx, a complete re-imagining of the notion of property itself. Having examined Marx's quite perceptive analytical analysis, let us turn to a considerably more controversial aspect of the Marxist philosophy — the concept of property and the notion of the coming revolution. Perhaps the most controversial of the prescriptions advocated by Marx and the Communists is the abolition of private property. For Marx, there were many who had, through no fault of their own, become incredibly wealthy. They had inherited property and wealth from ancestors who had created the wealth, but the heirs had neither the ability nor the vision of their forebears, choosing instead to enjoy the fruits of the labor of others with no efforts of their own to be productive. After the revolution, wealth would accumulate only by contribution of the worker to society. In the meantime, as long as profit was a feature of the economic system, that profit (or *exploitation*) would need to be redistributed to the workers.

In Hollywood, one would be hard-pressed to find cinematic offerings that advance a clear and unambiguous advocacy of Marx's views. The encounters with Joseph McCarthy and the affiliated House Un-American Activities Committee all but guarantees a certain furtiveness even now. However, the tools of Marxist analysis of film are profoundly useful in discerning the meanings, the texts and subtexts, the violence and the intrigue, and, indeed, even at times, the comedy of the most common diversion of twenty-first century America — the cinema. As I have argued here, it is important to distinguish between the arm-chair Marxist analysis and the thoroughgoing examination of a text, even if that text is a movie. The former is likely to lead to nothing more than trite water-cooler reflections. The latter is likely to provide deep insights, including ones that trouble the conscience of the 21st century viewer about the existence of those who suffer the oppression of the bourgeoisie, and the power and systematic and systemic manipulations of the proletariat that the capitalistic economic structure necessarily embodies.

Works Cited

Joe Versus the Volcano. Dir. Patrick Shanley. Perf. Tom Hanks, Meg Ryan. Warner Home Video, 2002. Film.

Monty Python and the Holy Grail. Dir. Terry Gilliam. Perf. Graham Chapman, John Cleese, Eric Idle, Terry Jones, Michael Palin. Python Pictures, 1975. Film.

Ocean's Thirteen. Dir. Steven Soderbergh. Perf. George Clooney, Brad Pitt. Warner Bros., 2007. Film.

Sweeney Todd: The Demon Barber of Fleet Street. Dir. Tim Burton. Perf. Johnny Depp, Alan Rickman, Helena Bonham Carter. Paramount, 2007. Film.

Part I: The Pre-War/Silent Era

Marx and Metropolis: The Farce of Religion in the Face of Dystopia
Mary K. Leigh

In many works of fiction, both literary and cinematic, one may find examples of working class revolutions. The idea of the dominant society oppressing the rest of its people is demonstrated in a number of socio-political situations from workers' unions to institutionalized racism. In his 1927 film *Metropolis*, Fritz Lang introduces his audience to a dystopian world in which a utopian vision has gone awry, producing a tyrannical ruling class which enslaves the workers who eventually rebel against their masters. It is tempting to read any working class revolution in accordance with the philosophy of Karl Marx, aiming to reverse the enslavement of the working classes and restore humanity and equality to all individuals. However, Lang's *Metropolis* does not present the accomplishment of this vision. The revolution in *Metropolis* is, in fact, a failed revolution in that it does not follow the Marxist principles for the uprising of the proletariat in any way that will garner success. In basing their violent uprising in religion, which has been co-opted by the masters, and in emotional rhetoric, the proletariat fails to win their freedom from the dominant capitalist society. The seemingly sentimental ending of the film, therefore, is exactly what Marx warns will happen if the revolution is not undertaken fully and with the right ideals in mind—the masters are still in charge, and the proletariat have placed their trust in a member of their own society who has demonstrated complicity with the ruling structure.

The creation of a dystopia instead of an intended utopia is a concept often discussed in terms of social philosophy and literature. These ideas must be clearly defined, however, as they take on many nuanced meanings depending upon the argument in which they are employed. As M. Keith Booker writes in the introduction to *Dystopian Literature: A Theory and Research Guide*, dystopian literature consists of "literary works that critically examine both existing conditions and the potential abuses that might result from the institution of supposedly utopian alternatives" (3). This definition extends to film as well given that both literature and film create imaginative worlds that allow the audience to explore social critique. John Huntington further delineates the differences and similarities of utopia and dystopia: "Dystopia (the bad place) is ... utopia in which the positive ('more perfect principle') has been replaced by a negative. Though opposites on the surface, utopia and dystopia share a common structure: both are exercises in imagining coherent wholes, in making an idea work" (124).

As social critique and the implementation of radically new social systems to create a coherent whole are concerns of Marx, it is important to examine the Marxist aspects of utopia and dystopia, especially as *Metropolis* appears to present elements of the dystopian as well as Marxist social critiques. Fredric Jameson, a contemporary Marxist scholar, notes in *Archaeologies of the Future: The Desire Called Utopia and Other Science Fictions* that utopia has "always been a political issue" (xi). The term utopia came to be "a synonym for Stalinism," and it is thus not surprising that the association became more of a dystopia, "betray[ing] a will to uniformity and the ideal purity of a perfect system that always had to be imposed by force on its imperfect and reluctant subjects" (xi). It is this meaning of utopia that Marx himself rejects in *The Manifesto of the Communist Party*. Jameson connects the Marxist revolution with the repressive enforcement of one vision of utopia:

> The Utopians not only offer to conceive of such alternative systems; Utopian form is itself a representational mediation on radical difference, radical otherness, and on the systematic nature of the social totality, to the point where one cannot imagine any fundamental change in our social existence which has not first thrown off Utopian visions like so many sparks from a comet [xi].

As such, Marxism has nothing to do with oppression or a forced giving up of the self; it is concerned with overthrowing even these attempts at utopia in order to achieve a radical change focused on the humanity of all.

In Section III of *The Manifesto of the Communist Party*, "Socialist and Communist Literature," Marx and Friedrich Engels describe different forms of reactionary socialism, which will be more closely related to the type of revolutionary action seen in Lang's *Metropolis*. In outlining "Petty-Bourgeois Socialism," they note the ineffective nature of this type of revolution:

> In its positive aims, however, this form of Socialism aspires either to restoring the old means of production and of exchange, and with them the old property relations, and the old society, or to cramping the modern means of production and of exchange within the framework of the old property relations that have been, and were bound to be, exploded by those means. In either case, it is both reactionary and Utopian [29].

Returning to the old system of property relations is impossible as the historical context of society has moved beyond those means of production, yet the modern means are not overthrown in this case, but simply modified to fit into the old pattern. This revolution will ultimately fail because the proletariat is not attempting to create a new system, only modify an older one that did not work either.

Determining and explaining the system in place in *Metropolis* requires a bit more careful analysis than a traditional work of literature as the film is silent. Through the use of subtitles and intricate set design as well as stage direction, Lang creates a striking vision of dystopia along the lines of the repressive social system described by Marx and Engels in *The Manifesto of the Communist Party*. As Marx and Engels write, "Society as a whole is more and more splitting up into two great hostile camps, into two great classes directly facing each other — Bourgeoisie and Proletariat" (15). Lang's vision takes Marx's concept of class antagonism and the division of society to an extreme in order to demonstrate its destructiveness, a common way of creating a dystopia.

The most complete version of the film that now exists, due to the loss of the original production and having only edited copies remaining, opens with a view of machinery. As the machines work ceaselessly, the image fades into that of scores of workers, thereby creating a link between the worker and the machine. The class distinction is immediately noted in the opening subtitles, explaining the differentiated living spaces of the workers and the masters: "As deep as lay the workers' city below the earth, so high above it towered the complex named the 'Club of the Sons,' with its lecture halls and libraries, its theaters and stadiums" (*Metropolis*). The workers live underground in conditions that provide only for their continued existence; the masters and their children live above ground, enjoying the fruits of the workers' labor in many ways, including an artificial playground representing the Garden of Eden: "Fathers for whom every revolution of a machine wheel meant gold had created for their sons the miracle of the Eternal Gardens" (*Metropolis*). These class distinctions are characteristic of the bourgeoisie and the proletariat as defined by Engels in the 1888 edition of *The Manifesto of the Communist Party*: "By bourgeoisie is meant the class of modern capitalists, owners of the means of social production and employers of wage labour. By proletariat, the class of modern wage labourers who, having no means of production of their own, are reduced to selling their labour power in order to live" (14). Thus, the theoretical class distinction described by Marx and Engels in the nineteenth century manifests in a futuristic society in *Metropolis*, intending to demonstrate to the audience a dystopia as social commentary.

The proletariat of the city of Metropolis works for ten hours a day to provide the power for the city above, to which it has no real access being unwelcome in the world of the masters and sons. These working conditions engender commodification and alienation, two of the most important experiences of the oppressed wage laborer. Booker describes Marxist commodification as objects being "judged not according to their 'use value' but according to their 'exchange value'" (*Literary Criticism*). This extends to the worker as Marx and Engels relate: "The modern working class, developed — a class of labourers, who live only so long as they find work, and who find work only so long as their labour increases capital. These labourers, who must sell themselves piecemeal, are a commodity, like every other article of commerce" (18). When Freder appeals to Joh Frederson, his father and master of the city of Metropolis, to see the workers as people, he finds that they mean nothing more than numbers to the masters. Freder asks, "And where are the people, father, whose hands built your city?" to which his father replies, "Where they belong" (*Metropolis*). Freder immediately comprehends something that his father does not, "In the depths...? What if one day, those in the depths rise up against you?" (*Metropolis*). Foreshadowing the coming attempt at revolution, these opening scenes between father and son demonstrate the commodification of the workers and their growing alienation from their labor and society, an alienation that will prove unstable for the masters.

The alienation of the worker is outlined in two components in Marxism — alienation from one's labor and alienation from society. Alienation from labor results in the worker feeling no attachment to the work produced: "Owing to the extensive use of machinery, and to the division of labour, the work of the proletarians has lost all individual character, and, consequently, all charm for the workman. He becomes an appendage of the machine" (*Manifesto* 18). The workers of Metropolis embody this type of feeling. When one of the workers collapses from exhaustion in Freder's arms, the worker's concern is the machine: "...the machine ... someone has to stay at the machine!" (*Metropolis*). The worker collapsing from exhaustion also demonstrates Marx and Engels' warnings regarding the increased demands from the commodities known as wage laborers: "In proportion as the use of machinery and division of labour increases, in the same proportion the burden of toil also increases, whether by prolongation of the working hours, by the increase of the work exacted in a given time or by increased speed of machinery, etc." (18). The product of the workers' labor in Metropolis is to power the city above and to prevent the destruction of their underground city by flooding. It is a calculated move by the masters to make the continued existence of the proletariat dependent upon their enslavement to the machine, which in turn provides the power to allow the aboveground dwellers to live in luxury.

By making the proletariat's very life dependent on their giving up any notion of independence or selfhood, the bourgeoisie alienates the worker from society as well. This alienation is best understood through the discussion of exploitation found in *The Manifesto of the Communist Party*: "It (the bourgeoisie) has resolved personal worth into exchange value, and in place of the numberless indefeasible chartered freedoms, has set up that single, unconscionable freedom — Free Trade. In one word, for exploitation, veiled by religious and political illusions, it has substituted naked, shameless, direct, brutal exploitation" (16). In forcing workers into labor as their only cause for existence, the bourgeoisie effectively alienates the workers from society at large. As Booker writes, "Individuals become estranged from society as a whole because they participate only in a small portion of it as a result of their specialized work activities" (*Literary Criticism* 73). The explosion of the M-Machine captures the exploitation and alienation in Metropolis. Following the explosion, Freder envisions the machine as a monster, with the subtitles telling the audience that what he sees is Moloch, an ancient god who required human sacrifice for appeasement. In the vision, Freder sees workers forced into the mouth of Moloch, serving as sacrifices. Thus, the utter disregard that the masters have for the lives of the workers is encapsulated in a few cinematic moments: the workers are expendable sacrifices to the machine that keeps the masters in comfort and the workers in basic existence.

The reference to the ancient deity who, in certain traditions, required child sacrifice to be appeased, is used to convey the bleak situation of the workers and introduces the audience to one of the more complex, and at times, baffling, aspects of *Metropolis*— religion. The workers are consoled by a young woman named Maria, a member of their own class concerned with the welfare of her fellow proletarians. She preaches to them in an underground "cathedral," creating connections between their situation and those in the Bible. Being named Maria and advocating Christianity, she is immediately seen in relation to the Virgin Mary. Christianity is a tradition that focuses on the salvation offered by the coming of the Savior, the one who mediates between God and humanity; thus, Maria's reliance on the appearance of a mediator instructs the audience to look for the intercessor, or Christ-figure. Freder serves in this capacity. As the son of the Master of Metropolis who comes to be with the workers, one may see a parallel to the human incarnation of Jesus. Just as Jesus sacrifices himself for humanity, Freder offers his life to creating a more tolerable life for the worker, perhaps attempting to rescue them from the harsh judgment of the masters. He takes on the responsibility of a worker, assuring the worker he has just relieved of his toil, "Someone will stay at the machine ... ME! Listen to me ... I want to trade lives with you!" (*Metropolis*). Further, the film is full of religious symbols: Rotwang's house contains many images of the Star of David, a Jewish religious symbol, and Maria preaches before large crosses. The new Tower of Babel serves as locus of the masters in Metropolis, and one of the stories Maria relates to the workers is the Tower of Babel. All of these religious elements do not seem to come together in the narrative to produce any time of significant meaning; however, if one views them in conjunction with a Marxist interpretation, the meaning may be more easily ascertained.

The cycle of history has clearly brought the workers and the masters to the brink of revolution, which Freder has already intimated to his father. Maria first appears in the film bursting into the Eternal Gardens and asserting the equality of the workers with their masters, telling the working class children, "Look! These are your brothers! ... Look—! These are your brothers!" (*Metropolis*). Yet, religion has a tenuous role in a dystopian society, and Marx straightforwardly warns about the reliance on any religious tradition in achieving a successful revolution.

In his "Contribution to the Critique of Hegel's Philosophy of Right," Marx connects religion to the forces that disrupt the development of a class consciousness which allows the proletariat to conceptualize their oppressed position in society:

> *Religious* distress is at the same time the *expression* of real distress and the *protest* against real distress. Religion is the sigh of the oppressed creature, the heart of a heartless world, just as it is the spirit of a spiritless situation. It is the *opium* of the people. The abolition of religion as the *illusory* happiness of the people is required for their *real* happiness. The demand to give up the illusions about its condition is the *demand to give up a condition which needs illusions* [42].

In allowing religion to soothe the proletariat, Marx argues that the necessary revolution cannot take place. Religion creates an illusion which will blind the proletariat to the necessary demand to overthrow the oppressor to achieve equality and recognition of a worker's humanity. In fact, it is the position of Marx and Engels that religion must be abolished, along with all other social institutions in order to achieve revolution: "Communism abolishes eternal truths, it abolishes all religion, and all morality, instead of constituting them on a new basis; it therefore acts in contradiction to all past historical experience" (26).

The need to abolish religion in totality is based in the realization that each religious tradition is a product of historical epochs. In a draft of "The Communist Confession of Faith," Engels writes, "All religions which have existed hitherto were expressions of historical stages of development of individual peoples or groups of peoples. But communism is that stage of historical development which makes all existing religions superfluous and supersedes them" (40). As products of groups of people at different points in history, the multiplicity of religious traditions cannot be made to agree with one another in order to create a coherent philosophy. Instead of uniting people, the many views of religion create discord among them.

Perhaps the most dangerous element of religion to the Marxist revolution is that it is not immune to being controlled by the power of the state. As Marx writes, "Man makes religion, religion does not make man" ("Critique" 41). However, one should not read the concept of man as the individual, rather "man is the world of man, the state, society" (41). Thus, the state creates religion in the image of its requirements for social order, creating for itself its "universal ground for consolation and justification" (41). Further, he writes in critique of a German newspaper article, "The domination of religion is nothing but the religion of domination, the cult of the will of the government" ("Leading" 36). *Metropolis* offers its viewers these concerns in demonstrating that the utopia promised by even religion is corrupted to create a dystopia.

The connection between religion, dystopia, and Marxism is best relayed by Maria's telling of the story of the Tower of Babel. In attempting to build a tower to glorify themselves to God, the architects of the project oppress the workers who begin to build it: "The minds that had conceived the Tower of Babel could not build it. The task was too great. So they hired hands for wages" (*Metropolis*). Yet, the inequality of the workers to their masters creates a situation in which the work cannot be completed. As Maria continues, "But the hands that built the Tower of Babel knew nothing of the dream of the brain that had conceived it. One man's hymns of praise became other men's curses" (*Metropolis*). The hymns of praise of the architects, or utopian vision, have become the curses of the workers, or dystopia. The oppression of the worker through wage labor creating commodification alienates the worker from the utopian vision, resulting in a situation that requires a new system to lead the people to resolution, or, in Marxism, the revolution to Communism. Maria's conclusion to this story is that the workers require a mediator between themselves, who have obviously built and maintain Metropolis, and the masters, who were the architects. However, it is precisely because the revolution attempts to modify the old systems, meaning religion and capitalism, rather than overthrowing them that prevent them from achieving real equality.

In the concept of the mediator, Maria introduces the self-abnegating aspect of Christian religion. Following Maria's sermon, the workers plead, "But where is our mediator, Maria —?" (*Metropolis*). Maria's answer is to continue to wait for him, "Surely he will come," drawing on the religious parallel of waiting for the return of Christ as promised in the Bible to relieve all suffering (*Metropolis*). This continual waiting for someone else to relieve suffering rather than taking action themselves is one aspect of religion that Marx critiques in "The Leading Article of No. 179 of Kolnische Zeitung." In his essay, he questions the coherence of this view; why does one get angry at the abuse of one's right to selfhood, if he or she will not defend it? As he answers his own question, "But you have been told that the sufferings of this life are not to be compared with the bliss of the future, that suffering in patience and the bliss of hope are cardinal virtues" (35). However, even to the workers of Metropolis, this view is hard to accept: "We will wait, Maria!... But not much longer—!" (*Metropolis*). The inability of the workers to calmly await their salvation demonstrates the validity of Marx's view; the demand for a new system of equality will eventually outweigh the ability of religion to promise a better life in death.

Even when a mediator, Freder, is found, it is clear to that he will be rather ineffectual in exacting radical change. He has already failed to do anything but raise the suspicion of his father in advocating for the working class. When he trades places with the worker, he is very nearly overcome by the work. In even his early plan to trade identities with a worker to achieve some form of revolution from the depths, he is thwarted by his inability to fully understand the workers' position. He simply did not take into account the temptation of the aboveground world with its wealth and freedom. All of these aspects imply the likely futility of a revolution based in religion.

Just as the religious foundation of revolution seems that it might be ready to attempt something beyond the theoretical, the conflict of multiple religious traditions becomes evident. In the plot of the film, Maria is kidnapped by the scientist, Rotwang, who is intent on creating a Machine-Man, which will also allow Frederson, the Master of Metropolis, to "sow discord between them [the workers] and her" (*Metropolis*). This plot development serves two purposes in a Marxist reading of revolution. First, Maria, a symbol of the Christian tradition in her symbolic representation of the Virgin Mary, is held captive in a house full of religious symbols of the Jewish tradition—the Star of David. This juxtaposition of religious symbols points to the irreconcilable nature of the two religious traditions. Second, Maria as a symbol of religion, is co-opted by the state to serve its own goals.

The literal struggle that Maria faces in Rotwang's capture of her and imprisonment in his house symbolizes the metaphorical struggle between competing religious systems. He traps her in the cathedral, carrying her away from the realm of Christianity into the basement of his home through a series of tunnels that connect the two. This physical connection of the two spaces is important as it may be seen to symbolize the connection of the two traditions, with Christianity coming out of the tradition of Judaism. In her captivity, Maria is not able to provide guidance to the workers. In fact, her absence and re-emergence as tool of the state causes the revolution to occur without the right motivation and planning. The association of Rotwang with Judaism is not made overt at any point in the text, but it is the association of the space of captivity with another religious system that reveals the Communist message — only by eschewing religion altogether will revolution have the ability to be successful.

The goals of the state are not met, however, by simply removing the impetus of the workers' organization. Frederson devises a plan to use the newly-created Machine-Man with the likeness of Maria to convince the workers to revolt openly; as Rotwang explains, "Joh Fredersen wants to let those in the depths use force and do wrong, so that he can claim the right to use force against them" (*Metropolis*). Further, the Maria robot is given instructions by Frederson intended to cause the rebellion: "I want you to visit those in the depths, in order to destroy the work of the woman in whose image you were created!" (*Metropolis*). The Maria robot performs wonderfully, rejecting Maria's message of peace:

> [Y]our mediator has not come.... You have waited long enough! Your time has come! Who is the living food for the machines in Metropolis—!? Who lubricates the machine joints with their own blood—?! Who feeds the machines with their own flesh—?! Let the machines starve, you fools—! Let them die—!! Kill them — the machines—!! [*Metropolis*].

In co-opting the likeness of Maria, Frederson is able to do more than undermine a leader. He is now able to use religion to his advantage, leading the workers to feel even more justified in taking violent action against their oppressor as their peaceful and religious leader now appears to be in favor of the ill-advised plan. Thus, in basing their revolutionary tendencies in the ideas of a charismatic religious leader, the workers find themselves enacting a revolution that will win them little when their leader is controlled by the state, even if it is through technological means.

Maria's forced coercion by the state serves as the culmination of the power of the dominant class over the workers. In her capture, Maria is immediately alienated from her labor, preventing her from continuing her work in the depths. More devastatingly, in using technology to create a robot with her physical likeness, she is alienated from her own body as well. This Marxist analysis combines with the critique of religion as social revolution in the commodification of Maria (in the form of the robot) as an erotic dancer. She is used as a weapon of the masters, enticing men and becoming the opposite of everything for which the real Maria stands. The Maria robot dances for the sexual stimulation of the wealthy, perhaps an ironic symbol of Christianity's tendency to reduce powerful, and potentially dangerous, women to the role of prostitute. As the subtitles relate during the Maria robot's dance, "For her — all seven deadly sins!" (*Metropolis*). In undermining Maria as an individual and as a religious symbol, Frederson attempts to assert total dominance over the workers, demonstrating his ability to seemingly defeat the best example of the reverent worker striving for peaceful revolution.

Without Maria, or even the mediator as yet unknown to the workers, Freder, the uprising continues at a frantic pace, losing coherence with every action. The revolution that began inappropriately from a Marxist perspective falls apart spectacularly. The workers storm the machines without regard for the consequences of their actions. At the base of the Heart Machine, the workers are confronted by Grot, demanding that they understand what they are doing: "Have you gone mad —?? If the Heart Machine is destroyed, the entire workers' city will be flooded —!!" (*Metropolis*).

In their emotional frenzy fueled by years of oppression by the masters and repression by religion, the workers have forgotten a crucial consequent of their actions — the welfare of their children. Although a woman declares that the revolution involves all of the working class, "Not one man — or woman — remained behind —!" (*Metropolis*), the children have been left behind in the city that will now be flooded by the actions of their own parents. In forgetting their children, the workers embody total enslavement to the masters; they have become dehumanized to the point that they respond as a mob, forgetting their own familial bonds and individual lives. The image of the M-Machine as Moloch reaches its full symbolic potential; in their attempts to destroy the machines, the workers are sacrificing their children to the masters.

The ending of the film sees the children saved and the workers supposedly united by their mediator, Freder, with the masters. Yet, there are immediate signs that the workers and the masters have not reached anything like a real understanding. The Master of Metropolis stands before the workers and is not overthrown. His power is still recognized; in fact, the uniting of workers with masters only further underscores the continued system of power relations. Maria pleads with Freder, "Head and hands want to join together, but they don't have the heart to do it.... Oh, mediator, show them the way to each other" (*Metropolis*). The head of the power structure is still Joh Frederson; the workers remain as the hands, or laborers. The man the workers have chosen to represent them is Grot, the person who has shown the plans of the workers' revolution to Frederson all along and who tried to save Frederson's machines that enslave the workers by warning the master to lock the gates. The seeming moral of the film is shown when Freder joins the hands of Grot and Frederson: "THE MEDIATOR BETWEEN HEAD AND HANDS MUST BE THE HEART!" (*Metropolis*). In short, the heart, representative of love and charity, must be involved in the decisions made by the head, or masters, for the hands, or workers. It is perhaps most telling of all that the decisions are still being made by those who were in power from the very beginning. While there may be recognition of responsibility, there is no promise of equality. The workers are just as likely to be exploited, although perhaps not quite so egregiously, in the coming system as they were in the old one as power has not truly shifted at all.

It is possible, then, that the film's conclusion is not one of endorsement but perhaps critique. A revolution undertaken through half-measures will yield, at best, only half successes, as Marx warns in Section III of *The Manifesto of the Communist Party*. Religion is a half-measure, seeking to blend social systems rather than overthrow them all to reach equality. Marx bluntly notes the ineffectuality of Christianity, and its complicit attitude toward oppression, in "The Communism of the Paper *Rheinischer Beobachter*":

> The social principles of Christianity ... know, when necessary, how to defend the oppression of the proletariat, although they make a pitiful face over it. The social principles of Christianity preach the necessity of a ruling and oppressed class, and all they have for the latter is the pious wish the former will be charitable.... So much for the social principles of Christianity [83–4].

In wishing for there to be a mediator to serve as a locus of love and charity between the workers and the masters, Maria's form of revolution becomes ineffectual, just as Marx predicts. One is left with the workers demonstrating something very similar to "the pious wish the [masters] will be charitable." Rather than allowing the masters to remain as the head with Freder, the son of the master but sympathizer of the worker, as heart, it should be as Marx concludes about the ultimate freedom of the proletariat: "The *head* of this emancipation is *philosophy*, its heart is the *proletariat*" ("Contribution" 58). Only when this type of revolution has been accomplished will the workers actually break free of their dystopian world to find themselves moving toward a utopia.

Works Cited

Booker, M. Keith. *Dystopian Literature: A Theory and Research Guide*. Westport, CT: Greenwood Press, 1994. Print.
_____. *A Practical Introduction to Literary Theory and Criticism*. White Plains, NY: Longman, 1995. Print.
Engels, Friedrich. "The Communist Confession of Faith." 1848. *Marx/Engels Selected Works, Vol. One*. Moscow: Progress, 1969. 98–137. Print.
Huntington, John. "Utopian and Anti-Utopian Logic: H.G. Wells and His Successors." *Science Fiction Studies* 9.2 (July 1982): 122–146. Print.
Jameson, Fredric. *Archaeologies of the Future: The Desire Called Utopia and Other Science Fictions*. London: Verso, 2005. Print.
Marx, Karl. "The Communism of the Paper *Rheinischer Beobachter.*" Comp. Reinhold Niebuhr. *On Religion*. New York: Schoken, 1964. 82–86. Print.
_____. "Contribution to the Critique of Hegel's Philosophy of Right." Comp. Reinhold Niebuhr. *On Religion*. New York: Schoken, 1964. 41–58. Print.

———. "The Leading Article of No. 179 of Kolnische Zeitung." Comp. Reinhold Niebuhr. *On Religion*. New York: Schoken, 1964. 16–40. Print.

Marx, Karl, and Friedrich Engels. *The Manifesto of the Communist Party*. 1848. *Marx/Engels Selected Works, Vol. One*. Moscow: Progress, 1969. 98–137. Print.

Metropolis. Dir. Fritz Lang. 1927. Paramount Pictures, 2003.

Metropolis: *Proletarian Triumph or Opiate of the Masses?*
ALAN WILLIAMS

Fritz Lang's 1927 silent film *Metropolis* has been rereleased several times since its original premiere, usually in a variety of edited versions with a host of different musical soundtracks. In 2001, a digital restoration of the film, restoring all but a quarter of the original print, entered UNESCO's Memory of the World Register, which described it as "without doubt famous testimony of German silent film art, a testimony that made history." In February 2009, a press release from Friedrich-Wilhelm-Murnau-Siftung, the current copyright holder of the film, announced that an even more complete version of the film had been discovered in Buenos Aires the previous year, and after a lengthy restoration process, a new version of the film containing an additional 25 minutes of restored footage premiered in 2010. Of the estimated 153 minutes of the version of film that originally premiered in 1927 Berlin, an estimated 149 minutes is now available to contemporary viewers. But interest in *Metropolis* is not limited to restorations of the original film; in an article by Ed Meza on *Variety's* website, film producer Thomas Schuehly announced that he had acquired the rights to remake the film, which the article described as "[o]ne of the most groundbreaking films in cinematic history." The article continued by describing that the cultural influence of *Metropolis* "is evident in classic works that have spanned the 20th century, from James Whale's *Frankenstein, Dr. Strangelove* and *2001* to *Blade Runner, Gattaca* and *The Matrix*."

Given the enduring interest in the film, evidenced both through the desire to remake the classic and through the proliferation of influences the film has had on popular culture since its initial release, it is not surprising that *Metropolis* has been the frequent subject of critical inquiry almost since its premiere. It is also no surprise that the film's heavy-handed moral message ("The mediator between the brain and the hands must be the heart") has been one of the primary foci of these examinations. This paper continues the discussion of the film's popularity by looking at *Metropolis* through a Marxist lens, beginning with an examination of the socioeconomic condition of the German film industry at the time *Metropolis* was made; continuing through an examination of those same conditions as they applied to the production, editing, and distribution of the film, and finally examining the content of the film itself.

By 1924, during the period of the Weimar Republic, Germany's economy had recovered from its post–World War I inflation and reached a period of stabilization. The German and American governments signed the agreement known as the Dawes Plan, in which American banks loaned Germany the money to pay war reparations and "effected Germany's incorporation into the financial system of the Allies" (Kracauer 131). During this period, Germany's industry increased dramatically; however, this dramatic increase brought an increased stratification of the labor system. Though the number of unskilled laborers doubled in this period, the number of white-collar workers increased fivefold, becoming an important new layer in the socioeconomic hegemony of postwar Germany. But white-collar workers were not necessarily better off than their blue-collar counterparts; inequality in trade between Germany and other nations rapidly reversed the growth of industry, and its implosion created a massive wave of unemployment.

The economic circumstances before and during the Weimar Republic affected the development of the German film industry as well. Kracauer relates that despite the heavy inflation before the stabilization period, Germany's film industry had been enjoying a modicum of success. Movie theaters were filled to capacity, as people "eagerly spent their money, which was lost anyway, on every pleasure available" (132), including films. Despite this domestic market boom, however, German film studios had to rely heavily on the practice of exporting films, where licensing deals nearly paid for the entire production costs of an average film. However, when the stabilization of the German economy brought with it a severe curtailment of film exports, many German studios folded as their box-office receipts dwindled. The domestic market was simply too small to keep studios and distributors afloat.

The timely intervention of Hollywood, however, saved the remnants of the German film industry from further collapse. As Germany's economy stabilized, American film studios began investing in the German film market, purchasing and building several new German movie theaters, and establishing film distribution agencies of their own. In response to this invasion of American culture, the German government required that a new film must be produced domestically for every foreign film released in the country, giving rise to "quota films." Quota films were usually movies shoddily made for the sake of receiving certificates that enabled film distributors to import another foreign picture. In the international market, these quota certificates were important to the foreign film distributors, particularly distributors affiliated with studios in the United States, and so the Americans began working with the German studios to produce domestic films in exchange for the quota certificates. Arguably, this created a shift in the exchange-value of German films; they were no longer measured in terms of the income they generated, but rather in the quota certificates they could earn for American films to enter the country. Out of this situation arose a deal between Germany's Universum Film (Ufa) and two American studios, Paramount and Loew's Incorporated (MGM). The American studios agreed to loan Ufa a considerable sum of money in exchange for the studio's quota certificates and the use of Ufa's theaters. Despite the millions loaned Ufa, however, the studio was once again on the verge of collapse by 1927, and one of the major factors contributing to Ufa's near-collapse was the production of *Metropolis*. Fritz Lang's vision of the film required production on a grand scale; Ufa, already under pressure to repay its domestic debt to the Deutsche Bank and to meet its new obligations under the agreement it had signed with the Americans, nearly went bankrupt.

Metropolis itself, however, represents an unusual circumstance in German film. According to commentary and behind-the-scenes material on Kino Video's 2002 release of the restored film, the grand scale of *Metropolis* owes its existence to the Ufa-Paramount-Loew's agreement. Although American studios were mostly interested in German films for their quota certificate potential, these studios took a special interest in Lang's epic. His reputation as a director extended as far as the United States, to where he would later flee after Hitler's rise to power, and American studios were interested in bringing him to the U.S. to direct films for them. As a result, they agreed to distribute the film not only in Germany but also in the U.S. itself in order to introduce audiences to Lang's work before he began directing U.S. films, thus improving his marketability. Several sources suggest that this is the reason Ufa, despite its financial woes, allowed Lang to go ahead with his grand-scale piece.

Unfortunately, after the Berlin premiere of *Metropolis* in early 1927, the American-based film distributors, deeming the movie too long for audiences to sit through, subsequently cut approximately one-fourth of the finished product before distributing it to either German or American audiences. The film's complex storyline was cut down to "streamline" it and reduce running time, and entire subplots, such as Rotwang's unrequited love for the long-dead Hel (which provided the reason for creating Futura in the first place), disappeared from the film, though the novel from which the screenplay emerged (written by Lang's wife, Thea von Harbou) retained these elements. Over the decades between its original release and its restoration, *Metropolis* endured further cuts for television, producing several versions of the film that affected both the plot and the impact of the film's imagery. The film became a casualty of mass-market culture, its value dwindling as it was reduced to not one, but several, shadows of its former self so that television stations and cable networks could neatly fit the film into a two-hour time slot and still leave room for commercials. Despite these setbacks, however, the film endured, perhaps in part because of the grand scale of its influence on popular culture, as exemplified in this essay's introduction, and perhaps because it is considered the last German Expressionist film.

The cinematic movement known as German Expressionism began with 1920s *Das Cabinet des Dr. Caligari* (*The Cabinet of Dr. Caligari*) and, according to many sources, ended with *Metropolis*. In an online article, Michelle Strozykowski succinctly describes this movement as "united by highly stylized visuals, strange asymmetrical camera angles, atmospheric lighting and harsh contrasts between dark and light." In another online article, Neal McLaughlin further explains that the early German Expressionist films were characterized not only by the strange visual styles but also by "intellectual" plots dealing with issues of madness, insanity, and monsters (e.g., *Nosferatu*), but later in the movement, German Expressionist artists "began a campaign to denounce the corrupt upper-class as well as to depict the despair and struggle of the common man." However, another significant aspect of German Expressionist film was that despite its distorted view of reality, it also created a sense of escapism. Films were momentary diversions from the dreary realities of blue-collar laborer and white-collar employee alike. In other words, German culture, the film industry in particular, commodified escapism. Films of this era often focused on a two-part formula of escapism:

> On the one hand, the film-makers pretend to tackle the social problem [of class inequality] by harping on the sufferings of the proletariat; on the other, they evade the social problem by giving one particular worker (who is not even really of that class) a lucky break. The design is obviously to trick the spectator into the illusion that he, too, might be upward bound, and thus make him stick to the "system" [Kracauer 144].

If it is true that "[t]he ideas in of the ruling class are in every epoch the ruling ideas" (Marx and Engels 172), then given the rampant unemployment and general discontent permeating the Weimar Republic, it follows that the ruling class would want to keep its workers docile by feeding them escapist fantasies and instilling in workers the idea that they, too, may someday rise above their lowly status. Moreover, it follows that German Expressionist films, by reifying both the reality outside the film and the desire to escape the reality, contribute to an "opiate of the masses" perception of the films themselves.

It is out of this milieu that *Metropolis* emerges as both an example of

Kracauer's two-part formula and an example of the commodification of reality and escapism. The materiality and socioeconomic conditions precluding the filming of *Metropolis* called for an epic movie that provided escapism for the masses, but Lang's cinematic work and immersion in the German Expressionist movement dictated that his film deal with reality, albeit a distorted view of reality. In particular, as an example of later German Expressionist film, *Metropolis* participates in the "campaign to denounce the corrupt upper-class as well as to depict the despair and struggle of the common man" through plot elements and imagery that depict the struggles of a future society where the proletariat and the upper class have become polarized.

The plot of *Metropolis* focuses on Freder, the son of the city's master engineer and administrator, Joh Frederson. Freder enjoys a life of ease among the upper levels of the city's skyscrapers until the day a young woman named Maria arrives with a group of proletarian orphans in tow to show them "how [their] brothers live." Intrigued by Maria and the plight of the workers, Freder descends into their world (literally—the workers live in catacombs beneath the city) and exchanges places with one of the laborers, gaining a firsthand look at their situation. In the meantime, Frederson, learning of his son's apparent defection, turns to an old ally, the mad scientist Rotwang, for help. Rotwang takes Frederson into the catacombs and shows him how Maria, preaching the story of the Tower of Babel, has helped inspire the workers to organize a revolt against the upper class—a revolt of which Frederson has already learned. Frederson orders Rotwang to kidnap Maria and replace her with Futura, a robot Rotwang has actually created to become a facsimile Hel (unbeknownst to Frederson), Frederson's late wife and Freder's late mother, and the woman whom Rotwang loved and desired despite losing her to Frederson.

Rotwang performs the kidnapping and substitution, and Futura, masquerading as Maria, foments discord among the workers and, in an opulent exotic dance number, sparks a fight between the workers and the young men in the club where she performs. The fight becomes a riot, and in the process the catacombs are flooded, destroying the homes of the workers and the machines they have tended for their masters. Freder rescues Maria, Rotwang dies, and in the end, Freder convinces his father to reconcile with labor (in the form of the workers' supervisor). The film ends with the slogan "The mediator between the brain and the hands must be the heart," an apparent appeal to management and labor alike to exercise compassion in their dealings with one another. On the surface, the film appears to end in a victory for the proletariat. Siegfried Kracauer, however, argues the converse is true:

> On the surface, it seems that Freder has converted his father; in reality, the industrialist has outwitted his son. The concession he makes amounts to a policy of

> appeasement that not only prevents the workers from winning their cause, but enables him to tighten his grip on them. His robot stratagem was a blunder inasmuch as it rested upon insufficient knowledge of the mentality of the masses. By yielding to Freder, the industrialist achieves intimate contact with the workers, and thus is in a position to influence their mentality. He allows the heart to speak — a heart accessible to his insinuations [163].

In other words, the upper class has reasserted its control over the proletariat through a "politics of compassion" that can basically be boiled down to this: "We, the privileged, understand the oppression you, the underprivileged, experience, and we empathize with you." Like the Weimar government's desire to keep the white-collar employees and blue-collar workers happy through escapism, Kracauer's argument posits that Frederson, after the end credits roll, will do nothing more than offer platitudes to the workers.

Critics have described Kracauer's analysis as "reductive ... to contemporary critics more used to seeing contradiction and ambiguity in filmic texts" (Desser 80). However, this reductiveness may reflect the simplicity of the plot, which some have described as "silly" (Meehan 33) and "familiar and trite" (Heldreth 214). But rather than depicting a failed proletarian revolution, perhaps the plot of *Metropolis* simply is what it is. In interviews given decades after the premiere of *Metropolis*, Lang looked back on his German films as "big films," as he described them to Lloyd Chesley and Michael Gould, with epic storylines and the broadly-painted, archetypal characters prevalent in German Expressionist film. The archetypal nature of the film's *dramatis personae* suggests that, rather than treating Joh Frederson as an individual with the level of cunning Kracauer ascribes to him and rendering his motives at the end of the film suspect, perhaps it is more accurate to view the final scene of the film as a true reconciliation between the proletariat and the upper class. Karl Marx would be proud.

Plot, however, is not the only aspect of *Metropolis* that reflects the struggle of worker versus upper class. The imagery throughout the film is rife with visual contrasts between the two classes. One example of this imagery can be found in the material conditions of the film's locales:

> The cityscape in *Metropolis* is divided between high and low: the city dwellers who live above the ground are contrasted to, and in conflict with, those who dwell beneath the streets.... Scenes of upper-class life revolve around pleasure, even debauchery; scenes of the workers reveal mechanized, depressed figures who seem barely human [Desser 82].

The buildings above ground are opulent skyscrapers, filled with clubs, spacious offices, and rooftop gardens among which the idle upper class cavorts in unbridled leisure. The unskilled laborers of the metropolis, by contrast, dwell underground in catacombs whose appearance suggests the collapse and burial of a prior civilization, in favor of a new hegemony that consigns the workers who keep the city running—the proletariat—to a state of ever-decaying ruin while the upper class enjoy all the conveniences of modern living.

Yet an anomaly exists in the city, found between the skyscrapers and the catacombs in the form of Rotwang's home. Situated on the ground level of the city, Rotwang's home is neither ancient catacomb nor futuristic skyscraper; rather, it resembles a medieval cathedral, complete with a secret passage to the catacombs beneath. Its location, situated between upper-class opulence and lower-class squalor, suggests that Rotwang is what is left of the middle class in this future city. He serves as an interface between Frederson's shiny upper-class world and Maria's dingy lower-class one. He can easily lay a finger on the laborers' collective pulse even as management comes to him for advice and execution of orders. The image of Rotwang's home as an anachronism in the city also suggests that the middle class is itself an anachronism in this polarized society. As the gulf between the haves and the have-nots has widened, it seems the middle class has been all but swallowed whole by the resultant yawning chasm. But the medieval nature of Rotwang's home also suggests a decaying, festering wound in the hegemony of the metropolis, and in the movie's plot, the wound reopens and threatens to infect the whole city as Rotwang plans to take revenge on Frederson for stealing Hel from him.

The imagery of Rotwang's home includes a gigantic bust of Hel herself right next to the laboratory where the scientist has created Futura. The almost religious fervor with which Rotwang worships Hel, and his desire to recreate her through Futura, appear through the juxtaposition of Hel's shrine and the laboratory containing the robot, and exemplifies the tension of science and religion. In a sense, both are addictions—opiates—for Rotwang, providing a counterpoint to how Maria's story of the Tower of Babel, based in religion and told through a striking series of visuals, calms the laborers' discontent enough for them to initially seek peaceful resistance against the city's masters. Rotwang's dual addiction also provides a counterpoint to Frederson's obsession with science and the running of the machines that power the city—the only capital he acknowledges, since he treats workers' lives as disposable.

In the metropolis, laborers have been dehumanized, descending towards the absolute nadir of the proletariat, carrying to an extreme the notion that the laborer "is nothing else, his whole life through, than labour-power, that therefore all his disposable time is by nature and law labour-time, to be devoted to the self-expansion of capital" (Marx and Engels 373). In the case of *Metropolis*, however, the self-expansion of capital (which seems to mean the expansion of the laborer's own capital in Marx) seems to take second place to expansion of the upper class's capital. But the capital of *Metropolis* includes machines that play a vital role the film. The M-Machine that runs the city serves as both consumer and manager, draining the physical energy of the laborers through exhausting work and measuring the exchange-value of the workers' labor in terms of the needs of the upper class. As Freder gazes upon the M-Machine, he sees it as an altar on which the proletariat is sacrificed for the upper class. Freder experiences the exhaustion of serving as a slave to M-Machine when he trades places with an injured worker and runs the massive power distribution dial, a machine that resembles a clock and requires a human worker to manipulate the dial's "clock hands" to regulate the flow of power to the places that need it (designated by the lights to which the worker must align the dial's hands). The energetic randomness of manipulating the "clock hands" suggests the proletariat's loss of leisure time, the need for labor to be productive twenty-four hours a day in opposition to the forty-hour work week Henry Ford instituted in the United States. The machines must be continually fed, and their fodder is the souls of the lowest classes of the city.

Another prominent machine in *Metropolis* is the robot Futura, originally created by Rotwang to become a faux Hel. In a scene that suggests all technology — all production — must bow to the needs of the privileged, Joh Frederson co-opts Futura for his own plans. Frederson orders Rotwang to kidnap Maria and substitute her with a disguised Futura, who will use Maria's influential position among the workers to squelch the budding workers' revolt. Immediately, Futura-as-Maria eschews the mother-nurturer role that Maria has occupied among the workers and instead foments discontent among the workers. However, Rotwang's modification of Frederson's orders — instead of disorganizing the workers, she is to incite them to attack Frederson and his cohorts — brings a redefinition of Futura's role. The robot becomes a vamp, exercising her sexuality in a provocative dance number that demonstrates how, when "the space of sexual culture has become obnoxiously cramped" (Berlant and Warner 557) for the lower class of the metropolis, the reaction is to rid the cramp by a stamping of collective feet. In her role as vamp, Futura represents the commodification of sexual desire in the film; her use-value as an object of lust is insurmountable — a commodity measured in terms of its ability to bring out the worst in man. However, Futura's role as the vamp in one sense represents a reversal of the use of escapism to control the masses, for her sexually-charged gyrations in the dance scene, rather than providing a distraction from the dreariness of life, sparks fights among the men watching her perform and then uses the eruption of those fights to goad the laborers into revolt. To the workers who are unaware of her duplicity, Futura-as-Maria is a member of the proletariat, calling for the workers of the world (or at least the metropolis) to unite. However, Futura merely serves Rotwang's goal of inciting a riot that will presumably lead to Freder's death as a form of revenge on Frederson. In this respect, Futura undermines the proletariat, standing in for the middle class that traditionally sparks revolutions for the sake of demolishing the upper class.

At this point, let us step back and examine the contradictions this exploration of *Metropolis* has brought forth. On the surface, it appears that the movie is classic Marxist tale of proletarian triumph over oppression, for the workers in the end reconcile with management and it seems a new era will emerge where laborers' value is again appreciated. However, Kracauer has argued the converse — that the end is a false reconciliation that has merely given management the power to further manipulate labor. Moreover, unlike Marx's vision of united workers taking down the existing socioeconomic structure and replacing it with an equitable one, the revolt appears to have been sparked by what remained of the middle class (Futura and, through her, Rotwang), which is the traditional model of revolution and not what Marx had in mind. And what does the destruction of the workers' homes in the catacombs entail for the future of the city? In other words, if this was a proletarian revolution, who won? More to the point, is *Metropolis* about a proletarian revolution in the first place?

I submit my answer to the final question is no, this is not about a proletarian revolution. Rather, *Metropolis* is about the death of the middle class. Looking at the restored version of the film, which includes title cards inserted to describe missing scenes, the original version of *Metropolis* included a far greater focus on Rotwang than subsequent recuts of the film retained. In fact, Rotwang's role in the story, in the restored film, is even more central than previously shown. He is a bitter man; he names Frederson the source of his embitterment and acts to revenge himself upon not only Frederson, who won Hel's heart, but also Freder, child of Frederson and Hel's union. Frederson further robs Rotwang of the chance to find succor in an ersatz Hel by commanding the scientist to give Futura the image of Maria. It is no wonder that Rotwang, driven to a state of loneliness and robbed of the chance to reify the image of his lost love, gives Futura instructions to incite a revolution that the scientist hopes will kill Freder and rob Frederson of his precious city. Drawing upon the German Expressionists' preoccupation with themes of madness, Lang explores what happens when the last member of the middle class loses everything he cares for and goes insane, ending Rotwang's downward spiral with the scientist's death — a death that signifies the end of the middle layer of the socioeconomic hegemony of *Metropolis*. Furthermore, in casting Rotwang as the supreme villain of the piece, Lang painted the middle class — the bourgeoisie — as the true bringers of discontent, catalyzing the film's climatic revolt.

This may seem like a stretch, but let us consider Lang's casting choice for Rotwang. Lang chose Rudolph Klein-Rogge to play the scientist; he had previously worked with Klein-Rogge in the successful *Dr. Mabuse* film series, and the name was familiar to the German public. Klein-Rogge's performance overshadows the other principals in the film so much that Rotwang and the exotic Futura are remembered beyond anyone else in the film. (Indeed, Futura is mostly remembered in her robot form, which only briefly appeared in the movie in comparison to her appearance as the false Maria, which suggests that as a human being, even Brigitte Helm was forgettable.) Lang's choice of a colorful, well-known (to German moviegoers) character actor as the über-antagonist ("über" because he plays against both sides) of the film surely could not have been merely a ploy to bring in German audiences; it seems clear that Lang wanted to draw attention to the middle class.

But Rotwang is not merely a villain; the additional scenes in the restored version of the film flesh out the character as a tragic figure as well, living a life in which he is well provided for materially (despite living at ground level, he doesn't appear to be underfed) but lacks intangibles such as love. His choice of residence reflects the idea of the middle class as a timeworn concept that has lost its usefulness, stagnating in past glory, even while his super-science shows that looks can be deceiving. Rotwang has been driven mad by the loss of his intangible desires, and even when he tries to (literally) reify his love for Hel, he is stripped of that, too. It is ironic, then, that audiences reportedly cheered at Rotwang's death, then. They were in essence cheering the destruction of the middle class and condoning the further stratification of the hegemony, and they were totally unaware of it.

Perhaps it is this level of complexity, fueled by the question of who benefits in the end, which underlies the endurance of *Metropolis* as a cultural icon and a representative of German Expressionist film. Coupled with the striking visuals, the deceptively simple plot, viewed through a Marxist lens, reveals a number of avenues for interrogating issues of hegemony and the possibility, let alone the success, of a proletarian revolution. While watching the film is an enjoyable undertaking, critical analyses of the film (like this one) raise new questions of whether Lang's decision to move away from "big films" after making *Metropolis* robbed moviegoers of the chance to view more films that would complicate their own perceptions of the world around them.

Works Cited

Berlant, Lauren, and Michael Warner. "Sex in Public." *Critical Inquiry* 24 (1998): 547–566. Print.

Das Cabinet des Dr. Caligari (The Cabinet of Dr. Caligari) Dir. Robert Wiene. Perf. Con-

rad Veidt and Werner Krauss. Decla-Bioscop AG, 1920. Image Entertainment, 1997. DVD.
Chesley, Lloyd, and Michael Gould. "Fritz Lang: The Lost Interview." *MovieMaker* 10 Feb. 2004. Web. 28 Apr. 2009.
Desser, David. "Race, Space and Class: The Politics of Cityscapes in Science-Fiction Films." *Alien Zone II: The Spaces of Science-Fiction Cinema.* Ed. Annette Kuhn. London: Verso, 1999. 80–96. Print.
Faraci, Devin. "*Metropolis* Reborn." *Cinematic Happenings Under Development* 2 July 2008. Web. 28 Apr. 2009.
Friedrich-Wilhelm-Murnau-Stiftung. "Restaurierung des Stummfilmklassikers Metropolis Angelaufen." *Murnau-Siftung* Feb. 2009. Web. 28 Apr. 2009.
Heldreth, Leonard. "Clockwork Reels: Mechanized Environments in Science Fiction Films." *Clockwork Worlds: Mechanized Environments in SF.* Ed. Richard D. Erlich and Thomas P. Dunn. Westport, CT: Greenwood Press, 1983. 213–233. Print.
Kracauer, Siegfried. *From Caligari to Hitler: A Psychological History of the German Film.* Princeton: Princeton University Press, 2004. Web.
Marx, Karl, and Friedrich Engels. *The Marx-Engels Reader*, 2d ed. Ed. Robert C. Tucker. New York: Norton, 1978. Print.
McLaughlin, Neal. "German Expressionism: 1910 to 1940s Germany." *Virtualology* 2000. Web. 28 Apr. 2009.
Meehan, Paul. *Tech-Noir: The Fusion of Science Fiction and Film Noir.* Jefferson, NC: McFarland, 2008. Print.
Metropolis. Dir. Fritz Lang. Perf. Alfred Abel, Gustav Frölich, Brigitte Helm, and Rudolph Klein-Rogge. Universum Film (Ufa), 1927. Kino Video, 2003. DVD.
Meza, Ed. "Metropolis finds new life: Schuehly to remake sci-fi classic." *Variety* 9 Dec. 2007. Web. 28 Apr. 2009.
Strozykowski, Michelle. "Info on German Expressionist Films: The Techniques and Influence of *Metropolis, Nosferatu, M* and Others." *Suite101.com* 27 May 2008. Web. 28 Apr. 2009.
UNESCO. "*Metropolis*—Sicherungsstück Nr. 1: Negative of the Restored and Reconstructed Version 2001." *Memory of the World Register* 14 May 2008. Web. 28 Apr. 2009.
Von Harbou, Thea. *Metropolis.* Norfolk, VA: Donning, 1988. Print.

Love in the Time of Capitalism: A Marxist Feminist Reading of Modern Times

BROOKE BELOSO

> I was riding in my car one day and saw a mass of people coming out of a factory, punching time-clocks, and was overwhelmed with the knowledge that the theme note of modern times is mass production. I wondered what would happen to the progress of the mechanical age if one person decided to act like a bull in a china shop.—*Charlie Chaplin on* Modern Times *(New York Times interview, 2 February 1936)*

Some see the opening of the *Modern Times* sequence "Dreams of Everyday Life" as the image of love: A husband leaves for work, lunchbox in hand. His wife follows him a few steps into the yard to kiss him goodbye not once, but twice. She waves as he departs, then skips joyfully back into the house. At first glance, it seems that even the Little Tramp and his gamine, watching from the curb, witness this sequence as such. They imagine themselves into the snapshot, further embellished by juicy steaks at the dinner hour. Emerging from the reverie, the Little Tramp vows to his gamine, "We'll get a home, even if I have to work for it."

And yet, because work is precisely what the Little Tramp does not do, the two never get a home; they never *are* this image of love. In this essay, I take this image of love to be a representation of the sex/gender system[1] endemic to modern capitalism — an image of the patriarchy part and parcel of what Walter Benjamin terms "the inhospitable, blinding age of big-scale industrialism,"[2] in its requisite production and reproduction of labor-power. In shutting their eyes to this experience by living "no place — anywhere," I suggest that the Little Tramp and his gamine occupy a space analogous to that which Walter Benjamin assigns Henri Bergson's philosophy, in relation to capitalism: "An experience of a complementary nature in the form of its [capitalism's] spontaneous after-image." Ultimately, I argue that seeing the

Little Tramp and his gamine as an *after*-image of patriarchy in the age of capitalism offers spectators a clue to a change in the structure of their sexual experience; processing *Modern Times*, we "fix it [Chaplin's film] as a permanent record" of a radically different definition of love in the time of capitalism (157).

Dreams of Everyday Life Under Capitalism

In her attempt to isolate the origin of the oppression and social subordination of women perceived by many as endemic to modern capitalism — the origin of such dreams of everyday life wherein men perform wage labor outside the home while women perform unpaid labor at home — Gayle Rubin (qua Marx) asks:

> What is a domesticated woman? A female of the species. The one explanation is as good as the other. A woman is a woman. She only becomes a domestic, a wife, a chattel, a playboy bunny, a prostitute, or a human dictaphone in certain relations. Torn from these relationships, she is no more the helpmate of man than gold in itself is money.

Seeking to map out these relationships whereby women become domestics, wives, chattel, playboy bunnies, prostitutes, or human dictaphones in her essay, "The Traffic in Women: Notes on the 'Political Economy' of Sex," Rubin enumerates multiple Marxist analyses of this oppression and social subordination of women, from the argument that women are a reserve labor force for capitalism, to the argument that their unpaid housework transforms raw goods into products for consumption by (male) wage earners. But in her estimation such analyses inevitably fall short because, while more or less accurate in their descriptions, they nonetheless fail to explain why the division of labor under capitalism has from the start consistently been drawn along the line of sexual difference (they fail to explain, for example, why men have by and large not become domestics, wives, chattel, playboy bunnies, prostitutes, or human dictaphones).

In the interests of addressing this failure, Rubin returns to Marx and Engels. First, in terms of the needs of the (male) worker living under capitalism which must be met in order to produce and reproduce labor, Rubin notes that in addition to needs determined according to biology and physical environment, in *Capital, Volume I*, Marx circumscribes "a historical and moral element" that gives rise to additional needs determined by cultural tradition — wherein "wife" can and does figure as a necessity (171). Rounding out this circumscription, Rubin turns to *The Origin of the Family, Private Property, and the State*, wherein Engels clearly separates the "relations of production" from the "relations of sexuality," asserting that the social organization under which people of a particular historical epoch and a particular country live is determined by both kinds of production [the production of the means of existence and the production of human beings themselves]: by the stage of development of labor on the one hand, and of the family on the other [71–72].

For this reason, as Rubin determines from this juxtaposition of Marx and Engels, it is of utmost importance "to maintain a distinction between the human capacity and necessity to create a sexual world, and the empirically oppressive ways in which sexual worlds have been organized" (168). One therefore does well to not presume that patriarchy — which, as Rubin pointedly notes, long predates capitalism — is indistinguishable from big-scale industrialism simply because the two are coeval. Implicit in Rubin's jeremiad is the suspicion that such presumption renders invisible those cracks in the patriarchal façade of modern capitalism through which one catches glimpses of alternative sex/gender systems.

The Patriarchal Façade of Modern Times

But before one can detect cracks, one must be able to see the façade. Charlie Chaplin's 1936 *Modern Times* offers up just such a façade of patriarchy. In the opening sequence of *Modern Times*, we see many, many men. We see men in suits and hats shuffling out of a subway opening. The film cuts to these men hurrying along city sidewalks to their factory jobs, where they punch their timecards and "man" their stations at Electro Steel Corporation. While an officious male President supervises from within his panopticon, a multitude of men in various states of attire ranging from the bare-chested watchman (hailed by his boss as "Man!") to the overall-clad Little Tramp industriously commit their manual labor to the interests of corporate profit. With the exception of a lone female secretary ("a human dictaphone"), whom we see performing such menial tasks as bringing the president a glass of water and opening the door for a salesman, capitalism is for all intents and purposes an all-male operation.

Every other representation of capitalist political economy that *Modern Times* presents spectators is similarly all male, from street vendors to law enforcement to sales teams, to the shipyards to the Jetson Mills, to the multi-storied department store, to yet another factory, to every strike and breadline. The film leaves one to presume that women work in the home, as does the "Mrs." figure in the afore-mentioned image of love — cooking, cleaning, catering to the whims of work-weary husbands, and (in time, as the romantic narrative unfolds) caring for children. Although women shop, dine in certain restaurants offering "Tables for Ladies," and accompany their husbands on certain excursions (the minister's wife, for example), we never see women working outside the home — except, that is, for the gamine.

In the context of *Modern Times*, the gamine cracks the patriarchal façade of capitalism. We first meet the gamine as she shamelessly steals bananas to feed her motherless sisters and unemployed father. Watching as she rushes home to proudly present the booty to her hungry family, spectators quickly realize that the gamine is the breadwinner of this house. In successfully displacing and replacing her family's nominal patriarch, the gamine outs the proverbial wizard from behind his curtain. But the gamine and her sisters soon lose not only their father — who meets a violent end in a strike — but also their house, when the State mandates that she and her orphaned siblings enter into foster care. Powerless to do anything but flee, the gamine does just that, choosing to instead live "no place — anywhere." Which is precisely where and how she meets the Little Tramp — a human being similarly and repeatedly cast into the shadows of capitalism in his many and varied efforts to enter into its blinding light.

The Little Tramp, a Little Misfit

Precisely why the character played by Charlie Chaplin — the Little Tramp — repeatedly finds himself cast from the bright lights of industrial capitalism to its shadows is essential to understanding how it is that he and his gamine together come to occupy a space analogous to that which Benjamin assigns Bergson's philosophy, in relation to capitalism, rather that the "Dreams of Everyday Life" inhabited by "Mr. and Mrs." For while the gamine has been cast into the shadows in the wake of her father's progressive disenfranchisement vis-à-vis unemployment and violent death in the midst of a workers' strike — forcibly expunged from the wageless workplace of the home reserved for female relatives of working men — the Little Tramp shuffles onto the scene from a diegetic nowhere.

But it becomes readily apparent that this diegetic nowhere — whatever it may have been — has ill-prepared the Little Tramp for the exigencies of modern times, a.k.a. capitalism. We first meet the Little Tramp on the assembly line of Electro Steel Corporation, where he performs his perfunctory duties more-or-less to the satisfaction of the president, observing his all-male operation from afar. Soon enough, however, the president decides that the section to which the Little Tramp belongs is not working fast enough, and he orders the bare-chested watchman, "Section 5, speed her up, 4-1!" This instantaneous acceleration, followed by yet another — "Section 5, more speed, 4-7!" — and another still — "Section 5, give 'em the limit!" which the Little Tramp cannot accommodate, is the first in a series of motifs suggesting that the Little

Tramp's inability to enter into the blinding light of big-scale industrialism has everything to do with his inability to meet the demands of a socioeconomic structure whose singular objective is to extract surplus value from labor to produce capital. In the context of such a structure — wherein his time is the entrepreneur's money, inasmuch as he makes capital use of his time — the Little Tramp is singularly unable and/or unwilling to fill the space of this time with ever greater numbers of bodily repetitions befitting such robotic contraptions as the Bellows Feeding Machine; for the Little Tramp, a qualitative, individual experience of time does not readily convert into that quantitative, mechanistic experience of time required by mass reproduction.

Nor does it for Bergson, whose philosophy largely addresses this very gap between time as a lived, bodily experience and time in its abstracted, calculable sense. Like Bergson, the Little Tramp pauses in the gap between these two very different experiences of time — and, invariably, these pauses cost him his job. As the opening credits of *Modern Times* foreshadow (the second hand of a clock winds ever closer to the hour, juxtaposed with a herd of sheep hustling to slaughter), the compliant subject of modern capitalism is first and foremost bound to a particular conceptualization of time wherein the extraction of surplus value from labor depends upon the degree to which he is willing and/or able to suspend what Bergson terms "pure memory," and wholly devote himself to "habit-memory." As we shall see in a further exploration of Bergson's philosophy, the worker in the age of big-scale industrialism who succumbs to the tyranny of factory whistles, alarm bells, and time cards suspends — at least for the duration of the workday — the experience of lived, bodily time.

Habit-Memory and the Time of Capitalism

In his analysis of *Matter and Memory*, Walter Benjamin suggests, "It is ... not at all Bergson's intention to attach any specific historical label to memory. On the contrary, he rejects any historical determination of memory" (157). But this suggestion stands in stark contrast to the assertion that ensues: that Bergson's philosophy "evolved, or rather, [arose] in reaction to" the age of big-scale industrialism. This is to say that Bergson's effort to develop a uniquely a historical conceptual apparatus for memory is itself historically determined by capitalism. In order to grasp this reading of Bergson, one must insert the wage-laborer into Bergson's conceptual apparatus for memory, perhaps best captured in this passage from *Matter and Memory*:

> It may be said that we have no grasp of the future without an equal and corresponding outlook over the past, that the onrush of our activity makes a void

behind it into which memories flow, and that memory is thus the reverberation, in the sphere of consciousness, of the indetermination of our will [70].

Bergson suggests that this "onrush of our activity" assumes one of two forms: First, there is habit-memory—the sort of kinetic memory one acquires by repeating a series of actions over and over again. Whether one learns to walk or to sing a song by heart, habit-memory is "set in motion as a whole by an initial impulse, in a closed system of automatic movements which succeed each other in the same order and, together, take the same length of time" (90). Habit-memory may be distinguished from the second form of activity —"pure" memory—in that it does not mediate, or alter, the onrush of activity in whose midst one finds oneself; rather, it simply perpetuates, or repeats, it; simply put, habit-memory "prolongs their [its] useful effect into the present moment." (For this reason, Bergson is reluctant to accord the process of habit-memory the name "memory" at all [93].) Needless to say, habit-memory serves many useful functions—from remembering how to tighten the nuts on an assembly line, to remembering to use the "In" door when entering a busy restaurant kitchen to pick up your customer's dinner, to remembering which lever disables a dangerous piece of machinery.

But habit-memory, taken to the extremes required by modern capitalism's strident injunction to "increase your production and decrease your overhead," radically distorts the way in which one might otherwise experience the world. For example, if the image of, say, nuts on a conveyor belt, in its repetition of a past sequence of events triggered by the very first nut I ever learned to tighten, makes of my present a closed system within which I automatically repeat this sequence-of-events again and again in a perennial *now*, then my experience of time as "a wholly qualitative multiplicity, an absolute heterogeneity of elements which pass over into one another" is indefinitely suspended by an out-of-time wholesale transplant from the past (Bergson, *Time* 229). (Chaplin parodies this phenomenon first in the factory sequence in which the Little Tramp's co-workers furiously chase him down, only to be thwarted in their efforts when he sets their assembly line going with a flip of the switch, thereby automatically summoning them back to their respective worker duties, and again when the Little Tramp cannot will himself out of the habit-memory of the assembly line, going through the motion of tightening nuts on a fire hydrant and the buttons on women's dresses.) In other words, in the grip of habit-memory, my present is cannibalized by my past; or, if you will, my past is indefinitely prolonged into my present.

Pure Memory and the Time of the Little Tramp

But as Bergson notes, one can never fully dispense with habit-memory. Were one to do so, one would be unable to walk, talk, or find one's way from the bedroom to the bathroom in the night; one would be effectively reduced to the status of a newborn infant, for whom each moment is brand spanking new. However, human beings tend to experience time on a spectrum ranging from habit-memory to pure memory. Where habit-memory merely *acts* the past in response to present stimuli, pure memory *imagines* the past, calling forth uniquely personal, highly contextualized memories that speak to present needs in a way that enables one to shape his/her reception and mediation of oncoming activity. Habit-memory sets the Little Tramp's body in motion in response to an initial impulse, automatically twisting nut after nut after nut; pure memory requires that he "call up the past in the form of an image ... to withdraw [himself] ... from the action of the moment." In order for pure memory to come into play, Bergson argues, "we must have the power to value the useless, we must have the will to dream" (94).

If the assembly line best captures habit-memory, the dream best captures pure memory in that it is, by definition, beyond reach of present stimuli of habit-memory.[3] For all practical purposes, dreams are useless. And while, as Bergson notes, "a human being who should dream his life instead of living it would no doubt thus keep before his eyes at each moment the infinite multitude of the details of his past history," the ability to dream — to shut one's eyes to habit-memory and instead summon those uniquely personal memories that, by Bergson's account, make for character and intuition — is indispensable if one is to mediate oncoming activity in a way that would not indefinitely prolong it as one's present (201). Only in this way — dredging up the real moments of a personal past to mediate rather than repeat present perception — can we "grasp in a single intuition multiple moments of duration," thereby "continuing and retaining the past in a present enriched by it" (303). To experience life in such a way that one's present generates ever-widening circles of connections to one's past, Bergson concludes, is "to touch the reality of spirit" (313). Just as the telescope collapses great distance at the twist of a hand, the person who can see a multitude of past moments in the present telescopes time (216).

But dreams, spirit, and a telescopic understanding of time are no good for capitalism. Even a moment of daydreaming — say, in the bathroom, over a smoke, at lunch — incites the ire of the president of Electro Steel Corp. , who orders the Little Tramp to "quit stalling! Get back to work! Go on!" For the corporate head whose sole interest in the worker is to use him to "increase your production and decrease your overhead," there is no such thing as "off the clock." Time and again, the Little Tramp gets into trouble for dillydallying, dawdling, and daydreaming — figuratively (and, once, literally) throwing a monkey wrench into the whole works. In the spectrum ranging from habit-memory to pure memory, the Little Tramp registers on the side of pure memory: he cannot remember a song or a lever to save his boss's life, much less his own job. Further, the Little Tramp consistently interrupts the habit-memory time of big-scale industrialism with his own irrepressible character and intuition, not hesitating to stop the show in order to scratch his armpit or pick at his nails, or to look away from such duties as the night watch of a department store to join the gamine in eating cake and ice skating into the wee hours of the morning. In the blinding age of big-scale industrialism, wherein, as Richard Glasser observes

> time was spatialized in order to satisfy the general need for security. Future possibilities were directed into a restricted number of channels. This conception of things, which determined the future both as regards time and space with the greatest exactitude, might be symbolized as a railway system and a timetable [288].

The Little Tramp's will to dream, touch the reality of spirit, and telescope time persistently derails the train of modern times.

Derailing the Dreams of Everyday Life Under Capitalism

Walter Benjamin makes a similar case for Bergson. Of the title, *Matter and Memory*, Benjamin suggests that "it regards the structure of memory as decisive for the philosophical pattern of experience." Affirming this suggestion, Benjamin further adds that, apropos of Bergson's 1896 work:

> Experience is indeed a matter of tradition, in collective existence as well as private life. It is less the product of facts firmly anchored in memory than of a convergence in memory of accumulated and frequently unconscious data.

With this synopsis, Benjamin enters into Bergson's understanding of what it would mean to understand one's private life not as a logical, readily accessible, and infinitely repeatable sequence of events[4] but instead as a singular memory-image impregnated by those pieces of one's past that meet the needs of one's present—"so to suggest to us that decision which is most useful" to oneself now (*M&M* 303). As such, authentic causality derives not simply from a set of remembered facts, but rather from a convergence of matter and memory described in Bergson's earlier work, *Time and Free Will*, as "a wholly qualitative multiplicity, an absolute heterogeneity of elements which pass over into one another " (229). As Gilles Deleuze notes, "Bergsonian duration is defined less by succession than by coexistence" (60).

Benjamin maps Bergson's contrasting descriptions of private life according to habit-memory and according to pure memory onto, respectively, private life according to a capitalist logic and private life according to a pre-capitalist logic. Where a naïve spectator might deem the private life, or "image of love," of Mr. and Mrs.—a starter home in the suburbs where Mrs. cooks and cleans all day while Mr. works 9-to-5 at the local factory—an effect of a romance narrative wherein a co-ed's joyful mission is to bag a boy to bring home the bacon and help her to get a bun in the oven, a Benjaminian-Bergsonian reading sources it from present demands that these two work, both inside and outside of their home, to produce and reproduce labor-power. Similarly, where Mr. and Mrs. conceive of themselves as occupying the trajectory of this romance narrative of their own volition simply because they are "in love"—dating, getting engaged, getting married, setting up house together, etc.—according to a Benjaminian-Bergsonian reading, the private life afforded by such a narrative cannot be extricated from the exigencies of modern capitalism.

In this vein, and in accordance with Rubin's articulation of the relationship between patriarchy and capitalism, an experience of womanhood is "less the product of facts firmly anchored in memory," than of the convergence in one's memory of "accumulated and frequently unconscious data." In other words, "woman" is a singular memory-image impregnated by those pieces of the past which best meet present sexual needs born of a particular social transformation of biological sexuality into products of human activity. Given the overriding objective of modern capitalism — to use capital to extract surplus value from labor to produce ever more capital — the sexual needs any woman living in "the inhospitable, blinding age of big-scale industrialism" experiences will have been wrested from biology for the express purpose of creating and expanding capital vis-à-vis the exploitation of wage-laborers. If, then, one is to imagine—to call up from the uniquely personal accumulated and frequently unconscious data of one's own past (and not simply repeat that closed system of automatic movements constituting a romance narrative that perpetuates the gender-stratified division of labor that has characterized and continues to characterize capitalism)—a sex/gender system that would not conflate the relations of production with love and romance, then one must be able, like Bergson, the Little Tramp, and the gamine, to shut one's eyes to the blinding age of big-scale industrialism. At which moment one begins to think photographically.

Thinking Photographically

To grasp what Benjamin meant by suggesting that in Bergson's philosophy one sees the spontaneous after-image produced by shutting out the experience of the blinding age of big-scale industrialism — that Bergson thinks photographically — one must remember that the image, intersection of thing and representation, foregrounds Bergson's entire discussion of time in *Matter and Memory*. Every image — including the body (also an image) — is for Bergson continually orienting in a particular way toward every other image, "like a compass that is being moved about," or a camera focusing on one particular part of the whole of the universe (10, 171). Moreover, because "[human] perception ... consists in detaching, from the totality of objects, the possible action of my body upon them," "images outrun perception on every side" (304–305). One might think of the image as an emulsion lifted in the process of making a Polaroid transfer: one peels away from a material object a necessary surface, but discards the remainder. As such, there is inherent to every perception a "necessary poverty" born of the discarded remainder that we fail to perceive in our singular orientation toward that "slice" of matter upon which we act.

For Bergson, this orientation is at once and always indivisibly spatial and temporal, and always in flux. The body is but a "central telephonic exchange" for receiving and transmitting, in varying intensities, other images in motion. An oncoming image acts in such a way that its movement is diffused along the multitudinous nervous networks of the body, to be channeled onward in a delayed release, or transmitted along rapid-response channels in its mobile journey through a universe that happens to traverse the body in question. Bergson thus likens perception to the passage of light through different media that sometimes reflect and sometimes refract it, according to their respective densities (*M&M* 29–30). For this reason, "if you abolish my consciousness," Bergson writes, "matter resolves into numberless vibrations, all linked together in uninterrupted continuity, all bound up with each other, and traveling in every direction like shivers" (276). But where there is consciousness, there is memory — a means of receiving and preserving the images in whose company one finds oneself, and of using accumulated images to mediate oncoming images.

In Chapter I of *Matter and Memory*, "Of the Selection of Images for Conscious Presentation. What Our Body Means and Does," Bergson offers photography as a metaphor for the way in which we have perceived and largely continue to perceive this reception and preservation of images — for our understanding of human consciousness. He writes:

> The whole difficulty that occupies us [in the application of this metaphor] comes from the fact that we imagine perception to be a kind of photographic view of things, taken from a fixed point by that special apparatus which is called an organ of perception — a photograph which would then be developed in the brain-matter by some unknown chemical and psychical process of elaboration.

The difficulty for Bergson in thinking photographically lies precisely in its requisite fixity, for such fixity requires that one convert qualitative experience into quantitative experience. To take a photograph is to simultaneously capture a moment in time and to take this moment out of time. This, Bergson argues, is what we do when we imagine that we represent to ourselves the real movement of time and space he terms *durée*. The best we can hope for is to filter this movement through our consciousness such that it registers upon us as if we were "the black screen ... behind the [translucent photographic] plate ... already taken, already developed in the very heart of things and at all points of space" (31–32). Understanding human consciousness as that which would register a moving still of the universe places heightened emphasis on the after-image as the intersection of the storehouse of uniquely personal memories that is individual consciousness with any given object of perception. Thus it is that Bergson concludes that an after-image consists of "images photographed upon the [perceived] object itself, and with memories following immediately upon the perception of which they are the echo" (125). That which consciousness registers, it registers as an after-image.

Thinking Sex Photographically, in the Durée

Despite the fact that, as Martin Jay notes, "there is little evidence that he [Bergson] thought very deeply about the body as a gendered, libidinally charged source of desire" (192), Bergson's argument is that the body is "an instrument of action, and of action only ... [and] in no sense, under no aspect, does it serve to prepare, far less to explain, a representation" (*M&M* 299) provides a useful way of thinking sex. For if one accepts Bergson's understanding of the lived experience of the body as the center of perception, rather than merely peripheral to and/or receptacle of external perception, and if one further distinguishes biological sex (matter) from the products of human activity (memory), then one begins to perceive "sex" less as the inevitable outcome of the past than as a particular and potentially paradigm-shifting convergence of "accumulated and frequently unconscious" data with an object perceived in the present. For women to experience themselves as second-class citizens, according to Bergson's logic, would therefore be to mistakenly "identify our selves with the external images available to others in the social world, rather than with the internal experience of individually endured time, the private reality of *durée*" (Jay 197). Patriarchy is therefore nothing more (and nothing less) than "images photographed upon the [perceived] object itself," but *not* the object itself. Theoretically, then, different images can be photographed upon "the object itself ... with memories following immediately upon the perception of which they are the echo" that do not further cannibalize the present with the patriarchal past.

But how to derail the train that is the habit-memory of patriarchy and open up new channels in our experience of sex? How to dismantle any constellation of ritual practices within a system so highly invested in reproducing itself? To put it in Chaplin's terms: How to act like a bull in the china shop that is patriarchy in modern times? For although patriarchy is likely, per Rubin's assertion, not endemic to capitalism, it has been and continues to be synchronous with it. And inasmuch as capitalism protects and defends the status quo, reifying any and all social systems that conserve and increase capital by substituting the habit memory of a perennial present for the pure memory that might remind us that what *is* is not what *must be*, the inherited, gender-stratified division of labor that is patriarchy cannot change unless and until its participants close their eyes to big-scale industrialism. Like the gamine, who of necessity pays little or no heed to the division of labor drawn along the line of sexual difference, occupying such "male" roles as breadwinner, waiter, and homesteader and paying her own way in the world (when she's not stealing), and like the Little Tramp, who assures her with a smile, "We'll get along" without the trappings of private property, women and men must crack the façade of patriarchy on which capitalism has long relied for the production and reproduction of labor-power. Indeed, if we are to take the Little Tramp and the gamine as any indication, one's ability to crack this façade and to glimpse alternate sex/gender systems through the cracks may be absolutely contingent upon the degree to which one is personally invested in the survival of capitalism. And it is only when someone throws a monkey wrench — be this wrench figurative or literal — into the works that the structural inequality of the sex/gender system at the disposal of capitalist political economy echoes through human consciousness in the form of ever-stronger after-images.

If we are to understand the way in which the structure of sexual experience changes, we must seek not only ever more occasions to look away from the blinding age of big-scale industrialism — as do the Little Tramp and his gamine, who finally turn their backs on the dreams of everyday life under capitalism, trading them for the symbolic *durée* of the open road — but also the permanent records of after-images of capitalism as manifested in and through patriarchy that others have seen.

For despite Bergson's conviction, as summarized by Mary Ann Doane — that "movement cannot be reconstituted from immobilities" (174) — such testaments as *Modern Times* alert us to the necessary poverty of our perceptions and remind us, as they reflect back to us our inability to represent real, embodied time — our inability to partake post facto "of duration, of waiting — of the gap between stimulus (sensation) and response" — that the sex-gender system we act is a far cry from the sex/gender system we are capable of imagining, given time (76).

Notes

1. In her essay "The Traffic in Women: Notes on the 'Political Economy' of Sex," Gayle Rubin uses "sex/gender system" in lieu of "patriarchy," which she feels "ought to be confined to the Old Testament-type pastoral nomads from whom the term comes" (168). However, for the purposes of this essay, I wield the term in its more connotative sense, as "broadly" defined by *Merriam Webster* as "control by men of a disproportionately large share of power," for lack of a better term.
2. For the purposes of this paper, I assume Benjamin's use of the phrase "big-scale industrialism" to be more or less synonymous with capitalism.
3. By this definition, then, the "Dream of Everyday Life" is not really a dream, but rather habit memory.
4. "Science assures me that all phenomena must succeed and condition one another according to a determined order, in which effects are strictly proportioned to causes." This is for Bergson "the reef upon which all idealism is wrecked" (*M&M* 300–01).

Works Cited

Benjamin, Walter. "On Some Motifs in Baudelaire." *Illuminations*. Ed. Hannah Arendt. New York: Schocken, 1988.
Bergson, Henri. *Matter and Memory*. Mineola, NY: Dover, 2004.
_____. *Time and Free Will: An Essay on the Immediate Data of Consciousness*. Trans. F. L. Pogson. Mineola, NY: Dover, 2001.
Deleuze, Gilles. *Bergsonism*. Trans. Hugh Tomlinson. New York: Zone, 1988.
Doane, Mary Ann. *The Emergence of Cinematic Time: Modernity, Contingency, and the Archive*. Cambridge: Harvard University Press, 2002.
Engels, Frederick. *The Origin of the Family, Private Property, and the State*. New York: International, 1972.
Glasser, Richard. *Time in French Life and Thought*. Trans. C. G. Pearson. Totowa, NJ: Rowman & Littlefield, 1972.
Jay, Martin. *Downcast Eyes: The Denigration of Vision in Twentieth-Century French Thought*. Berkeley: University of California Press, 1993.
Marx, Karl. *Capital, Vol. I*. New York: International, 1972.
Modern Times. Dir. Charles Chaplin. Perf. Charles Chaplin, Paulette Goddard. United Artists, 1936.
Rubin, Gayle. "The Traffic in Women: Notes on the 'Political Economy' of Sex." *Toward an Anthropology of Women*. Ed. Rayna R. Reiter. New York: Monthly Review Press, 1975.

Part II: The Post–War Era

"*She look like a wrong one to you?*" *BloodyMoneyBody*— Marxist Subversion in Hitchcock's Psycho *and Frear's* The Grifters

GREGORY BORSE

Alfred Hitchcock's *Psycho* (1962) begins with a sequence that, famously, has been regarded as one of the most ingenious red herrings MacGuffins in American modern cinema. The story establishes, apparently, that the film (heavily advertised at the time as a vehicle for the award-winning actress Janet Leigh) is about a woman who steals $40,000 from one of her employer's clients to flee town with her lover, a divorced man who works and lives in a hardware store outside of Phoenix, Arizona, and who cannot afford to pay alimony and start a new life with her. Forty minutes, give or take, into the movie, the woman, Marion Crane, is dead and the money, along with her body and all evidence of her existence, disappears into a swamp in the trunk of her car behind the Bates Motel.

But before that surprise, Leigh's character, Marion Crane, rather impulsively takes the cash that she is to deposit in the bank, packs her bags, and leaves town with the idea that she will surprise her lover, Sam Loomis, and the two will begin a life together—away from the stifling convention of Phoenix—in California. Along the way to meet Sam (who is unaware of her plans), she encounters a police officer who becomes suspicious of her and who follows her to a used car lot where she trades in her car, along with some of the cash she's stolen, for a different vehicle.

At the car lot, she acts increasingly nervous because of the interest the police officer obviously takes in her activity—as he leans against his cruiser, arms folded across his chest, watching her through mirrored sunglasses from across a busy city street. The car dealer remarks that he doesn't remember when *he* was pressured into a sale by a customer. Marion asks how much the car she's chosen will be along with her trade-in. The car salesman becomes suspicious himself and asks if she can prove the car actually belongs to her. She replies that she thinks she has the necessary paperwork. Satisfied that she has produced the required documents, the salesman hands her the keys, just as the patrolman enters the parking lot. Marion leaves so quickly that she almost forgets her suitcase, which is thrown into the car by the mechanic that had given her trade-in the once over. Marion leaves the lot, obviously in a hurry, and, after a series of camera shots and voice-over rendering her anxiety and paranoia, the camera settles on a mid-distance shot of the men she's left behind — the car salesman, the mechanic, and the police officer — watching as she drives away:

> CAR DEALER'S VOICE: Heck, Officer, that was the first time I ever saw the customer high-pressure the Salesman! Somebody chasing her?
> PATROLMAN'S VOICE: I better have a look at those papers, Charlie.
> CAR DEALER'S VOICE: She look like a wrong one to you?
> PATROLMAN'S VOICE: Acted like one.

At this point in the film, contemporaneous audiences were to be forgiven for having thought the main plot had to do with Marion's wanton flouting of social convention in her sexual affair outside of the confines of marriage, the theft of the cash from her employer's office, and her attempt — as she seems to be pursued, as she imagines, by the authorities — to secure a new life for herself far away from the stifle of convention. Of course, after it begins to rain so hard that she has trouble keeping the road, Marion pulls off the highway and books a room (under a false name) in the Bates Motel, and the plot device of Marion's theft of the money is revealed for the MacGuffin it is, the "real" story actually begins.

But the substance of the conversation between the car salesman and the patrolman is revealing of another theme pursued in the film: that of the individual who chafes against bourgeois social expectations. Marion's behavior makes her "look like a wrong-one." The men — and the women — in the film so far seem enamored, suspicious, and fearful of Marion, even while each is comfortable enacting the role reserved for her or him according to the late 1950s conventions depicted. And while Marion seems anxious that she is in for a world of trouble in consequence of the theft of the money, up to this point, she seems determined to see her plan through. But such chafing is not limited to Marion. The conversation between Norman Bates and Marion in the parlor off the Motel's front office, over a dinner of cheese sandwiches and milk, reveals that Norman chafes against expectations too — seeing them as a kind of prison:

> NORMAN: No. People never run away from anything. (A pause) The rain didn't last very long. (Turning suddenly) You know what I think? I think we're all in

our private traps, clamped in them, and none of us can ever climb out. We scratch and claw ... but only at the air, only at each other, and for all of it, we never budge an inch.
MARION[1]: Sometimes we deliberately step into those traps.
NORMAN: I was born in mine. I don't mind it anymore.

Norman has capitulated to the status quo—represented by the voice of his mother, expressing her frustration that he fails not only to live up to the expectations society holds out for him but, apparently, for *her*. And at just the moment that Marion realizes that she's made a mistake, as a result of her conversation with Norman, she is literally *erased*—not merely from the landscape that the film's plot occupies, but from the *film* itself. Norman watches her shower through a hole behind a painting in his parlor and then dons a wig and one of his mother's dresses and shows up to stab Marion to death—in one of the deservedly most famous scenes on film in history.

I was born in mine. I don't mind it anymore.

Such a line cannot be given to Norman Bate's film doppelganger, Roy Dillon, (played by John Cusack), of Stephen Frear's *The Grifters* (1990). From the opening shots of the film, Roy is a decidedly unhappy player in the materialistic world that functions as the landscape of his own psycho-drama—one that, like Norman's, ever pits his mother's expectations against a son's hopes for independence. At first blush, there is not much to recommend a comparison between the two films. After all, *Psycho* is rightfully counted as perhaps the first "slasher" film while Frear's *The Grifters* is consciously *neo-noir*. Yet Frear's film, and perhaps Jim Thompson's novel, upon which it is based, seems to have consciously incorporated elements of Hitchcock's film within their own settings and plotlines. *Pscyho* begins in Phoenix, Arizona, and moves to California. *The Grifters* takes place mostly in Los Angeles and La Jolla, California, but makes a crucially important detour to Phoenix, Arizona. In addition, the latter film's two female leads—Lilly Dillon (Roy's mother, played by Angelica Huston) and Myra Langtree (played by Annette Benning) appear not only disturbingly like body-doubles of each other (with their platinum blond hair and tight fitting dresses and nearly matching jewelry throughout the film) but as body-doubles for Hitchcock's Marion Crane, who is the epitome of their physical types. Indeed, Lilly and Myra are mistaken for each other at important points in the story and, in effect, trade places with each other toward the climax of the film.

Roy Dillon shares characteristics with Norman Bates too. Each is a decidedly unimposing male specimen, diminutive in stature and physically unthreatening. And each, crucially, is locked in an Oedipal struggle with his mother in a world that has been emptied of the threat of a father—who ought, according to the Freudian theory, stand in the way of the son's repressed desire for sexual union with the mother. Each film, I would argue, is so explicit about this Freudian content that it is rather pointless to pursue a critique along such lines. In fact, in response to a review that pointed up the Freudian elements in Hitchcock's film, the director is reported to have scoffed: "The stupid idiots! As if I don't know what I'm doing. My technique is serious. I am consciously aware of what I am doing in all my work" (Sandis). Likewise, what is the point of pursuing a reading of *The Grifters* along such lines when its climax explicitly exploits the Freudian sexual tension between Lilly and Roy, already obviously established earlier in the film, in order to advance its own plot and Lilly's own successful attempt to get Roy's money?

The Grifters invites comparison to *Psycho* explicitly in a line spoken by Roy after he agrees to a meeting with his mother. Hanging up the phone, he ruefully says, "Well? Who's a boy gonna talk to, if not his mother?" which seems to echo Norman Bates' comment to Marion: "A boy's best friend is his mother." Later in the same conversation, however, Norman notes, wryly: "A son is a poor substitute for a lover." Roy's reflexive laughter following the speaking to himself of a line that echoes Norman's psycho-drama reveals a dark cognizance of his own similarity to Norman Bates who explicitly "talks" to *his* mother by mimicking her voice in his pathological "conversations" with her. Rod S. Heimpel noticed many similarities between the two films and published, in 1994, in the *Canadian Journal of Film Studies* an article entitled, "Hitchcock's *Psycho* in Stephen Frear's *The Grifters*," which convincingly argues that Hitchcock's film stands as "intertext" for Frear's film. Heimpel's interest is in establishing the ways in which Hitchcock's text is imbedded in and transformed by Frear's film — without examining the question of direct influence of the one film or filmmaker on the other. Indeed, Heimpel goes out of his way to argue that his interest in the two films is wholly indifferent to the question of pure influence, and he goes some way at the beginning of his article to explain the differences in approach of "influence" readings and "intertext" readings. Whether one is interested in looking at the *Grifters* as a result of "influence" (direct or indirect) or "intertext," Heimpel's article establishes a clear connection between the two, regardless of theoretical point of view.

Heimpel's essay articulates nicely the uncanny similarities between the principal female characters in the two films. Marion and her sister Lila (Vera Miles) share physical similarities to each other which, though less dark, are mirrored by those same similarities between Lilly and Myra in Frear's film. Both sets of female pairs also share a kind of triangular relationship with their principal male counterparts. In the case of *Psycho*, Lila serves as a surrogate for the erased Marion in her relationship with Sam Loomis. In *The Grifters*, Lilly literally erases Myra in killing her (we will return to this shortly) and steps into her identity and, temporarily, into her relation to Roy as his potential lover. Heimpal also notes the linguistic game-playing in the seemingly deliberate echoing of names between the two films and raises the issue of the reversal of the "crime of passion" versus the "crime of profit" that seems to take place from one film to the other.

I am interested, however, in the relationship especially between the women in the film and money and the ways in which both films articulate cultural and social anxieties related to women literally *in* and *on* the market. For while most critics of Hitchcock's film have taken him at his word that the entire plotline of Marion's stealing the $40,000 was a MacGuffin, I would argue that it is precisely Marion Crane's relationship to money (and sex) that precipitates her demise and that her murder only masquerades as an accidental victimization as the result of an Oedipal crisis on the part of Norman Bates. Likewise, I'd argue that the Oedipal elements in *The Grifters* are also a put-on, explicitly and implicitly, to cover for the sub-textual theme of the shifting relationship(s) between women, sex, and money and the market that trades in all three. Crucially, Roy's own death might be said to be the result of his refusal to embrace the prize of the grifter's world: money.

A classical Marxist/Feminist reading of *Psycho* would no doubt link Marion Crane's death with her flouting of the expectations regarding women in society within the 1950s milieu presented in the film. Marion's platinum blonde hair and purposefully provocative dress, her casual attitude about her post-coital state of undress in the opening scene of the film, her illicit affair with the divorced Sam Loomis—even and perhaps especially the fact that their lovemaking takes place in a cheap hotel *during the daytime*, underscores the ways in which Hitchcock aimed to scandalize the audiences that showed up to see *Psycho* in 1960. And as if to ensure that the symbolism of the opening scene is not lost on the audience, Hitchcock follows it up with a conversation between Marion and her female counterpart back at the real estate office, Caroline (played by Alfred Hitchcock's daughter, Pat Hitchcock), which, while ostensibly about headaches, includes a veiled reference to what the "proper" relationship is between women and sexual encounters: Caroline offers Marion a pill and describes how her own mother's doctor had given her the pills to ease the first night of her honeymoon — even offering that her husband was "furious" when he found out she'd taken "tranquilizers." The message is clear: For women, sex is reserved for marriage and is understood *not* to be pleasurable, but a duty to be suffered. Obviously, Marion does not share such an attitude regarding a woman's prerogative to engage in sexual activity. She engages in sex for pleasure, outside of marriage, and in the middle of the day. Marion's listlessness and boredom in the office is offset by the mousy Caroline's engaged perkiness. Caroline is perfectly content to play the role reserved for her; Marion chafes against it. Thus, Marion represents the rising independence and power of the female as she transitions out of the traditional role of passive housewife/mother/secretary of the 1950s, to the sexually liberated independent *individual* woman of the 1960s. But in her attempts to liberate herself, Marion must contend with the male-dominated world's efforts to stop her from behaving in ways that undermine its authority — which operates through the domination and imprisonment of women.

Likewise, the women in *The Grifters* flout the norms of the landscape in which they move. Lilly, the far more "dangerous" of the two, represents the liberated woman who moves according to her own will and determination. She is the woman who needs no man. Myra, in contrast, prays on men for profit and her own pleasure by exploiting their willingness to trade money for her sexual favors. In a sense, then, Lilly and Myra are the inheritors of a way forged by women like Marion Crane in the 1960s. Yet these two latter women operate still within a male-dominated world that continues to view women as objects and slaves and in which the dominant values are still bourgeois in the Marxist sense. Indeed, the risks each woman is willing to take to make her own profit is in acting in ways that undercut the status quo and threaten to upset the order established by male-domination and bourgeois values.

This sub-text is reinforced in *Psycho* when Marion's boss and his client appear at the beginning of the film. Marion's boss, George Lowery (Vaughn Taylor), represents a typically upright and uptight male of the 1950s while the client, Tom Cassidy (Frank Albertson), represents his crass and disruptive male counterpart, the "cad" misogynist. A little drunk and very boastful, Cassidy upsets Lowery's desire for propriety — and reveals that such propriety is discomfited by open misogyny precisely because it threatens to expose the ruse of propriety itself, which is meant to conceal the misogyny of the entire culture in the first place. Hence, Lowery attempts to move Cassidy away from the two women and into his private office and is shown to be markedly disturbed by Cassidy's willingness to flash a wad of cash in front of them, equating the possession of money with "happiness." For Cassidy, the cash is a stand-in for male power and the phallus and his gesturing with the money in Marion's face leaves very little doubt as to this symbolism. Furthermore, the money itself, which Lowery obviously views with distaste (telling Marion to take it to the bank so that it can be exchanged for a "clean" cashier's check), is being used as the means by which Cassidy traffics his own daughter on the marriage-market. He happily recounts how he has earned it illegally (or at least has hidden it from taxation) and is using it to buy a house for his soon to be married daughter: the price he must pay to the groom for taking his daughter off his hands in marriage.

The link "money = happiness" seems to entice Marion into taking the money, and this choice constitutes the upping of the ante in Marion's flouting of convention — it is the transgressive act that precipitates the bourgeois male world's counter-offensive. Her other transgressions are tolerated so long as they remain hidden and do not seriously threaten to upset the status quo (wanton women, according to this formula, are tolerated because they make themselves available to men — like Sam Loomis — for whom extra-marital sexual activity is seen as necessary and permissible). The film makes clear that Marion has internalized all of these conventions as it allows the audience to hear her thoughts as she imagines how Caroline and Lowery and Cassidy and others will respond to her absence and the theft of the money when they are inevitably discovered the following Monday. Her intuition regarding that response will later be confirmed by the private detective, Arbogast (Martin Balsam), who is hired by Lowery's firm to find out what happened to her (and *not* get the authorities involved, to insure that Cassidy's indiscretions are not discovered along the way). He suggests to Norman that money is sufficient motive for him to have had something to do with Marion's disappearance. As the audience at this point knows, Arbogast is close in his suggestion that Norman is somehow involved but wrong, apparently, about his motive. Likewise, after Arbogast disappears, Sheriff Campbell (John McIntire) suggests to Lila and Sam that the detective might have solved the mystery and absconded with the money himself.

But this suggests another formula: "money = female body." In the post-coital scene that opens the film (as Heimpel's article also notes), the conversation between Marion and Sam links money, sex, and marriage in focusing on who "pays" for what in the market that trades in women. Sam complains that he has to work to pay his father's debts even though his father is dead and that he also has to work to pay alimony for a woman who "isn't there." Marion reminds Sam that she "pays" too, saying, "They also pay who meet in hotel rooms," foreshadowing her "paying" for her crimes against the status quo in the famous shower scene after she "meets" Norman Bates in his little hotel room. This is reinforced by the fact that Marion's disappearance is treated in terms of her having taken the dirty stand-in for the female body, cash money (suggesting that she can control how and when she is possessed). In fact, this suggests that the response by the male world masks its deep fear of losing that control, and exposes the "money=happiness" formula as a lie. Cassidy flashes his big wad of cash and boasts that his spending it will guarantee happiness that, logically, is constituted by his *getting rid* of a female body, his daughter. But he must *spend* the cash in order to procure such happiness. Hence, the male compulsion is to amass as much capital as he can so that he can spend it (himself) freely without threatening his position of power.

In fact, his power is measured in terms of the amount he can waste and still retain his phallic potency. Hence, Marion's theft of the $40,000 is a preemptive castration — she takes the male embodiment of power and conceals it on her person (*in* her person?) and becomes free to determine her own movements within the landscape — with it, she no longer *needs* the man. In fact, she now becomes the means by which she herself will *purchase* happiness *for* a man — a reversal that the patriarchy is clearly not prepared to tolerate.

Similarly, Myra's flouting of her sexuality and her willingness to trade sex for money is made obvious. She fails in her opening scene in the film to convince a jeweler to trade money for sex, but the theme for her character is established. Later, she successfully trades sex for owed rent and likens her body (during sexual intercourse with her married landlord) to a luncheon special at a diner: "Today's Special: broiled hothouse tomato under generous slice of ripe cheese!" Here, Myra's apparent liberation is in her accepting her body as a commodity to be traded on a market. But it is also a capitulation and manipulation of the male habit of objectifying the female body. Her relationship with Roy reveals her to be the initiator of their sexual encounters, reversing the roles reserved for men and women in bourgeois society.

Lilly too, acts to subvert the bourgeois status quo in her skimming money from her boss, Bobo Justus (Pat Hingle). And when Myra reveals her theft to Justus' crime syndicate, Lilly must "erase" herself from his world if she is to survive. And while Lilly is willing to wear the seductive attractions of the female form in her dress and hair and her jewelry, she remains, until the end of the film, an asexual person. Lilly's independence from male-domination is a result of her superior intellect, her willingness to defend herself at all costs, and her stealth. But her concern for her son's well-being leads to her failing to tilt the odds at one of Justus' racetracks and he incurs a loss that moves him to punish Lilly for her indiscretion. He threatens to beat her with a pillowcase filled with oranges (a technique, it is explained in the film, that injures internal organs without leaving bruises on the body), but settles instead with burning her on the back of her hand with his lit cigar. Once again, we see the cigar wryly used as a stand-in for the phallus and the symbol of male domination and control. In addition, we see that Bobo has "branded" Lilly — explicitly claiming her body as his own. His punishment of Lilly too is telling: it is physical. Like Norman's killing of Marion Crane, any disturbance to male order is to be literally written upon the female body.

What, then, is all of this symbolism indicative of? According the tenets of Marxist theory, the bourgeoisie is able to control the proletariat without much effort so long as the latter is duped into desiring to participate in its own exploitation. In these terms, Caroline, and even Lowery and Cassidy, in

Psycho, represent elements of the Bourgeoisie and Proletariat that have succumbed to the veneer of freedom offered to them so long as they play their appointed roles. So long, that is, as they follow the rules (or at least do not too strenuously or publicly break them). Marion, then, obviously, is a great threat to the status quo and must be stopped. But as Lowery's own nervousness suggests, something darker ruminates below the surface. It is not merely that Marion appropriates male power in taking the money, it is that she threatens to expose the real reasons for the entire ruse in the first place. And that ruse has to do with real individual freedom — which, ultimately, is expressed in unbridled and unregulated (by outside forces) self-determination. And given the repeated suggestions of the connections between power, freedom, money, sex, and the female body, the actual threat of the female to the male within this construct, embodied by Marion's transgression, becomes clear: the pleasurable "spending" of male potency in the sex act is *absorbed* by the female body which then *takes it away, appropriates it, and turns it into something else, thereby eclipsing and erasing the illusion of male power.* So long as there is no serious threat that male potency may be employed by the female herself, then her function within the controlling male system may remain benign — she may, like the proletariat in the Marxist bourgeois system, remain a "useful tool" for the exercise of male power. But once she takes what men have to spend and then acts independently, she has freed herself from male dominance and threatens to ascend to the position of power that the male currently occupies.

This male fear of female dominance is, of course, made rather plain in the character of Norman Bates who seemingly has been fully "absorbed" by his mother's personality — and even his act of killing her has failed to protect him from such absorption and emasculation. Over against the view that Hitchcock's films are generally misogynistic, but leaving aside this thesis for other of his films, I'd argue that it is not Norman's mother who is absent from beginning to end of *Psycho,* but Norman himself. As Hitchcock seems to hint through the dialogue of the psychiatrist at the end of the film, Norman is never "really there." He is dominated by his mother from beginning to end and constitutes the embodiment of that which terrifies the male world more than anything: the male body occupied and controlled by the female. But even the psychiatrist's speech is a kind of MacGuffin: it satisfies the characters' and the audiences' need for a satisfactory explanation for such a bizarre set of events. At the same time, however, it must be counterposed to the voice-over narration the audience is offered after the psychiatrist's speech. This narration is in *Norma* Bates' voice, not Norman's. And it shows that it is she who has been in control the entire time — that Norman has ineffectually attempted to expose her by attempting to make it *seem* as if *she* and not *he* is guilty of the deaths attributed to him. Hence, she says, she had to expose him, to protect herself. Yet, just before the fade to Marion's car being towed out of the swamp into which it was sunk, the camera focuses on Norman's smiling face, as his mother's voice triumphantly intones that her not lifting a finger to kill the fly that has settled upon Norman's hand will "show them" that she is innocent. Observant viewers will also notice, just before the fade to the car-swamp scene that functions as the final image of the film, that Hitchcock inserted an "Easter Egg" in *Psycho* in the form of the superimposition of the image of Norman's mother's putrefied corpse's face intermingled with his.

In light of this triple ending to *Psycho*, a few observations deserve to be made. First, the psychiatrist's explanation at the end is not really an explanation of aberrant behavior but an attempt to return all of the witnesses to these episodes to the status quo of bourgeois male-domination of the female proletariat world. Presumably, Lila will be satisfied by this explanation of her sister's death and will return to playing her "proper" role as a woman. Sam Loomis will return to his mundane life and either begin a conventional relationship with Lila or find some other woman with whom to construct a "normal" life. Fairvale, California, will return to convention — the sheriff and his wife will continue to go to church on Sundays and keep order in the sleepy little town. Phoenix, Arizona, will largely ignore the event as outside of its own little purview, and Marion's absence in the little real estate office will be rectified by the hiring of a new "girl."

Second, the voice-over (and Norman's smile, along with the death-mask) that serves to "confirm" the psychiatrist's explanation gives the lie, in a sense, to the possibility of its significance. If Norman's behavior is to be understood as his response to being "thrown over" by his mother for another man, which motivates him to kill her and her lover; and then "keeping her alive" by acting as she'd never died, even to the extent of stealing her corpse, dressing in her clothes, and speaking for her out of "guilt" for the monstrous crime he'd committed, then Norman's actions really don't make very much sense at all. If, on the other hand, Norman's killing his mother was his final attempt to throw off the possibility of being dominated by the female and even *that* failed, then it makes sense that in the aftermath of that failure, Norman's actions might be explained in terms of his continuing attempt to thwart his *mother's* desire to appropriate *his* body in order to control and spend male potency through sexual conquest.

Hence, when sexual desire is aroused in Norman's body, so horrified is he at the possibility of his *mother's* exercising it, he destroys its object. In a sense, then, the crisis within Norman/Norma is one of transgenderism, and *Psycho* is a drama that illustrates the panicked and violent response to the possibility that what functions as the "norm" might be exposed as a way to mask the real desires that serve as the actual motivations for human action just below the surface.

Third, though it might go unnoticed, the final shot of the film — the towline hooked to and pulling up Marion's car, trunk-first, from the swamp — is perhaps much more significant than at first appears to be the case. We have seen an examination of one of Marion's two cars earlier in the film, when she first encounters the patrol officer on the side of the highway before she trades her car in for the one that is made to disappear in the swamp by Norman Bates. At that point in the story, it is revealed that Marion has pulled to the side of the road because she was too exhausted to continue, and has fallen asleep. The patrolman, seeing the seemingly empty car, u-turns after passing it and pulls up behind her car and parks. He approaches the driver's side window and peering in, spies her sleeping in the front seat. After a testy exchange — during which she asks if she's "broken any laws" (which she knows she has) and he tells her that she's acting suspiciously, the patrolman demands Marion's license and registration. After she retrieves these items (attempting to conceal the money and other papers in her bag), the patrolman walks to inspect her license plate. Though there is no hint of what he sees in the final script of the film, in the movie itself, Hitchcock provides a shot of the plate from the patrolman's point of view: it reads "ANL 709."

While this makes the "money is dirty" connection, perhaps, rather explicit, it also suggests what's really being concealed by the propriety of the status quo. The patrolman in costume and demeanor is clearly the most hyper-masculine type of male in the entire film. He is large, imposing, anonymous behind his mirrored sun-glasses, intimidating, and costumed in the apparel that serves as the image of the power of the male bourgeois state to impose its will upon the "helpless" female. He even uses his night-stick to wrap on Marion's window, startling her awake. Marion Crane, at the moment, being a woman alone, immediately arouses his suspicions. He suggests to her that she is in danger simply by being alone; that she should have found a motel in the area "just to be safe." He is incensed by her rejection of the suggestion that she needs protection or that she has done anything wrong in traveling alone and acting according to her own desires. But the shot of the license plate itself is perhaps Hitchcock's own Freudian slip — since it suggests that the male dominance (and fear) of the female body also masks his fear of nascent homoerotic desires. That is, fear of the real logic of the status quo as expressed through money/body/power: If happiness can be bought through the expenditure of male power (money/sexual potency) but in being "spent" on the female body must also be risked (i.e., to the power of the female body to absorb and appropriate male power for itself), then one way to spend it without risk is to refuse to risk it through male/female sexual encounters that might result in procreation.

This complicates the idea that the Norman/Norma Oedipal psychodrama is the ultimate MacGuffin in *Psycho*. But given the various kinds of male characters represented in the film, we begin to see a continuum for the protection and sustenance of the status quo with Lowery at one end as the image of propriety and Norman at the other end as his polar opposite and image of ultimate deviancy — the male who threatens to expose the entire enterprise for what it really is. The psychiatrist hints that Norman does not dress up in women's clothing for any kind of sexual thrill or satisfaction. And, as far as this goes, this may be true. But, remember, the psychiatrist's information — the very foundation for his explanation of Norman's "condition" — he received by his own admission "from the Mother" since Norman no longer "exists." So, how can we credit the psychiatrist's Freudian explanation of Norman's condition with any validity since he's admitted that he's received the "stuff" being analyzed from Norman's "Mother" (who is, in fact, dead)? That is to say, there is no *evidence* that Norman poisoned his mother and her lover — even if he did steal her corpse. All we have is Norman's speaking in his Mother's voice *telling* the others that that is what he did. And, of course, we have the final view of Norman's own face, smiling devilishly at the camera (and us) in such a way that undercuts our trust in the account offered by the psychiatrist.

The crisis to the system, it is true, is precipitated by the transgressions effected by Marion Crane, but these bring the world to Norman Bates' door and reveal him to be an even darker threat to male dominance — and the materialist status quo which pretends to protect the special status of money and regulates who *spends* and who *pays*— because he now *is* the fully integrated male/female who acts *freely*: without reference to any accepted social convention or role. He is the monster of male nightmare: the individual who acts without reference to or regulation by some outside social force or order that is imposed precisely because freedom itself is a threat to its stability. Just as Marion Crane is a threat to male power, Norman Bates is a threat to male identity itself, having fully integrated his female persona and allowed it free reign in controlling his actions. The psychiatrist must offer a misogynistic explanation for Norman's apparent psychotic behavior to preserve the illusion of normalcy — but the explanation hides what the bringing up of Marion's car from the swamp at the end actually reveals: that it is the careless rejection of the most precious and potent symbols of the status quo that is the most threatening thing to the system. For look carefully at the final image and what is revealed by it, what is concealed by it, and what it contains: an automobile — one of *the* symbols of American status and individual potency and freedom; Marion Crane's body — the female whose own power to eclipse the male must be dominated because its independence is such a threat; Marion Crane's "important papers"— the documentation of her "official" and public identity, the loss of which is an erasing of her very prior existence; the $40,000 — the "dirty money," the sign of male potency and the reified "fiat" currency of a market that "spends" male power in order to trade in, dominate, and control the threatening female body.

All of these symbols, of course, were gathered together and erased by Norman/Norma as completely meaningless if one does *not* capitulate to the notion that one's freedom can be circumscribed by *any* power outside the self. And if the ultimate expression of male power is in the conventions of male/female relationships illustrated in Marion's office at the beginning of the film, then the ultimate expression of the violation of the status quo (and thus, real freedom) is Norman's assimilation of his Mother within himself (a reversal of the heterosexual norm, whereby the male "puts himself into" the female) and Norma's dominance from within his body (a reversal of the male dominance of the female according to status quo social norms of the time depicted in the film). Finally, one might wonder, given the implications of this explanation, why Marion — being a transgressive figure herself — would end up being a target of Norman/Norma. The answer lies in the quiet conversation between Marion and Norman/Norma at the very beginning of their encounter. During that encounter, two different theoretical explanations for why people behave as they do are offered by each character.

Norman opines, "You know what I think? I think we're all in our private traps, clamped in them, and none of us can ever climb out. We scratch and claw ... but only at the air, only at each other, and for all of it, we never budge an inch." Marion counters that she thinks sometimes "people deliberately step into" their traps — referring obliquely to the trap she's stepped into herself. Norman responds by saying, "I was born into mine. I don't mind it anymore." Marion believes that peoples' traps are the results of their own choices. Norman indicates they are the result of circumstances beyond one's control. Marion then switches the topic to Norman's mother's rough treatment of him (she thinks she's overheard her berating him for inviting Marion up to the house for dinner). After Norman explains his mother's apparent behavior as rooted in the loss first of her husband (Norman's father, when Norman was 5 years old) and then a lover she'd taken who convinced her to build the motel — who died in a way too unpleasant to discuss while Marion is eating — he says, "Anyway, it was too much for her ... she had nothing left." Marion comments, "Except you," to which Norman responds, "A son is a poor substitute for a lover." This last line might be seen as Hitchcock's way of building his Oedipal MacGuffin, in the suggestion of the lack of a barrier between a son's sexual desire for his mother and its realization in the form of a dominating male figure who holds the threat of castration as a consequence of not keeping such desires repressed. Of course, if Norman/Norma is acting freely, the overheard conversation between him and his "mother" might be seen simply as his manipulation of Marion; a way to seem normal in the invitation to dinner and a cover for his deviancy in living with the corpse of his mother up in the house. The ruse, of course, forestalls any question of Marion's being introduced to his mother even as it allows Norman/Norma to lure her into his "parlor" as prelude to her imminent murder.

Marion suggests that Norman could leave if he was willing to put his mother "someplace." There follows a testy exchange and a change of heart for Marion:

> NORMAN: An Institution? A madhouse? People always call a madhouse "someplace." (Mimicking coldly) Put her in Someplace!
> MARION: I'm sorry ... I didn't mean to sound uncaring...
> NORMAN: (The coldness turning to tight fury) What do you mean about caring? Have you ever seen one of those places? Inside? Laughing and tears and cruel eyes studying you ... and my mother there? Why? Has she harmed you? She's as harmless as ... one of these stuffed birds.
> MARION: I am sorry. I only felt ... it seemed she was harming you. I meant...
> NORMAN: (High fury now): Well? You meant well? People always mean well, they cluck their thick tongues and shake their heads and suggest so very delicately that ... (The fury suddenly dies, abruptly and completely, and he sinks back into his chair. There is a brief silence. Marion watches the troubled man, is almost physically pained by his anguish.)
> NORMAN: (Quietly): I've suggested it myself. But I hate to even think such a thing. She needs me ... and it isn't ... (Looks up with a childlike pleading in his eyes) ...it isn't as if she were a maniac, a raving thing ... it's just that ... sometimes she goes a little mad. We all go a little mad sometimes. Haven't you?
> MARION: (After a long thoughtful pause): Yes, and just one time can be enough. (Rises) Thank you
> NORMAN: (Cheerfully, correcting): Thank you, *Norman*.
> MARION: Norman.
> NORMAN: You're not going to ... to your room already?
> MARION: I'm very tired. And I'll have a long drive tomorrow. All the way back to Phoenix.
> NORMAN: Phoenix?
> MARION: I stepped into a private trap back there — and I want to go back and ... try to pull myself out. (Looking close at Norman) Before it's too late for me, too.

Beyond Norman/Norma's impassioned response to the suggestion that "mother" ought to be locked away in an institution is the important revelation at the end of the conversation that Marion must go to sleep because she has a long drive *back to Phoenix* the next day. Norman/Norma responds "Phoenix?" and Marion explains that she's got to get herself out of a trap she's gotten herself into before "it's too late for me, too." I would suggest that this constitutes the clearest reason that Marion is murdered by Norman/Norma. This confirms Norman/Norma's suspicion that Marion is not what she first appears to be — a woman who has "what most girls never have" (in Norman's words), something "there's no name for," something that "puts a person at ease." Obviously, the entire conversation has been especially disturbing to Norman/Norma. Marion's letting slip that she's going back to Phoenix reveals that she lied to Norman when she registered and implied that she was traveling *from* Los Angeles by writing that as her hometown, next to what the audience knows is a false name — Marie Samuels. Norman's assumption is evident when he points out the "Bates Motel" stationary in Marion's cabin "just in case" she wants to make her "friends *back* home envious" (emphasis mine). In addition, Marion indicates, with the use of the word "too," that she believes that it is too late for Norman/Norma but not for her and, by extension, that Norman/Norma's circumstances are somehow wrong but also hopeless. I would contend that this, combined with the sense that (s)he has been lied to by Marion sends Norman/Norma into a murderous rage. Marion, for Norman/Norma, is not the "special" exception to the norm (s)he took her for in the first place but just another, typical, "woman," who has expressed a desire to go back to "society" to fix an error that might result in her *not* fitting in anymore. In essence, that which makes Marion transgressive to the status quo is what made her "special" to Norman/Norma in the first place; her decision to capitulate by freely going back to the status quo is what becomes for Norman/Norma an unforgivable transgression against her/his implied theory of real individuality/freedom — and it is for this reason that Marion must be punished.

In *Psycho*, then, womanhood or femaleness itself is revealed to be transgressive and the Norman/Norma persona is the epitome of the logical end of the reversal of the "normal" gendered and statused relationships between the sexes. In the Marxist-Feminist configuration, the male dominates the controlling bourgeoisie and tolerates the presence of the female only insofar as it functions as a tool of control and domination. Money is the stand-in for male dominance and can only be "spent" by males; females are the commodities males trade in and control. The female is the "body" (the proletariat) upon which male dominance is exercised and remains unthreatening so long as it is passive and victimized and can be used to produce in a controlled way more fodder for control (i.e., through male-controlled procreation). Once that female body resists or, worse, absorbs and then absconds with male power, it must be re-captured and re-subjugated. A "straight" Marxist reading of this configuration ends with the interpretation that Marion's death is her punishment for refusing to act according to the role reserved for her according to the male dominated power-structure. But the fact that so much of Hitchcock's *Psycho* is also already gendered, such a reading is deepened and supplemented by the intersection of the money/body/power nexus and the ways in which outwardly gendered persons are alternatively "free" or "imprisoned" both externally and interiorally. According to this more complicated view, the apparent "Oedipal" themes in *Psycho* (and later, in *The Grifters,* for similar reasons) are the real MacGuffin: a ruse to conceal the real issues at hand. Norman/Norma is *not* merely some instrument of the system that conveniently metes out the punishment due an agent that dares to flout convention; rather, Norman/Norma is a transgendered transgressive force who metes out its independent vengeance against a member of the system that denies his/her *right* to full autonomy. It is Marion's capitulation to the status quo that kills her — not her transgression, since the male system of dominance never catches up to her sufficiently to punish her. Rather, that male system, by the end of the narrative, intuits that Norman/Norma constitutes a far greater threat than Marion ever did and so seeks to re-normalize the entire episode by offering a "scientific" explanation for everything which itself, upon inspection, is made-up whole cloth. The psychiatrist conveniently credits Norman's mother's "voice" with a true account of what "really" happened and why and then spins it in a Freudian web that satisfies everyone with its apparent bizarreness—cleverly hiding that Norman/Norma represents exactly those desires for full autonomy that the "system" seeks to conceal.

The cad Cassidy equates money with "happiness" at the beginning of the film — and this constitutes a deception he has internalized as a result of his being a willing tool for a capitalistic system that privileges his desires at the expense of others' freedom (especially women). But, in the end, what character might we say is "happy"? I would contend that Hitchcock's last camera shot of Norman/Norma's face reveals the answer to that question: (s)he is.

It is obvious, from this point of view, to me, that the film *The Grifters* either traffics in or negotiates the same symbolic landscape of Hitchcock's *Psycho*. In both films, women are presented as problems to a male sense of specious order. Women function but they don't fit. They are necessary and dangerous for the same reasons— they might act on their own. The differences between the two films is that in the former the female activity is "new" and in the latter female actors (perhaps literally and figuratively) become the inheritors of the triumphs of their successful predecessors: they are women who have chafed — and they have embraced their status as "wrong ones." Marion Crane becomes, then, for Lilly especially and Myra to a lesser extent in *The Grifters*, a kind of Iphegenia who baptizes through martyrdom a future possibility of success and freedom for a sisterhood founded in her own sacrifice.

Just as Hitchcock's film manipulates its audience into believing that the film "belongs" to Marion Crane, Stephen Frear manipulates his audience into believing *The Grifters* is about Roy Dillon. But it is not. Or, at least, while it may begin that way, it ends up otherwise. In fact, the entire film might be seen as a contest between three characters to be the independent and dominate centers of their own stories. That contest inevitably leads to the violent altercations first between Lilly and Myra and then between Lilly and Dillon. And, of course, it is Lilly — not Myra and not Roy — who prevails.

Myra's attempt to kill Lilly and steal the money Lilly has stolen from Bobo Justus is fitting for a character whose apparent independence is exhibited in her wanton embrace of her status as an object of sexual desire: Myra understands that men want two things, money and sex. And Myra is willing to trade her sex for their money — feeling, always, that she has cheated them in the process and come out "on top. " Her weakness is her greed: her ways require participation in the "long con," and the long con requires partners. Roy was warned away from partners by his earliest mentor — who taught him that the greatest grift of them all is when one grifter is able to get one over on another. As a result, Roy refuses to trust anyone and contents himself with the short-con, tricking people out of minor amounts of money. The pay-offs are always low, but so are the risks. By contrast, Lilly has taken a position in a "racket"— a large and well-organized criminal enterprise. She exerts her independence from within the system by skimming money from her employer and explaining it to her boss by saying that she takes some but not too much, because, she says, Bobo wouldn't trust an employee who wasn't willing to take care of herself. *All* moneyed transactions in *The Grifters* are a form of theft. Capitalism is a kind of theft in which one profits at another's loss. According to this logic, the "grifter" is merely inviting participants in the system to hazard a chance to profit at someone else's expense. Every transaction poses risks for each participant and the gritty and unsentimental view of the grifter is as old as the market it trades in: *caveat emptor.* In the end, Myra and Roy fail (and give up their lives as a result) because each holds to a kind of fantasy that they alone can exist unstained by the grift. Lilly, however, ultimately resists the urge to sentimentalize her relationships and it is she alone who survives.

Myra is the most sentimental of the three characters. When Roy intimates that he's content "where he is" and won't partner with Myra, she says, "I gotta have a partner! I've looked and I've looked and, believe me, brother, I've kissed a lot of fucking frogs, and you're my prince!" Myra explicitly traffics in the terms of the fairytale: she is the princess in distress waiting to be rescued by her prince. It is Myra's explicit capitulation to the system — her "needing" a man — that spells her doom. It is her weakness. While she appears bold and independent and ruthless, she is ultimately vulnerable as a result of this *need* for a man. Roy, on the other hand, is undone by his lack of potency—expressed in his lack of ambition. As Lilly seems to intuit, Roy will ultimately be crushed by the grift because he "doesn't have the stomach for it"; that is, because he will not go for the kill, but contents himself with small victories in his effort to exist on the edge of the status quo as a "respectable young man," even as he makes his living stealing from members of that status quo. Roy's fantasy is that as long as he is alone, he can be "free" and independent—making his own decisions and doing as he pleases. What Lilly tries to tell him is that *no one* in the system is truly free. Unlike Myra, but like Roy, Lilly is ultimately concerned with one thing and one thing only: survival. Her view is coldly realistic: since the entire system victimizes everyone, then there is no sense in trying to beat it (Myra) or to participate in it without stain (Roy). Winners in the dog-eat-dog market that is capitalism (the ultimate grift) are willing to do anything to survive—and Lilly is a winner in these terms.

Lilly's "victory," however, is at Myra and Roy's expense—and the end of *The Grifters* is a fascinating reversal of just about everything in *Psycho*. After Myra informs an associate of Bobo Justus that Lilly has been skimming from him, Lilly flees La Jolla, California, and checks into a motel that recalls the Bates Motel. Its location is telling: it's on the outskirts of Phoenix, Arizona (the city in which *Psycho* begins). But, unlike the Bates Motel, the motel Lilly takes a room in (in the back, facing away from the highway) is entirely benign. Unknown to Lilly, however, Myra has followed her from California and pulls into the same motel after Lilly has checked herself into her cabin. Myra asks for a room too (and the motel clerk at first mistakes her for Lilly), and manipulates herself into one a few doors down from Lilly. After she is sure that Lilly must be asleep, she uses one of hundreds of keys on a ring she has to get into Lilly's room and attempts to strangle her. Lilly always carries a gun, however, and succeeds in shooting Myra in the face. Roy is then contacted to identify what authorities think is the body of his mother. He flies to Phoenix and laughs in the Medical Examiners office when he realizes that the corpse on the table is Myra's, not Lilly's. He confirms this by examining the back of her right hand and discovers there is no scar from Bobo's cigar. He leaves without revealing this fact and the authorities in Phoenix close their investigation into Lilly's apparent death, filing it as a suicide.

Lilly's quick-thinking ruse is ingenious but not foolproof. By leaving Bobo's stolen money in the trunk of her car and allowing the authorities to believe that Myra's body is hers (and by taking Myra's clothes and automobile—and likely checking out of the hotel room under Myra's name), Lilly has successfully made herself disappear from not only her official existence within bourgeois society, but from Bobo Justus' underworld. Just as Marion Crane's existence was literally erased by Norman Bates (he puts her body, her papers, and the money into the trunk of the car and sinks it in the swamp), Lilly has *erased herself* from the world and, in doing so, stands on the verge of real freedom and true independence. She has two problems, however— one she explicitly acknowledges and one that she does not. She needs money if she is to re-establish herself somewhere far away from her old identity and her associations with Bobo Justus. And Roy is the only one in the world who knows what she has done. Roy's knowledge, then, is the *real* currency of the world of the grift — not money.

In the end, money in *The Grifters* is a symbol of superior knowledge. As in *Psycho*, for some characters, it functions as a sign of male potency. But that sign, in *The Grifters*, is extended to include blood — literally and metaphorically. Kinship ties (clan ties, mob ties, etc.) and familial ties (including marriage ties or the lack thereof) are critiqued throughout *The Grifters*. Roy's relationship with his "too young" mother, Lilly (who had him out of wedlock when she was fourteen years old), is not "normal." Apparently always on the grift in some form or another, Lilly passed Roy off as her brother rather than her son. His resentment at this treatment is expressed in his calling her "Lilly" unless he wants to hurt her by calling her, sarcastically, "Mom." Lilly has not been undamaged by their abnormal relationship but harbors a mother's concern for the welfare of a son. But she has long since given up any right, in Roy's view, to act on those concerns and he views her with a mixture of contempt and resentment. Lilly, for her part, exhibits her guilt that Roy had such a rough upbringing, but masks it by demanding that he acknowledge that he "owes" her his life. Simultaneously, she actively tries to dissuade his relationship with Myra and to get him to give up the grift. Ultimately, Lilly fears that the world will ruin him. In a sense, she has a bit of the martyr in her: she rationalizes her own participation in the system by telling herself that it's to save her son.

Lilly's erasing of Myra from the world and the landscape of the film is a reversal of Norman Bates' erasing of Marion Crane from her world. Myra, in the end, constituted a real threat to Lilly's world, where Marion constituted only an imagined threat to Norma/Norman's. Nothing in the Bates' world would have been changed had he simply left Marion alone. Lilly, however, does not have a choice in killing Myra — who is shot as she straddles Lilly with both hands tightly around her throat. But in assuming Myra's identity and even her clothing and car, Lilly re-enacts some of the crucial aspects of Hitchcock's film: Norman dresses as his own mother when he kills. Norman gets rid of Marion by getting rid of her car and all official evidence of her presence not only at the motel, but in the world itself (as represented by the file of "official" papers she carries with her). Norman unwittingly throws the newspaper with the $40,000 in it into the trunk as well. Lilly re-writes each of these actions in the reverse direction: she takes Myra's life in an act of self-defense; she assumes her identity not to kill but to survive; she leaves Myra's body in plain view, assuming that it will be attached "officially" to her (Lilly's) identity as the renter of the motel room, the owner of the car, and all the money that will be undoubtedly found in its trunk. And, presumably, it works.

The only loose ends Lilly must attend to are back in Roy's apartment in Los Angeles. So she drives there and, walking through the lobby to the elevator, she is mistaken by the manager for Myra. She allows the mistake to stand, as it serves her purposes for people to believe that she is Myra. She breaks into Roy's apartment and finds his money ($40,000?) and attempts to abscond with it but is interrupted by Roy, who seems to be returning from some errand. There follows an uncomfortable exchange between the two in which it is revealed that Roy knows exactly what Lilly has done and attempts to use it as leverage to force her to get off the grift and live the "straight" life. The weapon he uses to force the issue is his refusal to give her the money to allow her escape. But Lilly will not accept being dominated by Roy, and attempts to maneuver him so that she can leave with his money. Roy reveals to Lilly that *he's* getting off the grift and when she tells him in no uncertain terms that she could never live the "square life," he says:

> Roy: I thought you'd be happy for me. After all, you–
> Lilly: Bobo isn't after you! Bobo's after me, and he's goddamn good! But so am I. I'm a survivor, Roy. I survive.
> Roy: I know you do, so that's why–
> Lilly: And to survive, my way, I need money. Bobo knows about the stash in the car, so I didn't dare touch it, not if Lilly Dillon's dead. So that leaves this.
> Roy: No.

Here, Lilly reveals her understanding of the grifter's life: it's about surviving. Lilly changes tact and goes to the kitchen to get two glasses of water. She re-enters the living room and brings a tray to Roy and, indicating the glasses, says, "Take whichever one you want." It occurs to Roy that Lilly might try to poison him. Taking one of the glasses he says, "You wouldn't do that," to which Lilly replies, "You don't know what I'd do, Roy. You have no idea. To live." Lilly tries to play on Roy's resentment at her being a "bad mother" (a thematic echo of *Psycho*) in an attempt to convince him that since he's going to lead a "square" (i.e., legitimate) life now, he doesn't *need* the money, saying, "If you keep it around, it'll just make you think how clever you are. It'll be a temptation to get back into the game." Roy answers her by saying, "Oh that's it! You're stealing my own money from me for my own good! How motherly of you, Lilly." Roy has hit the nail on the head: Lilly's motherly instinct is to protect her son from forces she thinks are too big for him to control; he resents his mother's attempts to stifle and control him. But the film is also explicit about the Oedipal forces just below the surface as well. Roy, like Norman Bates, lives in a fatherless world. The prohibition against sexual desire for his mother cannot be enforced. Myra, in her last scene with Roy, accuses him with using her as a substitute for sleeping with his mother, saying, as she leaves, "And you don't even know it."

Lilly preys on Roy's unspoken fears regarding his desire for his mother, asking him, "Roy... What would you do if I told you I really wasn't your mother? ...You'd like that, wouldn't you? You don't need to tell me.... Roy ... Roy... [walking toward him; standing too close, seductively] I have to have that money, Roy. What do I have to do to get it?" Roy reacts with a mixture of shock and confusion. He doesn't move — allowing Lilly to bend in close and kiss him on the lips. At the moment that Roy begins to seem to kiss her back, he jerks his head away and pushes her away. He lifts the glass to take a drink of water and Lilly hits him in the head with the attaché case with all his money it in. The clasp gives, the glass breaks, and money and tricks of the trade go flying. Roy has suffered a cut to his jugular vein from a glass shard and falls to the ground. Realizing what she has done, Lilly bends over her dying son and (as the script describes) weeps "grindingly." As the scene was shot, Lilly's agony is seen from somewhere above and behind Lilly as she leans over the dying Roy. The heaving of her body and the sounds she makes make the momentary scene suggest copulation — with Lilly on top of Roy.

Just as in *Psycho*, Frear makes the Freudian aspects of the Lilly/Roy/Myra triangle explicit, negating any real reason to pursue a "Freudian" reading of the film. Like Hitchcok, Frear's seems to have used the Oedipal angle as a kind of ruse. After Roy dies, Lilly grabs as much of the cash from the floor as she can. It is smeared with his blood. Hereby, Frear conflates money with blood as the sign of potency. And Lilly, in taking the money, reverses Marion Crane's "error" in *Psycho*. Lilly *refuses* legitimacy and the status quo. She refuses to play a role that has been reserved for her by anything or anyone. She refused to be a "good" mother for Roy. She refuses to live as a woman in society within the confines of "the Law." She subverts Bobo Justus' "control" over her movements by "killing" Lilly Dillon, killing her rival for her son's affections, and killing the one person with knowledge sufficient to have an advantage in the grift. Lilly defies the order of the capitalistic system: she enters into no *transaction*; rather, she *takes*.

That last shot in *The Grifters* is of Lilly leaving the underground parking lot of Roy's apartment building in Roy's car. She makes a right turn into light, late-night traffic on an unnamed boulevard in Los Angeles. From a high angle, the camera simply views the scene as Lilly drives through a green light and on. Her car fades into the lights of other cars on the road and literally disappears from view. She has erased herself from the grid and is now free to start over — to fashion for herself whatever life she chooses. She has reversed the tidy ending of Hitchcock's *Psycho* in which the removal of the car from the swamp will proved the "authorities" with all the evidence they need to "prove" their theory about what transpired at the Bates Motel and why. In the male-dominated bourgeois world of *Psycho*, every theory is a self-fulfilling prophecy. But in the world of *The Grifters*, Lilly manages to do something *new*. She's proven that she has the intelligence and ruthlessness to get what she wants. Not only does she survive, she succeeds. Marion Crane, in *Psycho*, is the victim of Norma/Norman Bates for capitulating to the status quo; for her decision *not* to make a life on her own by subverting the male-order that would consign her to her position as mere "woman." Norma/Norman, in turn, becomes a tool for that status quo, in that his/her apparent pathology serves as a convenient explanation for what has happened. The pulling the car from the swamp confirms and re-establishes the order of the status quo (though the death-mask on Norma/Norman's face and his/her smile suggest that resistance is ever just below the surface). Likewise, Frear's film ends with a shot that includes the back of a car — and one that contains all of the elements included in Hitchcock's film: a woman, money, papers that "prove" identity (Lilly reveals to Roy that she has Myra's credit cards — presumably, she'd have taken her driver's license and other "official" indications of identity as well, though the film is not explicit on this point). Significantly, however, Hitchcock's car is pulled passively from the swamp and contains a female *body*. Frear's car drives away under its own power, driven by a female *person* — indeed, by a person with the knowledge and ability to re-invent herself in any way she pleases.

Both *Psycho* and *The Grifters* masquerade as psycho-sexual thriller/dramas trafficking in Freudian vocabulary whose sub-text is psychological. Yet, since each film makes such "subtext" explicit, I argue that the apparent subtext is subterfuge to mask each film's critique of American society and the ways in which capitalism is for all within its power a means of control and manipulation. Hence, in each film, subtext really is text and that text masks different subtext. In *Psycho*, the psychiatrist's explanation at the end of the film is society's effort to avert everyone's gaze from the real danger that seeks to overturn the status quo. True, Marion is punished for having presumed to *not* play the role reserved for her — but Norman/Norma is the greater danger, in his/her capacity to reveal what motivates male dominance over the female in the first place. In *The Grifters*, likewise, sex is a subterfuge to mask the intersection of money/bloody/body in the ongoing war for dominance and control. The "grift" thereby is merely the acknowledgement that *all* moneyed transactions are inherently "dirty." In exerting her individuality, her life, over that even of her son's, Lilly acts to preserve that only thing that is *hers* — her life. She tells Roy repeatedly that he "owes" her — because she gave him his life, "twice" (once by bearing him, another by saving him from his stomach injury). She offers him a way to clear his debt: give his money to her. When he refuses, she takes it from him and takes his life (back) in the process.

In *On Literature and Art*, Lenin wrote that the freedom of the writer in bourgeois society is illusory. "The freedom of the Bourgeois writer," he writes, "is simply masked ... dependence on the money-bag, on corruption, on prostitution" (Habib). Lenin implies that the bourgeois system only offers illusory freedom. Hitchcock's *Psycho* seems to illustrate how such a system always punishes the individual efforts at freedom — in any form. In the end, the "system" wins and the status quo is restored almost too neatly. Significantly, all the blood in *Psycho* occurs in the first half of the film and then is wiped away. The ending of the film, in which Lila's death at the hands of Norman/Norma is prevented by Sam Loomis, is, quite literally, bloodless. *The Grifters*, however, pushes the bloodletting to the end of the film. And in linking the blood to the money Lilly desires — and to life and potency themselves — dissolves the illusion that there is some kind of wall of propriety that stands between the symbol of power (money) and its possession and efficacy (blood). Lilly instinctively *knows* that "freedom" in the system is masked "dependence on the money-bag, on corruption, on prostitution." But Lilly is not interested in changing the system: she interested in surviving it. In a sense, however, her final act *is* the proletariat rising up against bourgeois propriety and dominance to seize, in a sense, what has been stolen from her. Lenin's implication is that "freedom" within the reigning power-structure is either impossible or illusory — but Lilly's escape suggests an alternative.

Before the confrontation between Lilly and Roy at the end of the film devolves into violence, Roy suggests that his forcing her to go straight is what "she needs." And he seems to believe that he holds all the cards — since he doesn't really believe that Lilly will "do anything ... to live." He tells Lilly that even if she took his money it wouldn't last forever and she have to go back to the "racket" and then she'd be under the thumb of another Bobo Justus. By refusing to give her the money, Roy says, "you've got to go the square route. You could send me a card when you're settled, I could help you out sometimes." Lilly's response reveals her identification with Norma/Norman in *Psycho*. For Roy's suggestion is tantamount to asking Lilly to fully capitulate to the role reserved for a woman of her station — the "square" life in the "legit" world. And just as Marion Crane's admission of her error and her expressed desire to go back to the status quo ignites a murderous fury in Norman/

Norma, Roy's suggestion infuriates Lilly. She shouts, "That's what it is, isn't it? Keep me down. Your turn to be in charge. Have the power."

 Lilly says out loud what has been implied in both *Psycho* and *The Grifters*: that all relationships are moneyed relationships and all moneyed relationships are gendered. *Psycho* wants you to think it's a movie about money when it's a movie about sex; *The Grifters* wants you to think it's a movie about money when it's a movie about sex. But, taken together, they suggest something else as well: movies about money are always about sex and movies about sex are always also about money. *Psycho* suggests that the intersection of power, sex, and money is necessarily "dirty." *The Grifters* acknowledges this reality — but the character who, in the end, *makes* the world of the film her own does something the other female characters fail to do: she acknowledges the intersection of power, money, and sex and mixes them all together, *money/bloody/body* and, in doing so, makes a *clean* break.

Notes

1. In the original and final drafts of the script, Marion Crane's name was actually "Mary," but was changed to "Marion" after it was discovered that there was a real "Mary Crane" living in Phoenix, Arizona. I have changed the name to "Marion" to avoid confusion.

Works Cited

The Grifters. 1990. Second Draft: Donald Westlake. March 1989.
Habib, M. A. R. *The Johns Hopkins Guide to Literary Theory & Criticism.* Michael Groden and Martin Kreiswirth, eds. Baltimore: Johns Hopkins University Press, 1994.
Heimpel, Rod S. "Hitchcock's *Psycho* in Stephen Frear's *The Grifters*." *Canadian Journal of Film Studies* 3, no. 1, 1994.
Psycho. Dir. Alfred Hitchcock. Perf. Anthony Perkins. 1959. Film.
Sandis, C. "Hitchcock's Conscious Use of Freud's Unconscious." *Europe's Journal of Psychology* 3 (2009). Qtd. from Simmons, Jonathan. "The Pervert's Guide to *The Birds*." *Bright Lights Film Journal*, No. 69, August 2010. http: //www.brightlightsfilm.com/69/69birds_simmons.php.

Replicants and the Commodity Form: A Marxian Reading *of* Blade Runner

J. Eric Lambert

I love *Blade Runner*. Impossible to pigeonhole, the movie blends elements of dystopian science fiction, film noir, and rumination on self-consciousness and personal identity. Visually fascinating, moody, paced by a musical score at times ethereal and other times nostalgic, *Blade Runner* is also thematically complex and polyvalent, inviting viewers to reflect on questions of free will, memory and mortality, and concerns about corporate power and social inequality. To date (i.e., 2010), there have been eight film adaptations of novels or short stories by science fiction writer Philip K. Dick (hereafter PKD). The movies vary in quality and fidelity to PKD's work, but I believe *Blade Runner* is the most inspired and fully realized of them all. The film has such artistic integrity that it stands alone as a cultural work, justly meriting consideration in its own right, independent of the source novel. Yet *Blade Runner* preserves, even complements and enriches the philosophical vision of PKD's classic, *Do Androids Dream of Electric Sheep?*

In this essay, I offer a novel interpretation of *Blade Runner* that draws on Marxist theory. More exactly, I develop a new interpretation of the meaning of the Nexus 6 replicants, a reading that draws on what Marx called the "commodity form." But, as just mentioned, there are many perspectives from which the film can be viewed. For example, it could be seen as an allegory of race. Manufactured as slave labor for humans on the Off-world colonies, replicants are legally forbidden from returning to Earth and either denied a memory (created without memory) or else given a falsified memory, so that, unaware of their origins, they are more easily controlled. This interpretation is strengthened when a police officer calls the replicants "skin jobs," an epithet that stereotypes and distances them from biologically reproduced human beings. Or one could view the movie as a statement on inequality and state/corporate authoritarianism, depicted powerfully by a juxtaposition of the crowded and hardscrabble life on the streets, and the soaring, pyramidal corporate headquarters that dominate the skyline. Finally, the film can be seen as a philosophical reflection on personal identity. Is memory the glue that binds a person's identity? What if those memories are "implants"? *Blade Runner* prompts viewers to consider *what it is* to be distinctly human. Just what separates (and morally distinguishes) the human from the nonhuman?

To anticipate my later analysis of Marx, I want to begin with some observations about the concept of the commodity form. A commodity is an object made by human beings. It possesses *use value* (e.g., satisfies a need) as well as *exchange value* (that by virtue of which one object can be exchanged for another of equal value). Unlike natural objects, such as trees, stones, or rivers, commodities in a developed market society are, according to Marx, produced *for the purpose* of being exchanged; so that, although every commodity satisfies some human need, the essence of a commodity (the source of its value) is not what it helps us do but, rather, its *exchangeability* with other commodities. Said differently, in market societies the value of a commodity is established quantitatively and relative to other commodities (including cash, stock shares, natural resources, as well as a worker's skills).

Now, to say commodities are *manufactured* is to say they are made by human beings, so they are the product of human labor (effort, ingenuity, time). Marx refers to this as a society's available *social labor* and notes that the mass production of commodities requires an extensive and sophisticated *division of labor*, which increases the productive capacity as well as efficiency of that society. Controversially, Marx asserts that a commodity's exchange value is determined by the social labor time required to produce it, so that social labor—or the aggregate effort of social actors—establishes a *universal equivalence* among commodities: a standard, that is, by reference to which given commodities possess more or less value. The implication is worth spelling out. What establishes a commodity's exchange value, which is its *actual* value in market societies, is not some quality or feature of the thing itself, but the social labor time "accumulated" or "stored up" in the process of making the thing. The exchange value of a commodity is relative to other commodities; but since the true source of a commodity's value is human labor, what is in truth being exchanged is the human effort, time, and creativity embodied in the commodity. For this reason, Marx maintains that exchange value (or the *commodity form*) expresses a social relation: or rather, *is* a social relation and not a relation between things, as it appears to be when people exchange money for goods and services, for example.

We typically assume that a commodity is more or less valuable because of some quality it possesses. It costs *this* much because it has *these* qualities.

Such qualities constitute the thing's value, whether that value consists of sex appeal, youthfulness, or a commitment to world peace. (A Humvee is powerful, not the owner. And no human says "I love you!" as convincingly as a diamond.) When people experience objects as having qualities like power, earnestness, or sex appeal, they lose sight of the human origin of those qualities; they fail to note that *human agency* endows the object with those qualities.

Perversely, they come to think that objects have these qualities and that humans gain such values as they consume commodities. It is as though things had skills, virtues, and a sense of purpose, and humans a merely subsidiary and accessory role. In this way, people experience themselves as subject to the product of their own activity, just as humans are subject to the vicissitudes of hurricanes and cancer. When people confront the things they have made as though those things were (collectively) an external, independent agency, their experience of social reality (relations, practices, etc.) is *mystified*: distorted not only in reflection but also in practice. Marx's concept of the commodity form provides the lens through which we should understand the replicants in *Blade Runner*. They are the commodity form incarnate, an embodiment of the Truth of Capitalism, which is that objects of human labor appear to achieve independent agency, appear to turn and to confront their makers, the humans who, in the face of their own creation, feel less real, less assured of their own reality.

Because the film invites multiple readings, I do not propose that my interpretation is the definitive or single best way to understand the movie. Whatever guiding metaphor one adopts to make sense of the film, *Blade Runner* is too rich and complex to reduce to a single overarching frame. So while the reading I propose is compelling and amply supported by plot narrative and action, it is not the only plausible way of making sense of the film.

To appreciate fully the philosophical depth and substance of *Blade Runner*, it is necessary to have some familiarity with the source novel, *Do Androids Dream of Electric Sheep?* So after summarizing the film's plot, I briefly discuss the novel in order to identify an important contrast between the two. There are different versions of the movie, the 1982 Theatrical Release and the 1992 Director's Cut. I will refer to the Director's Cut, which is the version endorsed by director Ridley Scott, and offers the following advantages. The Director's Cut removes the final scene where Deckard (a police "bounty hunter" who "retires" replicants) and Rachel (a replicant who becomes intimately involved with Deckard) escape to green fields somewhere "in the North"—a happy ending, perhaps, but out of character with the rest of the film. The Director's Cut restores, on the other hand, Deckard's dream of the unicorn, a scene integral to the film's suggestion that Deckard is a replicant. The 1992 release in this way better preserves the philosophical import of the novel, while being the more cinematically forceful of the two film versions.

Commentaries on *Blade Runner* regularly note that the replicants are tragic figures, beings with whom viewers can identify and empathize. Biogenetically engineered androids, the replicants are manufactured to provide labor for humans who have relocated "Off-world." They have "incept" and termination dates, i.e., a built-in lifespan. The Nexus 6 (the latest model) are equipped with "memory implants" to serve as a buffer, a type of "cushion" for their elementary emotional responses. The replicants are biological beings possessing intelligence, emotions and memory, such that they begin to question their origins, develop an awareness of their mortality, and form a desire for "more life"—a desire to continue living, to persist in their being.

Consigned to work Off-world, a band of six replicants has hijacked a ship, murdered the crew, and returned to Earth. The reasons why are initially unclear, although we soon learn that the replicants have an interest in the Tyrell Corporation, the company that manufactures the Nexus 6 generation. Roy Batty, a "military model," is the leader of the group. He is astute, charismatic, and as physically powerful as he is graceful. Pris is a "standard pleasure model." Roy's mate, so to speak, she is at once seductive and sinister, girlish and eerie. Leon is a plain worker model. Strong, sturdy, resolute, he demonstrates little initiative but acts decisively once directed. Zhora is alluring and bold; womanly, in contrast to Pris' girlishness. She is also lethal, designed to be a "political assassin." On their return to Earth, one of the six replicants is killed trying to enter the headquarters of Tyrell Corporation. The final replicant is never overtly identified, though we can surmise that it is Rachel, who is introduced in the film as Tyrell's personal assistant. That is, the character "Rachel" ostensibly works for Tyrell, but we quickly learn that (though she at first has no idea that this is so) she is a replicant.

Some of the replicants have learned the truth about themselves: they are biological robots manufactured to labor for humans, performing dirty or dangerous work as well as those tasks that exceed human physical and mental abilities. And though it is unclear whether this is by intent or a brute biological limit, the replicants have a four-year lifespan. Once they attain awareness of their brief duration, they begin to experience fear, confusion, and pitched resentment and anger, a sense of injustice that they have been created only to be used as instruments, and then to die. They return to Earth to seek out Eldon Tyrell, the engineering wizard who conceived them, and demand that he give them "more life." But because they are dangerous and more powerful than humans, they are forbidden to return to Earth, on penalty of death. A special branch of police called "blade runners"—described as "bounty hunters," they are actually assassins—has the task of locating and "retiring" (i.e., killing) fugitive replicants. Rick Deckard, the film's protagonist and a skilled "blade runner," is abruptly (and unwillingly) called back into service, after having quit police work for reasons never spelled out. The action of the film then plays out like a classic detective story—Deckard hunts the replicants, who in turn pursue their quarry, Eldon Tyrell.

The dawning self-awareness of the replicants—the confusion, anxiety, and yearning that accompany it—is made more poignant by our knowledge that they were produced solely to live as slaves. Whether seen as a cautionary tale of authoritarianism or an existential dramatization of "the human condition," the movie clearly tries to elicit understanding and empathy in viewers. Though made by genetic engineers, the replicants love, fear, hope, and question the meaning of their existence, as (presumably) do their creators. In this sense, then, they are "like us." Indeed, as Tyrell, the "God of biomechanics" affirms, they are "more human than human."

The concern with empathy is presented very differently in the source novel, however, and much of the depth and weight of the film is lost if we fail to note the difference. The novel does not exhort readers to empathize with the androids (the novel refers to them as "androids," not "replicants"); it does not portray androids as having begun to develop empathy and thus as more "like us" than henceforth realized. PKD's concern in *Do Androids Dream...?* is diametrically the *opposite*: a warning, not an exhortation. In the novel, the androids are cast not as sympathetic figures but as "predators," lacking emotion as well as empathy. Physically and mentally gifted, androids feel no emotional connection to other living things. For this reason they are disturbing, alien, even loathsome to the humans who encounter them.

For PKD, empathy is a defining characteristic of the human. The utter lack of empathy, in turn, defines the android. Recall (in both novel and movie) the design and purpose of the V-K ("Voigt-Kampff") Test. Sensors are attached to the subject's body, including an optical device trained on the eye, at which time the subject is presented with various scenarios to which he or she is to offer a verbal response. Each scenario describes a type of suffering. The equipment registers and records spontaneous, pre-reflective physiological reactions (pupil dilation, a blush, etc.), which are then studied. The emphasis on *pre-reflective* reactions is important since, like sociopaths, the androids are adept at ascertaining the details of a situation and simulating what they conclude to be the appropriate emotional response. They are proficient at feigning empathy, at mimicking emotions they do not feel. By contrast, humans are *affective* creatures, defined not solely by intellect or reason but also by empathy with other sentient beings. Thus, the V-K Test distinguishes between human and android by registering the pre-reflective physiological signs of empathy with suffering creatures.

The worry expressed in *Do Androids Dream...?* is that humans are suffering a deadening of emotion, a "flattening of affect." Put starkly, PKD does not prompt readers to consider that the androids are becoming more like us, but that *we* are becoming more *like them*. Humanity is losing empathy, the ability to share in the joys and commiserate in the sufferings of others. This point is almost never discussed in connection with *Blade Runner*, and yet it forms a vital contrast between film and novel. On the first page, in the *first sentence* of the novel, PKD warns us of the enervation of human emotion: "A merry little surge of electricity piped by automatic alarm from the mood organ beside his bed awakened Rick Deckard." In the novel, the "Penfield mood organ" is an ordinary appliance, like an alarm clock or a coffeemaker. Everyone has one. Like other appliances, it has various settings that allow people to program in different moods, adjust for intensity and duration of the mood selected, set start times, and so on. One day Deckard's wife, Iran, opts for "a six-hour self-accusatory depression," which annoys Rick but suits her just fine. After a nuclear war in which most of the animals on the planet have died, radioactive fallout and ecological wastage have become the norm, and as many humans as could have left Earth for "a new life!" on the Off-world colonies, it seems *perfectly reasonable* to Iran to feel depressed. The apartment complex in which she and Rick live is nearly vacant, devoid of noises, voices, and activity. Emptiness reigns. Iran notes:

> Although I heard the emptiness intellectually, I didn't feel it. My first reaction consisted of being grateful that we could afford a Penfield mood organ ... then I realized how unhealthy it was, sensing the absence of life ... and not reacting.... That used to be considered a sign of mental illness; they called it "absence of appropriate affect." So I left the TV sound off and I sat down at my mood organ and I experimented. And I finally found a setting for despair.

Having dialed up the mood of despair, PKD remarks that Iran "showed satisfaction, as if she had achieved something of worth."

Notice what is established at the start of the novel. People have become so desensitized, so dehumanized that they no longer feel determinate emotions. They need machine assistance, technology, simply to feel. They use an appliance to produce moods, to generate an emotional connection to themselves, to others, and to their environment. The V-K Test was supposed to distinguish between android and human based on evidence of empathy, the ability to experience others as feeling beings. But already we learn that humans are increasingly unable to experience ordinary emotions and feelings, much less empathy. So the concern expressed in the novel is not that humans fail to recognize the degree to which androids (a human artifact) have become like us; but that we fail to see the degree to which the human world has been enveloped in thinghood, absorbed into the insensate domain of objects.

None of this shows (nor do I claim) that *Do Androids Dream...?* is a "Marxist" novel. Warnings about the instrumentalization of human relations, social inequality, and corporate domination are themes found in the Marxist tradition, articulated explicitly or by implication in Marx's writings and in the work of later Marxist theorists. But to criticize social inequality and corporate hegemony does not make a criticism uniquely Marxist, any more than condemnations of lying or infidelity make a rebuke Christian. Ingredient to a properly Marxist account of such trends would be an historical narrative linking tensions between the forces and the relations of production, on one side, to social conflict and qualitative historical change, on the other. While neither *Blade Runner* nor *Do Androids Dream...?* develops such a narrative, both film and novel express concerns about dehumanization, objectification, and a "flattening of affect," which are central themes in the writings of Marx and Western Marxism. And the claim that certain types of *social organization* can essentially distort subjectivity, relationships, and knowledge of social reality dovetails especially well with Marx's conceptions of alienation and commodity fetishism.

While *Blade Runner* reverses the evaluative scheme (urging viewers to see the replicants as *like us* rather than worry we are becoming *like them*), the reversal is incomplete. Initially, the film seems to express less suspicion of technology than does the novel. The replicants are sophisticated achievements of bioengineering; and their ability to communicate, question, and desire intimates that the boundary between creator and created is permeable, that human-made artifacts can not only simulate but also attain a form of self-awareness. And yet the film clearly hints that Rick Deckard is a replicant; that, in fact, he is uncertain of *what he is*; that his memories and personal identity are a composite of (artificial, manufactured) "implants."

Furthermore, as many commentators have noted, there is the portrayal of stark economic inequality, environmental devastation, police control, and sheer corporate might. With regard to the last point, recall that it is the *replicants* the police aim to control and regulate. The replicant-as-commodity, Deckard says in passing, can be "a benefit or a hazard." Nowhere in the film is Tyrell, the corporate magnate who engineered the advanced (and dangerous) Nexus 6, held accountable; and nowhere is the question of corporate responsibility for producing the replicants even raised. In fact, the goals of Tyrell Corporation are *in conflict* with those of the public and the police. Why is Tyrell Corporation designing replicants that cannot be detected by the police? If replicants are dangerous, why does Tyrell design them *in order to be* undetectable? But the police never pressure Tyrell to stop. Instead, they clean up the mess he creates as though the police were an extension of a private corporate security force. An additional observation worth noting at this point: consider the contrast between the office of Bryant, a police captain, and the headquarters and bedroom of Tyrell. Bryant's office is dingy, cluttered, dimly lit. It looks like a janitor's closet. Tyrell's headquarters and living space, by contrast, are in an actual pyramid: the building that houses his corporate headquarters and apartment is shaped like a pyramid and taller than any other building in the film. The rooms are spacious, elegant, *palatial*. Police live in run-down apartments and work in shabby offices, while corporate heads live and work in palaces.

Such considerations suggest that *Blade Runner* is not an uncritical paean to technological advance, nor a mere homage to or postmodern "celebration" of the blurring of subject and object, self and alter. It seems safer to say that the film is marked by a *fertile ambivalence* that resists univocal and overarching interpretations, and so can equally well be seen as an allegory of race, a reflection on personal identity, an allusion to burgeoning class-consciousness, and so on. But insofar as one reflects on *Blade Runner* from a Marxist standpoint, it is helpful to move beyond merely adventitious observations about social hierarchy, inequality, and the like, and try instead to examine the movie with distinctly Marxist concepts and arguments. As I show momentarily, Marx's explication of the commodity form provides an especially fruitful way of doing so.

Marx develops the concept of the commodity form most fully in volume one of *Capital*, a sprawling, often dense work that combines economic analysis, sociology, historical studies, and a theory of social knowledge. For the sake of readability, I refrain from close textual exegesis and instead approach the concept of the commodity form by examining two related concepts, i.e., alienation and commodity fetishism. For these two concepts help to unearth the *critical content* of Marx's analysis of the commodity form, which intends not only to grasp how a capitalist economy works but, equally important, to illuminate how economic practices can distort people's understanding of their own activity, social roles and relations, expectations and beliefs, and so on. In light of this analysis, I return to *Blade Runner* in the following section to show how the replicants epitomize and concretely embody the commodity form.

Alienation is an evocative concept. It can refer to a determinate (if vaguely conceived) *emotion*, as when a person feels separated from and unable to communicate with co-workers, neighbors, and the like. You feel a sense of disquiet, of unease. Or it can refer to a persistent dissonance or fracturing of *thought*, as when a person fails to see the reasons behind another's expectations or demands. You lack the words, the frame of reference for making sense of the circumstances and events affecting you. Less familiar to modern ears is an economic meaning of alienation, which refers to the *exchange* or *transfer* of goods. For example, a person "alienates" her labor when she exchanges her time and effort (i.e., her work) for food, healthcare, or oxygen.

Explicated in connection with his analysis of private property in the *1844 Manuscripts*, Marx's conception of alienation incorporates all of these meanings. Put differently, for Marx alienation characterizes a historically sensitive form of human experience. A way of relating to nature, society and oneself, alienation arises from (and is conditioned by) the economic activities by virtue of which a people survive and perpetuate their way of life. That is to say, Marx argues that alienation emerges when property (or the "means of production," such as land, energy, food production) is privately owned. For when a society's means of production are privatized, then those without property (the poor) are reduced to dependence on others (property owners) for the staples needed merely to survive. For this reason people "get jobs," seek paid work at least to be able to satisfy basic needs. But the voluntary appearance of employment is deceptive; or rather, the coercive nature of the work relation is "veiled" by the labor contract, which appears to situate worker and owner as free equals. In reality, however, if one does not own property, then she has few alternatives (hunger and homelessness?) to working for another.

Work done under such conditions appears voluntary, since one can refuse a particular job or change jobs, but is a form of compulsion. To accept a job in order to avoid destitution is not a meaningful "choice," or exercise of personal freedom. Marx therefore argues that when property is privatized, the labor of those with little or no property is alienated. For the worker must sell (i.e., "alienate") her labor power — her effort, time, creativity — in exchange for wages needed to survive. And the thing she makes is both owned by and conceived solely in accord with the plan and purposes of another, namely her employer. Irrespective of the industry — oil drilling, factory work, or coal mining — the rate and efficiency of the production process as well as the type of thing made, the target market, and the quantities in which it is manufactured, are decided not by those who perform the productive labor but, rather, by owners and their delegates. Such work is not experienced as intrinsically rewarding, since workers make few (if any) meaningful decisions about their working conditions; nor as expressive of human ingenuity or creativity, since workers have little (if any) practical input about *what* gets made and *for what* purposes.

Alienation thus characterizes the emotional and intellectual experience of the worker *as* a worker. Because the object of a worker's effort is owned by and conceived according to the plan of another, Marx describes the experience as a "loss of reality": i.e., as the *becoming alien* of the fruits of a person's practical agency. From this directly economic kernel (i.e., the work situation) another facet of alienation coalesces and ramifies, affecting a worker's social relations as well as her self-understanding. As she *lives* her dependence and vulnerability, feels it in her bones, so to speak, her values, beliefs and expectations assume an instrumental and strategic cast. She judges her worth (and that of others) in light of primarily economic criteria: independence, productivity, professional status, and achievement. The social conflict between labor and management is one manifestation of such alienation. A more subtle form manifests in hostility between workers, as when Hispanics in the U.S. are accused of "taking our jobs" or the poor denounced as "lazy and unmotivated." When people view others as rivals, obstacles or competitors, and view themselves as "owners" of "marketable skills" (among which is the ability to "sell oneself"), then alienation pervades society, structuring and saturating economic practices as well as social relations, moral beliefs, cultural attitudes, and public policy. The social world itself then appears to be (or rather, is unreflectively *experienced as*) something alien: a type of "second nature," independent of and indifferent to a person's will; indeed governed by its own laws, gravitational and seismic forces, destructive potentialities and vicissitudes.

Put differently, Marx contends that, in advanced market societies, people experience and think about social reality *as though* it were a type of supernatural realm. The market assumes the *form* of a supernatural reality. Just as people sometimes interpret personal misfortune or natural disaster as a consequence of "God's will," so do they try to explain job loss or economic crisis as a consequence of "market fluctuations" or "volatility," as though "the Market" possessed its own objectivity and autonomy, independent of human agency. People thus experience themselves as *subject to* (threatened or controlled by) "market forces," when in reality the market is a product of their own activity — a social reality that humans have historically, collectively constituted. But the *apparent* autonomy and objectivity of the market obscures the possibility (and so, the belief) that production and distribution can be *rationally organized* so as to satisfy basic human needs. Instead we "let the market decide," trusting (piously) that "market-driven solutions" will present themselves.

For Marx, this acquiescence before the seeming autonomy of the market, combined with a disbelief in the power of humans rationally to manage a social reality they create, is a form of superstitious awe, a radically estranged understanding of human activity and its relation to the world. It is *as though* humans exist in order to serve the market: to facilitate production, "grow" industries and profits, await opportunities and innovations. In this way, commodities (or objects produced and exchanged by humans) seem to gain volition and purpose, and humans to augment and gain direction from economic activity. Or rather, commodities (i.e., the market, the totality of commodities) seem to acquire human traits like intelligence or strength, while humans ossify into mere functionality or serviceability.

In volume one of *Capital*, a penetrating analysis of capitalist economy published twenty years after the *1844 Manuscripts*, Marx resumes and deepens the analogy with religion. As just argued, when property (including human labor power) becomes privatized, economic processes and outcomes assume the appearance of an independent "second nature"—a type of supernatural reality. But part of what this means, Marx now adds, is that human-made artifacts become idols. Commodities become fetishes, objects imbued with special powers, traits, and value. A fetish (a crucifix, say) is an object made of wood, bone, or plastic that embodies and personifies a deity or spiritual agency. On reflection, we know that the object is just a thing, something fabricated by humans, so that whatever meaning it contains is given to it by us. And yet *we believe otherwise*, as any Christian can attest who imagines a crucifix being dunked in a pot of urine. Reflectively, we say the object "represents" or "symbolizes" what we revere. But in practice, in actuality, we regard *the object itself* as the revered. In a precisely parallel fashion, we regard commodities as having virtues, merits, values, even emotional vagaries. "We are not aware [we do this]," Marx says, "nevertheless we do it." (Slavoj Žižek suggests that what Marx *should* have said is: In fact, we are aware we do this, but we do it anyway.) And so, in developed market societies, it is as though commodities achieve volition and purpose, "entering into relation both with one another and the human race." Commodities become agents that confront humans, who subsequently find their own purpose and meaning vis-à-vis the economic activity of things.

This gloss on the concept of commodity fetishism offers a vantage point for appreciating the import of Marx's analysis of the commodity form. What *explains* the "enigmatic character" of the commodity? Marx answers: "Clearly [the] form itself. The equality of all sorts of human labor is expressed objectively by their products all being equally values ... [such that] the mutual relations of the producers ... take the form of a social relation between the products." This answer is hardly illuminating, as it stands. But a quick review of the link between the *value* of a commodity and the *social labor* that creates it will help to clarify matters.

Recall the distinction cited above between an object's *use value* and its *exchange value*. Use value consists of what an object enables us to do (e.g., harness energy) while exchange value consists of the ability of an object to be exchanged for another object of equal value. The chief question, the source of the "enigma," as Marx puts it, concerns the nature of exchange value. If an object can be exchanged for another of equal value, then *by virtue of what* is this equivalence established? Marx's answer is as simple as it is controversial. What determines a commodity's value is not some quality of the thing, such as durability, versatility, luster or comfort. Instead, what determines a commodity's value is the amount of work—or the quantity of social labor as measured in time—required to make the thing. So when we speak of a commodity's value, we may *think* we are referring to some quality of the object ("It's shiny!") but, in truth, we are unknowingly pointing at, or perceiving in a "mystified" form, the social labor time "congealed" in the manufacture of the object. For this reason, the exchange of commodities (e.g., paying for a computer) is not what it appears to be: a simple transfer of goods, in which you give someone money and she gives you a computer. Physically, of course, this occurs. But what *actually* gets exchanged is not only—nor most importantly—the thing itself, but the totality of human insight, effort, learning, and fatigue packed into the thing's conception and realization. More simply put, what gets exchanged is labor power—human exertion—not mere things.

A worker's contention that she is oppressed should thus be taken literally. In a concrete sense, economic relations are power relations, and economic inequality a "veiled" form of social domination. Corporations do not just "command enormous wealth"; they control and command the activities, schedules, and life plans of workers as well. We may not be aware of this, and yet *we live it*. From a lived, subjective perspective, the market (or the totality of commodities, their exchange relations, production and distribution processes) does not seem to be *a human work*, an institution that is itself the objective form and materiality of human relations, practices, meanings and norms. Rather, the economy seems to possess its own autonomy, lawfulness, and purposes, which may enhance (a home purchase) or devastate (a subsequent home foreclosure) the quality of a given individual's life. But if economic relations are power relations, and people's struggles to maintain or improve their standard of living expresses (in "veiled" form) a social conflict, then the proudly heralded "freedoms" and "equality" of advanced capitalist societies are, for the poor and the working class, not concrete realities but merely formal, abstract incantations.

Matters are different for commodities, however. Whereas the capitalist has power over the worker, an asymmetry which entails they are not substantive equals, a given commodity is equal to every other commodity insofar as each is measured against a universal standard. Since commodities are equal simply by virtue of being a commodity, no commodity commands another and the moral norm of universal equality has been realized. Only among things, not humans. Commodities similarly enjoy a freedom of movement and social mobility often denied humans. No matter how humble their origins, commodities can enter any home, enrich any workplace, and assume any social role or variety of meaning. In our enlightened times, all agree that no thing is intrinsically good or bad. ("Guns don't kill!" etc.)

And so, as Marx says, "the mutual relations of the [human] producers ... take the form of a social relation between the products." It is as though commodities form relationships, acquire purposes, and turn to confront their makers. As we will see momentarily, this fetishism of the products of human agency, this alienation and "loss of reality" whereby human meanings and values are divested from the social world and instead animated by things, is depicted movingly in *Blade Runner*. In *Capital*, Marx affirms that "the life-process of society, which is based on the process of material production, does not strip off its mystical veil until it is treated as production by freely associated men [sic], and is consciously regulated by them in accordance with a settled plan." This statement should be kept in mind in the following section. As I indicated above, few characters in the film *know what they are*, know whether they are human or replicant. And the humans—or at least those we assume to be human—seem to have little moral orientation, so that Tyrell pursues biogenetic innovations without regard for social well-being (hardly a rational and "settled plan") and Deckard, insofar as he believes he is a police officer *and* a human, resentfully acquiesces to his orders, which direct him to locate and kill replicants.

"The eyes have it"

Such is the title of a PKD short story, in which a nondescript man riding the bus home from work finds a paperback on one of the seats, begins to read it, and discovers to his horror that it reveals an "invasion of Earth by lifeforms from another planet," aliens "masquerading as ordinary human beings." Naturally this disclosure is ciphered, threaded into descriptions of what appear to be normal goings-on at a dinner party. But there are clues which, properly decoded, unveil the truth: "*His eyes slowly roved the room*," the novel says teasingly; and then: "*His eyes fastened on Julia*." But what sort of being is it that has detachable parts! our anonymous worker muses. Surely the novel's author *wants* the secret to be found out; else why would he openly describe such unearthly, nonhuman powers as these: "*...Julia had given her heart to the young man ... her eyes followed him all the way down the road and across the meadow.*"

Blade Runner makes no allusion to this short story. Nor are there aliens per se, except, in a figurative sense, the alienation produced when humans are confronted by their creation. Yet if the replicants do not have detachable parts, they do have "parts" that were designed and made in accord with consumer specifications. When Leon and Roy accost Chew, an eye design specialist who subcontracts with Tyrell Corporation, Leon leaves the inquiries to Roy and explores Chew's lab. Reaching into a tank of liquid nitrogen, Leon's hand instantly freezes. Puzzled, he removes his hand from the tank, stares at it, then sniffs it curiously. Later in the film, Pris dunks her hand in a pot of boiling water, pauses, and removes a hard-boiled egg. Her attitude was playful. She was trying to charm — or to intimidate? — J. F. Sebastian, a brilliant but childlike genetic designer who worked closely with Tyrell Corporation, and so could provide the replicants the access they desired. So while there are no floating eyes or extractable hearts, there is nonetheless something alien, even uncanny about the replicants.

More substantively, eye imagery and pointed allusions to vision abound in *Blade Runner*. Many of the allusions refer directly or indirectly to Tyrell, as when a frightened Chew tells Roy he should talk to Tyrell ("I just do eyes!" Chew protests) and Roy contemplatively replies: "Not an easy man ... to see." Similarly, after Deckard tells Rachel she is a replicant and she presses for more information, Deckard suggests she question Tyrell. Flustered, Rachel blurts: "He wouldn't *see me*!" These two scenes tell us much about the social world depicted in the film. As much a scientific genius as a ruthless businessman, Eldon Tyrell chooses who to see and who not to see, what to notice and what to ignore. Subtle, scheming, playfully aloof, he is untouched by the suffering of the replicants and unconcerned by any threat they pose to humans. As noted above, the police *do not want* replicants to be indistinguishable from humans. Replicants are dangerous; even those who evoke sympathy in the film have murdered people. The police aim to maintain order, but that task becomes more difficult when every test they devise for identifying replicants is subverted by Tyrell's ambition to ensure replicants *cannot* be so identified. Like a "modern Frankenstein," Tyrell is not only unfazed by the threat created when replicant is indistinguishable from human, he is intrigued by the technical challenge it presents. His concern is neither moral nor humanitarian, but technical. He wants to refine replicants so that they are "more human than human," and the engineering puzzles and difficulties captivate him.

Tyrell's attitude toward the replicants, and his relation to the police and public, support a Marxist reading of the film. He wields such power that he plays by a different set of rules. The police do not hold him responsible for the "hazard" his corporation produces. Instead they solicit information from him about the nature of the threat so that they can better contain it, even though Tyrell knowingly modifies his product to circumvent their efforts. The manufacture and further development of the replicants, moreover, has become detached from its original end, which was to reduce the need for human labor in the Off-world colonies. That goal has been accomplished, but Tyrell cannot rest content. Marx insisted throughout his life that it is of the essence of capital that it grow and reproduce, which might require the destruction of surplus goods, the creation of "false needs," or the planned obsolescence of a thing otherwise adequate to its purpose. And so, replicants are designed with a four-year lifespan. On the one hand, such a measure prevents the replicants from developing a memory and an articulate emotional life; on the other, it guarantees corporate control over their product and facilitates "turnover," ensures the product "moves." Although there is neither a need nor a socially responsible reason for doing so, then, Tyrell feels driven to enhance the Nexus 6 by equipping them with memory implants.

Significantly, Tyrell is the only character in the film to wear glasses. And his glasses are huge, covering nearly a third of his face. "Corrected vision" is a peculiar phrase, suggesting that glasses repair whatever flaw impairs one's sight: your vision used to be blurry, but now you have glasses so the flaw is "corrected." Of course glasses do not repair or fix the flaw that causes poor vision. The flaw remains; glasses just compensate for it. Tyrell's vision is terrible. Despite his singular brilliance, he *does not see well*. The importance of his impaired vision, underscoring as it does the eye imagery resonating through the film, merits attention.

Vision historically connotes knowledge, or, perhaps better, understanding. In Plato's "Allegory of the Cave," wisdom is gained after ascending out of the cave's shadows into the clarity of sunlight, in which radiance the genuine value and meaning of things is illuminated. In different centuries and by various thinkers, moral conscience as well as the ability to reason has been likened to a "natural" or "inner light," which guides thought, decision and action. Everyday language seamlessly preserves the association of vision and understanding, as when I implore my lover to "see what I'm saying!" and she replies: "but you need to see things from my perspective first!" At such times, a "light comes on," and I have "a clearer idea" of what to do. *Moral* vision is a type of *attention*, a taking-notice-of that involves perceiving something's value, observing its relations to other things, grasping its uniqueness—in short, understanding why the thing *matters*.

A failure of vision, in this sense, would imply moral blindness, a degradation of one's ability to perceive, feel, and judge. The multifaceted value of an object might be reduced to its functionality; the value of a person, misshapen by strategic considerations that engender distrust, hostility, or simple indifference. As discussed in the last section, Marx's concepts of alienation and commodity fetishism account for such distortions in human relations and experience through an analysis of their origin in the commodity form. As economic activity is detached from social ends, the product of human agency appears to assume a life of its own, its own purposiveness. Social relations come to seem thing-like in character, a nexus of *means* disconnected from moral *ends*, while relations between objects come to appear social in character, or as relations governed by norms and values.

Tyrell has poor vision. He does not witness a world of fear, loss, hope and love. Rather, he surveys data: hypotheses, probabilities, efficiencies, as well as stock prices and advantageous chess positions. Like Frankenstein, he is emotionally stunted, a technocrat whose knowledge is amoral, purposeless, and therefore alien to human *cares*. Because he fixates on means divorced from ends, the problems he wants to solve are not human problems. Of course, this is not simply a character flaw of Tyrell. It is a flaw of the (capitalist and hyper-industrialized) social reality presented in the film. Tyrell is only a representative of a social type that is—as Marx would put it—"called into existence" by a particular form of socio-economic organization.

Deckard first meets Rachel in a Tyrell Corporation conference room. Unaware that she (or he himself) is a replicant, he mutters: "Replicants are like any other machine. Either they're a benefit or a hazard. If they're a benefit, they're not my problem." Deckard just wants to do his job; and his job does not include questioning the rationality of resource management or the moral quality of economic decisions. That is to say, Deckard's "internal life" is exhausted in his social function. It is not till the end of the film, when he suspects he may be a replicant, that he evinces doubt or uncertainty concerning his actions. And consider Roy's exquisitely ambiguous remark to Chew, the eye designer: "If only you could see what I have seen, with your eyes." (Don't take my word for it: see it with your own eyes! And: I've seen things, using the eyes you created in a lab.) Here, the commodity assumes human form, achieves subjective awareness. There is a vision that the commodity possesses and that humans lack. The object has become subject, and the subject object. Roy is eloquent. He acts on reasons. Chew sputters in half-sentences; stares dumbly, uncomprehendingly, at the idols before him.

In this connection, Slavoj Žižek's take on commodity fetishism is especially illuminating. In a capitalist society, where the commodity form structures and saturates social reality (norms, relationships, common-sense beliefs), it is as though commodities have experience *in place of* humans. For example, Žižek argues that a laugh track does not "tell us" when to laugh. On the contrary, it laughs *for us*, it laughs *so that we do not have to*. We are amused; but it is the thing that expresses our amusement *for us*. In like fashion, things see for us—they *bear witness* so that we do not have to. Think of the family vacation; perhaps the first trip abroad. Just as you would not forget to bring along your child, so would you not forget to bring a camera. Cameras see for us, as anyone knows who has poked a friend and said, breathlessly, "Wouldn't that make a great picture?" Observing some splendid vista—*snap!*—you form a memory of the site vis-à-vis the camera. In fact, you *judge* the site as "beautiful" from the viewpoint of how "nice a picture" it will make — later, when you stare at the photo with friends and tell them what a "wonderful time" was had. But when *you are there*, present at the base of the Aztec Pyramid of the Sun, it is the camera that looks, notices, captures color and reflection, and (literally) "takes in" the splendor. And so Roy says, "Chew, if only you could see what I have seen, with your eyes."

More striking still is the confrontation between Roy and Eldon Tyrell, Roy's Father and Maker. When Tyrell asks why he has come, Roy answers: "I want more life, *fucker.*" Tyrell then explains (or purports to explain: he may be lying) that the four-year lifespan is an insurmountable biological limit; attempts to extend replicant life beyond four years have failed. Yet Roy persists, demands to explore every experimental possibility for prolonging his life. Tyrell interrupts, proclaiming:

> But this, all of this, is academic. You were made as well as we could make you.... The light that burns twice as bright burns half as long. And you have burned so very, very brightly, Roy. Look at you — you're the Prodigal Son.... You're *quite a prize...*

Roy sits and lowers his gaze. Tyrell caresses his head. Haltingly, Roy begins: "I've done ... questionable things." Immediately Tyrell interjects: "Also *extraordinary* things! *Revel* in your time!" And with a tired smile, Roy finishes: "Nothing the God of biomechanics wouldn't let you in heaven for." He then stands, holds Tyrell's head in his hands to kiss him, and slowly crushes his skull, completing the act by driving his thumbs deeply into Tyrell's eye sockets.

Roy gouges out Tyrell's eyes. More than a vengeful murder, putting out Tyrell's eyes is a punishment, an evisceration, literally a moral disembowelment. Roy sought out Tyrell to gain more life; or at least understanding, perhaps comfort or absolution. Yet Tyrell is obtuse, utterly oblivious to the moral question Roy gropes to ask. He speaks unhesitatingly about the technical complexities of biogenetics, but is so blind to the concerns that *enliven* experience that he cannot recognize a moral plea, much less offer consolation or counsel. The encounter between Roy and Tyrell is the apotheosis of commodity fetishism, the actualization of human alienation from the world they have created. For we witness that it is *things* (the replicants) that question, ruminate, and struggle to choose and act. Humans do, too. But meagerly. Their vision is so marred that they dumbly observe moral behavior in replicants, not in themselves, as though replicants were the subjects and they the objects.

Elsewhere in the film, Leon catches Deckard unawares on the street. "How old am I?" Leon demands, wanting to know how long he has left to live. Deckard punches him in the face. Slamming Deckard against cars and into a garbage dumpster, Leon says: "Painful to live in fear, isn't it? Nothing is worse than having an itch you can never scratch." He then forms a "v" with his fingers, announces "time to die," and begins to press his fingers into Deckard's eyes. Rachel saves Deckard by shooting Leon in the head. What is vital to note here is that *so far as he thinks he is human*, Deckard's "sight" is flawed (hence the uselessness of his eyes). He has just killed Zhora and would kill Leon without qualm, had Leon not got the drop on him first. Like Tyrell, Deckard is emotionally abstract, morally inanimate. As I mention below, only when he learns *he is a replicant* does Deckard "see" clearly, for it is then that he *feels* the moral value of Rachel.

In *Blade Runner*, the replicants grow, mature, and evolve psychically. Humans react. In Ralph Waldo Emerson's words, it is as though "things are in the saddle," not people. Indeed, the replicants engender and propel the existential ambiguities and moral tensions that make the film compelling. I have argued that the force of the drama is strikingly elucidated in Marxian terms.

Marx always maintained that a society's material practices and relations shape the subjective attitudes, beliefs, and values of individual social actors, as well as the objective (or publicly shared) patterns of belief, expectation, justification, and entitlement that are sedimented in and expressed through social institutions. Stated more simply: *what we do* conditions what we think, believe, and value, not the reverse. To lose sight of the *historical nature* of social reality, or rather, to regard economic relations, social roles, and the like as fixed, merely given pieces of the world is—as Marx so strikingly puts it—to experience a "loss of reality," an alienation from self, others, and the social world. For then, instead of experiencing society as the work of human hands, the totality of practices, goods and services, tradition and law, it appears as a mysterious, self-originating monolith standing over against human beings, with its own weight and density, independent of human will. Marx insisted that people thus experience social reality not as their creation, but as *itself* a type of agency. "The Market" is as an earthly god, acting according to its own norms, values, and will.

The parallel with religion is deliberate and exact. People once explained natural disaster and death by invoking "the will of God." Today, they recommend "letting the Market decide" how best to remedy mass unemployment, global warming, the lack of affordable healthcare, and so on. Knowingly or not, such recommendations concede impotence, a powerlessness to address problems human activity has produced. So it is in *Blade Runner*, where objects exhibit human qualities such as loyalty and fear, and humans "act" in solely functional ways. Roy's defiance of Tyrell signifies the incarnation of the commodity form, wherein the object, for its own purposes and reasons, faces and commands its maker. Crystallized in this scene is the truth of alienation and commodity fetishism: object becomes subject, and subject object. And insofar as the human proves unworthy of the artifact — his idol — so is he destroyed, shorn of his sightless eyes.

Some find religious symbolism in *Blade Runner*, both in Roy's patricide of Tyrell and especially in the penultimate scene when, Christ-like, Roy saves Deckard's life, releases a dove, and then dies. I agree there are religious overtones, but feel these are best understood in light of Marx's conception of commodity fetishism. By killing his Maker, "the God of biomechanics," Roy's transubstantiation is complete — he is *as a god*. The powers of creative, rationally free humans have been transferred to the object of their labor; an inversion of reality parallel to the regularly heard claim that job losses were the result, not of human decisions to maximize profit, but of anonymous "market forces." But Roy is a god that has killed several people in his quest for "more life." And he saves Deckard only so that a witness remains to preserve his memory, fearing his experience will otherwise subside "like tears in rain." An ambivalent god is Roy.

As depicted in *Blade Runner*, people drink, trade, and scurry in a world that is polluted, hyper-industrialized, by turns congested and empty, and highly stratified (with corporations and police at the top, and then "little people," i.e., everyone else). In many ways it exemplifies the concern raised by ecologist and theologian, Thomas Berry, who warned that the "wonderworld" promised by economic development and technological progress could easily degenerate into a "wasteworld," unfit for the sustenance of living beings. The harder we bang the rock, the more insensible the ringing and sparks make us. In the world of the film, it is not a commodious place that human ingenuity has created. If *that* is the world humans have made, it is not clear that the master achievement of that world, namely the replicants, should be viewed sympathetically.

After being saved by Roy, Deckard lay in the rain, blinking, trying to recover his wits. Meanwhile Gaff (an assistant to Captain Bryant) has been watching, his hovercraft idling nearby. He shouts approvingly: "You've done a man's job, sir!" Turning and taking a few steps toward his vehicle, Gaff pauses and, clearly referring to Rachel, yells back to Deckard: "It's too bad she won't live.... But then — *who does*?" This apostrophe volatizes the existential vertigo pervading the film, as few people know *what* they are, or know whether they *are* who *they think* they are. Human or replicant? Free, unique individual — or product of some anonymous external agency? Even the irony of Gaff's congratulatory "You've done a man's job!" is as brutal as it is wryly amusing, since Deckard is not a "man" but a replicant, a suspicion confirmed when he returns to his apartment to check on Rachel and finds an origami unicorn on the floor. Earlier in the film Deckard had dreamed (or perhaps had a sleepy reminiscence) of a unicorn, galloping slowly in a meadow, coat gleaming with light. As the two hurry from the apartment — Rachel is a replicant and therefore in danger — Deckard notices a tin foil origami unicorn on the floor. Picking it up with thumb and forefinger, he examines it, nods, and smiles humorlessly.

He knows. What had seemed introspective, personal, part of the texture of his interiority, is an object of reflection for others, a piece of knowable, manipulable data. And that realization completely alters the mood and meaning of the film, intimating that Deckard's care and love for Rachel *does not* signify a moral lesson learned — say, that at last a human has empathized with a replicant, learned to accept replicants in spite of their difference. *Deckard is himself a replicant.* His concern for Rachel, indeed their mutual trust and regard, signifies the actualization, even the consummation of the commodity form. By film's end, objects are so "human" that only they feel and know love. Humanity is otiose.

The eyes have it, then. Only not human eyes, which have lost their light, but the eyes of objects, artifacts "masquerading as ordinary human beings." Just as Marx presciently saw, over a century ago.

Works Cited

Blade Runner. Dir. Ridley Scott. Perf. Harrison Ford. Warner Bros., 1992. Film.
Dick, Philip K. *Do Androids Dream of Electric Sheep?* New York: Ballantine, 1996.
Marx, Karl. *Capital: A Critique of Political Economy.* London: Penguin, 1993.
_____. *Economic and Philosophic Manuscripts of 1844.* Blacksburg: Wilder Publications, 2011.
Žižek, Slavoj. *Welcome to the Desert of the Real.* London: Verso, 2002.

"Somewhere That's Green": The Dream of the Middle Class in Frank Oz's Little Shop of Horrors

TRACI J. COHEN

In 1960 Roger Corman released the camp horror film *Little Shop of Horrors*. This film was one of the lowest budgeted films that Corman made; in total it cost the studio $27,000 (Gomery 59). Twenty years later Alan Menken and Howard Ashman came together to create a stage musical version of this film. The plot deviates from the original movie in many ways; it basically keeps the original concept of a man, Seymour Krelborn, who works at a flower shop and grows a man eating plant he names Audrey II. In order to keep the wealth he has earned, and the affection of the woman he loves, he continues to feed humans to the plant after his initial hesitation at the thought of killing another human being.

In 1986, four years after the Broadway musical's release, director Frank Oz released a film version of *Little Shop of Horrors*. The biggest difference between the Oz version and the Broadway version is the ending. The Menken and Ashman incarnation ends with Audrey II devouring both Seymour and his love interest, Audrey. This scene is promptly followed by the audience being told that one of the advertisers who had been interested in signing Seymour as a company spokesperson has distributed cuttings from Audrey II across the nation. The original Broadway ending was filmed and shown to test audiences; they quickly shot it down.[1] The creator rushed and changed the ending of the film: Audrey and Seymour survive, destroy the evil plant and live happily ever after in middle-class bliss.[2]

Although each incarnation alters the story slightly each telling has one central conflict: class. In all three versions Seymour and Audrey live on Skid Row. Skid Row is pictured stereotypically — people who live there are broke, life is a joke, and depression is the norm. The director creates a world where the misery of living on Skid Row causes Seymour to do anything to earn money, but it is not just his environment that causes him to struggle for monetary success. Seymour is in love with a woman named Audrey, and he hopes to gain wealth to impress her. On Skid Row the poor are pitted against each other to get the attention of those who live uptown. Seymour takes this struggle to the extreme, killing his fellow residents of Skid Row to increase his social status.

There has been little direct scholarship about the 1986 film by Frank Oz, and less still that discuss the class struggle that dominates the storyline. Marc Jensen briefly mentions the struggle between classes, stating it is obvious. Instead, he focuses his argument on the depictions of race in the film. Carol Strohecker does make mention of this film in her essay about the chorus in film, but the mention is brief, lasting only one line and would not further any argument about *Little Shop of Horrors* unless the discussion centered solely on the use of the Greek chorus in modern film. The general lack of scholarship could stem from the idea which Babington discuss, that some musicals are less worthy of a critical eye than others. Levine may argue that this text is considered "lowbrow" or popular and therefore mainly looked at as solely for entertainment.

I will be discussing the 1986 film directed by Frank Oz, and the scene "Somewhere That's Green" in particular, using a Marxist lens. By doing so, I plan to examine what the middle class is seen to be and how the hopes of joining the ranks of the middle class keep the lower class in line.

If I am to be discussing Marxism I should first attempt to answer the question, "What is Marxism?" I do not plan on attempting to fully define Marxism, but to explain this term in relation to how it relates to my primary source. I find Marxism to be a misleading term; it implies that when one discusses anything in terms of Marxist theory they will only discuss class struggles. This concept is not entirely incorrect, but there is more to Marxist theory than class differences. In discussing language, Karl Marx stated:

> Language is as old as consciousness, language is practical consciousness, as it exists for other men, and for that reason is really beginning to exist for me personally as well; for language like consciousness only arises from the need, the necessity, of intercourse with other men.

Here, Marx shows language as originating from a need for human interaction. The need for human interaction is the core of human nature and fundamental to Marxist studies. But, the issue of human interaction is not an explicit belief laid out in some studies. These articles will often discuss how film culture itself promotes a capitalist culture and how big budget Hollywood films will not strongly oppose the capitalist regime because the creation of film is part of this regime.[3] For the purposes of this essay, I will be using Marxism in terms of how capitalist culture can destroy a person's ability to connect with others as well as the emphasis it puts on material possessions.

The basic plot for the 1986 film is Seymour Krelborn (Rick Moranis) works at a flower shop, Mushnik's Skid Row Flowers. The flower shop is on the verge of closing when Seymour introduces a strange plant he discovers in the flower district. He names this plant Audrey II (voiced by Levi Stubbs) after the woman he is in love with, Audrey (Ellen Greene). Although Audrey II is a huge success, there is one issue — Audrey II lives off of human blood. Seymour soon exhausts the miniscule supply that he himself can give and risks the death of the plant that had gained him so much wealth and status. Audrey II convinces Seymour to kill other citizens of Skid Row to feed him, and, in return, promises Seymour that his wealth "will surely rival King Tut's." Seymour commits two murders before deciding that he can no longer take the lives of his fellow human beings. The film ends with Seymour killing Audrey II and moving with Audrey to a home in the suburbs.

Before the first murder of the film is committed, there is a scene in which Audrey expresses her desire to move to the suburb and live a middle class lifestyle. The first stanzas of the song emphasize the qualities about Seymour that Audrey may like, but the lyrics quickly lapse into a catalogue of all the items Audrey wishes to own. As the song runs through a very simple list that includes — a patio grill, a disposal, washer, dryer, and ironing machine — Oz shifts its angle to show a copy of *Better Homes and Gardens* that Audrey has begun to flip through. Contained within these pages are painted images of women gloating over large home appliances. Oz situates this shot so that Greene's physical person is isolated from the images in this magazine; the only part of her physical body that is seen at the same time as these images are her manicured fingernails.

After giving a brief introduction to Audrey's dream the shot fades to green and re-opens to show a cardboard cut out of a house in the background and a fake lawn in the foreground. Moranis pushes a lawn mower over the false grass before waving to Greene who is behind one of the windows of the cardboard house. The perspective of the shot changes and now shows Greene sitting in a living room, looking out the window. She begins to dance around the room, allowing the viewer to get a full view of the room in the background. According to Julie Prewitt Brown:

> Susan Sanaka points out that the formal living room is rarely used in the American home. Accordingly, we may notice a certain unlived-in look in the living room and the suggestion in its arrangement of furniture that things are on display. [...] The bourgeois interior is meant to be shown.

Brown claims the typical living room in America is not a place for living. Instead, it is an opportunity to display what and how much one may have.

Rooms like these are kept in an almost museum quality state of preservation. The living room Audrey inhabits is almost frighteningly antiseptic, with plastic covering all of the furniture so that it will remain in the state of pristine cleanliness. In this fantasy world nothing can possibly destroy the world she worked so hard to maintain. Covers are placed on the furniture because if these objects were to get dirty it would ruin the pristine fantasy. The preservation of the fantasy extends even to the most natural of things. Oz creates a world where one must stop the air from becoming contaminated. The air is "Pine-Sol scented" and the scene shows Greene spraying an abundance of chemicals into the air around her head. Oz has created an existence where all the naturalness has been removed from the air and has replaced with a chemical that society has told women they will need to keep their home in perfect condition.

In this shot, and the ones that follow, the room in the background is seen clearly within the frame. In each of these shots the set is staged so that the walls are covered with shelving to hold the many items that are owned. Other items which appear in the backgrounds of these sets are human beings. One of the shots of this scene shows Greene bringing out a large tray of snack to a table crowded by women who listen to a saleswoman as she attempts to sell them Tupperware. Greene smiles over her guests but, other than placing the snacks down for her guests, she has no interaction with them.

Actually, it is not until roughly three minutes into this five minute segment of the film that Oz allows Greene to interact with another human being. This is the first shot in this scene where Oz places Greene and Moranis in the same room. The two actors are in a room together sitting on a couch eating frozen dinners as they watch *I Love Lucy* with their two children. Everything in this shot stands in stark contrast to previous shots in the scene. The song makes a petite change in pitch and becomes pacato, or calm. Earlier stanzas and shots were more preoccupied with the objects one could own and display, but in this scene there is an intimacy that was lacking in earlier moments. Although there are still items on display in the background and there is an emphasis on the "big, enormous, twelve-inch screen," this moment is more about time with the family. Also, the emphasis on the television screen is important because this item is made to be something of more import than it actually is. Although the song may indicate the television set is the main focus of the room, the images on the screen tell a different story. The children are placed in the foreground which would indicate that they are the most important feature in this shot.

The staging of the background in this shot is also indicative of what's truly important. The setting is drastically more intimate and although this room may still contain objects on display, these objects are much more personal than what has been shown up until this moment. For example, in the background there are some hand-drawn pictures that are clearly meant to have been made by the children. Brown does have something to say about the display of familial artifacts: "In the family room other forms of preservation appear: family photographs and relics, such as a bronzed baby shoe [...] The bourgeoisie like to leave traces of themselves, even in the most private spaces." In other words, even the most private of spaces and items are used as commodities, they may not earn a person wealth, but it gives them a form of status. It causes people to look at how much someone has and to look at how perfect the family seems to be. In the case of Audrey, these personal artifacts seem to be hidden in a room that breaks from the others rooms in the house. The television room in this scene appears small, because of the amount of clutter in the frame. Pillows and toys are removed from their typical homes and are placed haphazardly on the floor. The room is clean but, unlike the bourgeoisie living room, it gives a distinct impression of being lived in. This is the place where the family gets together; it is the room of social interaction. The children who have, up until this shot, not been mentioned or even alluded to, take up the bulk of the foreground. The room is filled with toys for them, but some of the furniture, like a rocking chair and a couch, are placed so that the parents may be included in this section of the home.

Another way this moment breaks from the commodification of the home is that the characters are having frozen dinners. Within the first few stanzas there Audrey associates herself with icons of the dramatic time period—cooking like the great Betty Crocker and looking like the quintessential homemaker, Donna Reed. But this moment does not conform to the ideology of the 1950s where women must cook every meal and cook it well. This scene shows the possible reality of the situation, women will not suddenly be amazing cooks because they now live middle-class lives, and they will still probably cut corners and use items like frozen dinners. Granted that in the 1950s frozen dinners would have been considered a modern miracle, they still break away from the classic image of Mrs. Cleaver making home cooked meals for her family at every chance.

Throughout this scene there is a clear distinction between the public and private space. The audience is reminded of their role as voyeur by Oz. Oz sets up this reminder by having various shots reveal that the audience is looking through a window into the scenery, indeed, often looking directly through the outside window where Audrey is watering plants in a windowbox, setting up the dramatic structure of observing without interacting with the scene. The fourth wall remains symbolically intact.

At the beginning of the dream sequence in this scene we are openly allowed into the interior of the home, but the window is a main feature in the opening shot because at first Greene is seen only through the window, and when Oz shows Greene she is looking out the window that we were looking at her through only a moment ago. Also, when Greene is watering her flowers during the Tupperware party the camera pans out and the audience is again looking at Greene through another window. Although the audience repeatedly gains access through these windows, Oz still creates areas where we are given limited access or are completely denied access. It is in the shot that is set in the family room where the audience's capacity to act as voyeurs begins to change. The audience may be able to observe the family in their private space, but the audience almost acts as part of the family; we too watch *I Love Lucy* with them. Yet when Greene and Moranis enter their bedroom, the audience has a door closed on them so that they may not enter. Despite an overreaching theme of displaying the commodity, Oz makes a clear distinction between the public space and the private space.

It is the dream of the middle class that keeps one from actually achieving any sort of success. Greene is trapped with the semi-sadist dentist, while longing for Seymour whom she says is the greatest. She must have one pair or the other: the financial security of the former without the abuse or the decent guy and financial instability of Seymour. This leaves the audience to wonder why Oz would still allow Greene to stay with an abusive boyfriend, Orin Scrivello D.D.S., especially because Oz seems to know how badly she is being treated and that Moranis would definitely be an upgrade. One scene in the movie shows Greene claiming that she, as Audrey, is not good enough for Seymour, and some might say that because Oz has created a character that has been abused which causes the character to have low self-esteem are the cause of her staying with Scrivello and not dating Seymour. I do agree this is a viable reason and may play into Oz's decision to keep Audrey and Scrivello together, but if one were to look at the scene where Mr. Mushnik encourages Audrey to dump Scrivello she states, "He's a professional." And an earlier line has her telling Mushnik, "He's a rebel Mr. Mushnik, but he makes good money. Besides he's the only fella I got." The character Scrivello is one of the more successful men on Skid Row. So, despite his abusive nature, Oz has Audrey continue to stay with him, and to not even consider Seymour as a candidate for a romantic relationship. As long as Oz continues to have Audrey fantasize about the perfect life that Seymour, who at the time is completely broke, cannot give her, she will repeat the same actions and forever be stuck on Skid Row.

This film warns society against commodity fetishism. By obsessing on material possessions, one may not be able to actually realize their dreams of gaining these possessions. And if one were to actually succeed in gaining the middle-class dream that Oz presents us with, what then? Oz's film seems to tell the viewer that when one achieves this dream it will not be the material possessions that are important, instead one will crave interaction with other people. So, in the end, humans will continually search for a connection with their fellow man, even if they destroyed this connection to gain class status.

Notes

1. Oz previewed the original ending to a test audience and they were shocked and horrified: "They hated us when the main characters died," Oz said. "In the play, they're eaten by the puppet, but you know they're coming out again for a curtain call. But the power of movies is different. They really believed in those characters and they were angry" (qtd. in Jensen).

2. Class is a difficult term to pin down. In this case the middle-class is, as the name would imply, in the middle. They have less monetary resources than the upper class, but have more wealth than those in the lower classes. For more information please see the works by Arthur Marwick, Erik Olin Wright and Gary Day.

3. Examples of this are the texts by Walter Benjamin, James Kendrick, and Mike Wayne.

Works Cited

Brown, Julia Prewitt. *The Bourgeois Interior*. Charlottesville: University of Virginia Press, 2008.

Gomery, Douglas. *A History of Broadcasting in the United States*. Malden, MA: Blackwell, 2008.

Little Shop of Horrors. Dir. Frank Oz. Perf. Rick Moranis. 1990. Film.

Marx, Karl. *Manifesto of the Communist Party*. Blacksburg: Wilder Publications, 2008.

Apocalyptic Redux:
(Re)Vision and Recognition
in Terry Gilliam's Twelve Monkeys

JEREMY BURNS

In a discussion of Brecht and the concept of estrangement, Ernst Bloch suggests that estrangement "occurs as the displacement or removal of a character or action out of its usual context, so that the character or action can no longer be perceived as wholly self-evident" (121). Estrangement, in other words, introduces a measure of doubt into the well-worn familiar. Moreover, as Brecht and Bloch both knew, estrangement opens a space for reconsidering the contradictions of a given cultural situation. As Bloch puts it, "[T]he beholder achieves insight by means of the estrangement-effect which can turn into its dialectical opposite — the recognition or "Aha!" experience; insight into what is closest to the beholder grows out of his amazement at being confronted with what is farthest away" (124). To this end, Terry Gilliam's *Twelve Monkeys* (1995) is a film heavily invested in estrangement. In particular, Gilliam's ironic restaging of the heroic, apocalyptic narrative unfolds in such a way that the film calls into question the expectations of renewal and liberation often associated with the apocalyptic story. In the space created by this displacement, *Twelve Monkeys* draws attention to the importance of recognizing the present moment as a vital site of struggle, hope and change.

The repetitive dream sequence of *Twelve Monkeys* is one of the most discussed aspects of the film, and not without reason. The airport killing that repeatedly unfolds on screen — first as James Cole's (Bruce Willis) recurring dream and then as the film's ambiguous climax — foregrounds the critical importance of circularity and repetition in *Twelve Monkeys*. Indeed, the film recycles narrative, setting and imagery, and through its use of the (science fiction) narrative conventions of time travel and postapocalypse, it elaborates a complicated weave of returns and repetitions. There is, however, a particular strategy at work in the way the film continually revisits the past. Like Cole's recurring dream, each repetition in the film is also a revision, an opportunity to recognize something new.[1] The film articulates this strategy in a particularly significant scene, in which Cole sits in a darkened theater watching Hitchcock's *Vertigo* (1958).[2] Realizing that he has seen the film somewhere before, Cole turns to Kathryn Railly (Madeleine Stowe), the woman who is quite literally the girl of his dreams, and says, "The movie never changes. It don't change, but every time you see it, because you are different, you see different things." Cole's insight — that seeing something again means seeing it differently — illustrates the logic of the many repetitions and returns orchestrated in the film. In its unrelenting and estranging circularity, *Twelve Monkeys* illustrates what Bloch hints at in the passage that opens this essay: there is a fundamental distinction to be made between perception and recognition, between looking and actually seeing.

Twelve Monkeys follows Cole's misadventures as he travels in time between a postapocalyptic future and the "present" world of the 1990s. In the future year of 2035 — Cole's present — a pandemic virus has decimated the human population and driven the survivors underground to live in a dystopian, prison-like society, where they are governed by a mysterious group of scientists. These scientists send Cole back in time on a mission to collect evidence about the initial release of the virus, which the scientists suspect happened in late 1996. Ostensibly, a pure sample of the virus will allow the scientists in the future to develop a vaccine and reclaim the surface of the planet. What is central in this premise is the film's recapitulation of the key concerns of apocalyptic narrative, concerns that the film systematically revises.

Twelve Monkeys' restaging of the traditional apocalyptic narrative is, in many ways, the central repetition of the film, one around which the film's other concerns inevitably coalesce. Moreover, *Twelve Monkeys* inverts this narrative in order to illustrate the circularity, contradiction and paradox of what might be called apocalyptic desire. As Lee Quinby points out, "Americans have been taught to reside in apocalyptic terror and count on millennial perfection...this imprecise yet overpowering belief system is a way of life" (2). This "way of life" is inherently a historical and amnesiac — paradoxically, the present is always in crisis, but the future always assured. As Quinby goes on to argue, such an apocalyptic perspective on history lacks a necessary measure of skepticism that would engender social and political critique (2); furthermore, such an apocalyptic perspective tends to gloss over the very real historical blockages of contemporary life, the structural limits of possibility in the present situation. The apocalyptic narrative at the core of *Twelve Monkeys*, by contrast, refuses to indulge the millenarian themes of liberation and redemption and focuses instead on the disorientation, limitation and suffering of its protagonist. In this thematic shift, the film defamiliarizes the common tropes of apocalyptic belief and illustrates the importance of recognizing the limits of change (and the limits of hope) in the present moment. Only after such recognition may change really begin.

Twelve Monkeys' restaging of the apocalyptic narrative subverts both the diegetic trajectories of that mythic structure — its inexorable drive toward redemption — as well as its conservative ideological orientation. Apocalypse, in the conservative imagination, often betrays an ambiguous attitude toward catastrophe. As in Martha Bartter's witty essay, "Nuclear Holocaust as Urban Renewal," widespread catastrophe can be conceived "both as obvious disaster and as secret salvation" (148). Bartter goes on to point out, "This covert message is usually overlooked ... but it powerfully influences our cultural subconscious" (148). In fact, this "covert message" is a kind of apocalyptic desire — an eschatological expectation of social and political simplification via disaster — that has roots in the religious millenarian imagination. The same desire, however, also informs the ideological undercurrents of many modern apocalyptic fictions, as well as a vast array of political rhetoric.[3] Indeed, what is particularly interesting — and problematic — about such apocalyptic desire is that it becomes a means of preserving and reaffirming the static identity of the dominant order: "The apocalypse would be the *definitive* catastrophe — not only final and complete but absolutely clarifying. It would unmistakably separate good from evil, true from false. [It] would replace the moral and epistemological murkiness of life as it is with a post-apocalyptic world in which all identities and values are clear" (Berger 8, emphasis original).

In other words, imagining the apocalypse becomes a way of negating historical change and resisting political difference. For instance, as in Phillip Wegner's insightful reading of the apocalyptic ending of *Terminator 3: Rise of the Machines* (2003), disaster often appears from the conservative perspective as an opportunity for the regeneration of a firm identity. Wegner explains, "It is precisely [John Connor's] failure [to stop the apocalypse] that also turns out to be John's personal triumph, allowing him to retrieve the heroic destiny that had been lost ... [and to] take up the mantle of leadership" (79–80). The operative ambiguity in *T3* is simply that, without Judgment Day — the artificial intelligence led nuclear annihilation that the entire *Terminator* franchise revolves around — John Connor would be denied the very thing his identity has come to be based on, a kairotic experience of his own messianic destiny.[4]

The tendency to view disaster as "secret salvation" and as an opportunity for regeneration is famously satirized in Stanley Kubrick's comic masterpiece, *Dr. Strangelove or: How I Learned to Stop Worrying and Love the Bomb* (1964). Kubrick's film demonstrates the contradiction of imaginatively reaffirming the dominant identity through violence. In the denouement of the film, once it is clear that global nuclear annihilation is inevitable, Dr. Strangelove (Peter Sellers) outlines a ludicrously funny plan for the continued survival of the (American) population. Surrounded by the president and his military advisors (tellingly all male, all white), the doctor begins to outline a plan for surviving nuclear fallout and gradually repopulating the country. He explains (in Sellers' wonderfully campy faux German accent):

> Mr. President, I would not rule out the chance to preserve a nucleus of human specimens. It would be quite easy at the bottom of some of our deeper mineshafts. Radioactivity would never penetrate a mine some thousands of feet deep ... of course it would be absolutely vital that our top government and military men be included, to foster and impart the required principles of leadership and tradition ... actually, we would breed prodigiously ... with the proper breeding techniques and a ratio of, say, ten females to each male, I would guess that they could then work their way back to the present Gross National Product within, say, twenty years.

As Dr. Strangelove describes this plan, the men listening to him become increasingly aroused by his ideas. Predictably, they link the urgency of repopulation to a renewal of Cold War competition with the Russians: survival and frenetic repopulation efforts become not only a human, but also a patriotic duty. The catastrophe of nuclear war, in this instance, mysteriously reinvigorates the patriarchal and militant identity of the dominant order, and, as if to drive the point home, Dr. Strangelove miraculously springs from his wheelchair (Mein Führer, I can walk!), literally erect at the libidinal possibilities suddenly facing him.

Such affirmative negotiations of apocalypse, however, privilege the reaffirmation of identity over the reality of suffering that accompanies disaster. As Elana Gomel points out, "[apocalyptic] scenarios are shaped by the eroticism of disaster" in such a way that "all apocalyptic and millenarian ideologies ultimately converge on the utopian transformation of the body (and the body politic) through suffering" (405–406). To the minds of the privileged "top government and military" men in Kubrick's film, for instance, the postholocaust world that Dr. Strangelove describes is something of a perverse utopia — allowing them to openly exercise their sex- and power-drives. Tellingly, however, Dr. Strangelove's plan downplays the suffering of millions (and this is, of course, one aspect of Kubrick's film that gives its irony such teeth).

In *Twelve Monkeys*, on the other hand, it is precisely suffering that comes to be the film's central concern. The apocalypse is imagined from an inverse viewpoint, from the perspective of those excluded from redemption, from "utopia"— those who, like James Cole, are left to suffer for the benefit of the dominant order. This inversion serves to defamiliarize the apocalyptic story, and to open a space for the viewer to recognize and reconsider the ways in which such stories overlook suffering, elide violence and regeneration and imaginatively reaffirm the dominant identity without skepticism.

Cole's suffering body, in fact, grounds *Twelve Monkeys*' attention to the contradictions of apocalyptic desire and apocalyptic identity. Throughout the course of the film, Cole is repeatedly subjected to bodily harm and psychological trauma. In a surprisingly allegorical moment, he is mistakenly sent back in time into the trenches of a heated World War I battle. He arrives naked and confused and is wounded before suddenly being plucked out of time again and relocated to the 1990s, an antique bullet still in his leg. In this moment, Cole literally carries the wounds of history within himself, under the skin and impossible to ignore. His identity becomes as confused as his trips through time: he suffers doubt, disorientation, paranoia and fear, at one point, even celebrating with Kathryn the possibility of his own insanity, because even that is preferable to his reality. Through Cole's suffering body, the film systematically undermines the viewer's expectations regarding heroic redemption, liberation or clear identity.

In this sense, in *Twelve Monkeys*, the apocalypse is anything but clarifying. Rather than being reinvigorated in the wake of the disaster wrought by the virus, human society becomes increasingly inhospitable to everyone except those with power; identity becomes ever more tenuous and constrained. In this way, *Twelve Monkeys* presents a failed apocalypse in which the bio-catastrophe of the virus changes nothing, and nothing is transformed. Instead, the film focuses on the plight of those living in the postapocalypse and on the seemingly implacable powers that control, limit and punish them.[5] Moreover, in a critique that unfolds within the twists and (re)turns of *Twelve Monkeys*' postapocalyptic, time travel narrative, the film collapses the distinction between the present of its audience and the postapocalyptic future it presents, so that, in the end, it becomes possible to recognize the present as a postapocalypse of a different kind.

As many critics have pointed out, the basic premise of *Twelve Monkeys* resembles the postapocalyptic, "time-loop" scenarios of other popular science fictions films, most notably the *Terminator* films. Indeed, given that *Twelve Monkeys* was produced only a few years after the box-office smash *Terminator 2: Judgment Day* (1991), such comparisons are both apt and inevitable. Certainly this scenario has a diegetic complexity that lends a film a sense of urgency and makes it particularly engaging for viewers. James Berger explains, "The 'time-loop' ... is a perfect apocalyptic/post-apocalyptic plot line. Every action before the apocalypse is simultaneously an action after the apocalypse, and the event itself exists as a monstrous possibility made more or less likely by actions that, if it occurs, will never happen" (6). In other words, such puzzle-box narratives have at their core fundamental questions about human agency, as well as about the relationship between action and reaction.[6] In such scenarios, the conventional expectation is that the heroic protagonist will avert disaster and save the day. However, Gilliam's reiteration of the postapocalyptic, time-loop narrative echoes Cole's insight that "every time you see [something], because you are different, you see different things." *Twelve Monkeys* undermines the well-known conventions of the postapocalyptic, time-loop narrative, and, in this way, the film estranges the redemptive expectations associated with such narratives.

One such defamiliarizing revision has to do with the way in which *Twelve Monkeys* presents closure. There is an abiding tendency in postapocalyptic narratives to end in romanticized ways (Booker 85). This tendency is not dissimilar from the one being worked out in traditional apocalyptic narratives, in which, as discussed above, the end of the world often appears as a means of return to less socially and politically complex times. What is often overlooked in such romanticized endings, however, is the incongruity involved in symbolically recontaining the anxieties and traumas that postapocalyptic narratives engage in the first place. As James Berger points out, "postapocalyptic representations are simultaneously symptoms of historical traumas and attempts to work through them" (19); however, the integrative value of these narratives diminishes when the endings imagined in them — the putative answers to the problems being worked out — fail to offer anything new. Often, this is not strictly an ideological choice on the part of the author but is evidence that, as Fredric Jameson suggests, "our imaginations are hostages to our own mode of production (and perhaps to whatever remnants of past ones it has preserved)" (*Archaeologies* xiii). In other words, as the saying goes, it is easier to imagine the end of the world than to imagine the end of late capitalism (Jameson, *Seeds* xii). However, this imaginative bind may be read in either direction.

In *T2*, as Wegner points out, the impossibility of imagining the end of late capitalism comes to be represented as a figuration of its immortality, its "[ability] to reproduce itself into infinity" (74). Indeed, in *T2*, Sarah and John Connor succeed not only in delivering their world from disaster — or, it might be better to say *through* disaster — but also in sustaining the dominant order of that world.[7] In *Twelve Monkeys*, late capitalism is equally immortal, self-sustaining and painfully continuous; however, in Gilliam's film, the imaginative limitation of the characters, along with their disorientation and inability to recognize either their own limits or their opportunities for freedom, becomes a figure of the totalizing — and totalitarian — capacity of the system itself. Thus, while *Twelve Monkeys* repeats, in key ways, the narrative structure of *T2*, in this repetition, the narrative changes and takes on new meaning. Whereas *T2* envisions late capitalist culture as positive and progressive, *Twelve Monkeys* renders it much more darkly — as if to suggest the indefinite continuation of the dominant order is more dystopian than desirable.

In this light, it becomes significant that the time-loop at the center of *Twelve Monkeys* continuously foregrounds failure. James Cole is no John Connor; he has no messianic destiny, no redemptive future. Indeed, though the viewer does not fully realize it until the film's ending, Cole's death is prefigured in the film's opening sequence, when Cole first dreams about the airport killing. This sequence itself is a remake of the central scene of Chris Marker's *La Jetée* (1962), a photomontage composed almost entirely of still frames. In Marker's film, humanity retreats underground in the wake of nuclear war. Out of options and nearly out of hope, authorities and scientists in the human underground begin to send time travelers back in time in hopes of discovering a method of also sending travelers forward into the future, to find a way of improving the present situation (Del Rio 383). As in *Twelve Monkeys*, the goal of the scientists is not to change the past, but to open new possibilities for the present.

La Jetée follows one traveler as he returns to the past. This traveler is chosen because he has a particularly strong memory of the pre-holocaust world — a memory that revolves primarily around two images, one of a beautiful woman's face, another of a man being shot and killed at an airport. As he returns to the past, the traveler encounters and subsequently falls in love with a woman who looks inexplicably familiar. Out of his desire to be with this woman, the traveler refuses to obey the authorities of his present (and future). The viewer knows this woman to be the exact woman from the traveler's dream, but only too late do the implications of this fact become apparent. As he is meeting the woman at an airport, the traveler's dream (which is, paradoxically, also his memory) becomes a reality; he catches up to his own future and, suddenly seeing the woman's face in tableau exactly as it has always appeared to him in his dreams, he is shot (by an agent from the future) and dies.[8]

Cole's recurring dream is also a proleptic memory, one in which he (repeatedly) watches a man/himself be shot in an airport terminal and a woman (Kathryn) rush to his side. Cole's dream of his own death — a dream that becomes reality at the conclusion of the film — repeatedly prefigures his failure to either avert the apocalypse or to save himself. Like the iris of monkeys that fills the screen during the film's opening credits, Cole is seemingly locked into a circuit from which he cannot escape. Among other things, this closed loop reminds the viewer of Cole's disempowerment.

Likewise, the closed loop of the narrative echoes elsewhere in *Twelve*

Monkeys: the film makes it clear that Cole cannot save the (already-doomed) past. When the scientists in Cole's postapocalyptic world first return him to the past to collect information about the virus, they mistakenly send him to the wrong time. In short order, Cole finds himself locked in a mental ward, being questioned by a panel of psychiatrists (a group that offers one of many parallels between the present and the future). Asked to tell his story, Cole says to them — notably using the past tense — "Five billion people died in 1996 and 1997. Almost the entire population of the world." To this, one doctor replies, "Are you going to save us, Mr. Cole?" Cole's response illustrates the entire film's approach to apocalyptic redemption: "How can I save you? This already happened. I can't save you. No one can." In this exchange, the film forecloses the possibility of redemption. This, taken together with the film's continual return to the image of Cole's death and the moment of his failure, mark a shift in the film away from liberation and toward limitation. If, as in many apocalyptic and postapocalyptic films, the viewer is meant to identify with the survival and redemption of the protagonist, Cole's lack of power and, ultimately, his death provide the viewer with an altogether different experience — the experience of defeat. It is against this estranging turnabout that the rest of the film plays out.

In the place of an attention to future liberation or redemption — what Quinby calls "millennial perfection" — *Twelve Monkeys* examines the dynamics of power that govern and control the present. Thus, *Twelve Monkeys*' version of the postapocalyptic time-loop is drastically different from the version depicted in the *Terminator* films, which repeatedly invokes Sarah Connor's apocalyptic motto: "No fate but what we make." Significantly, in *Twelve Monkeys*, individuals alone do not make change possible; rather, possibilities for change are constrained by structural and institutional power relationships that govern and enclose the social and political situation. The film seems to bear this out: despite Cole's best intentions to stop the apocalypse and to free himself, he is prevented by forces beyond his control — indeed, beyond his recognition.

Elena Del Rio argues that *Twelve Monkeys*' "strong degree of closure erases the most disturbing aspects of its own circular time frame" (383). On the contrary, it is this very emphasis on narrative closure that drives the film's examination of social and political limitation. Furthermore, these limitations manifest in the film's peculiar attention to the control exercised over Cole's body. In both the future world of 2035 and in the "present" world of the 1990s, Cole's body is enclosed, locked away and meticulously monitored. Again, representations of Cole's suffering become a particular way of allegorizing his — and, by extension the audience's — oppressive situation.

In *The Ideology of the Aesthetic*, Terry Eagleton notes, "In the realization of [the] needs and capacities [of the body], that body ... opens out onto a shared social world, within which its own needs and desires will have to be weighed alongside those of others. It is in this way that we are led by a direct route from the creative body to such apparently abstract matters as reason, justice and morality" (208). In *Twelve Monkeys*, the representation of bodies is heavily implicated in the film's attention to the dialectic of freedom and control. Thus, it is not only the needs of the body — in particular its need to avoid exposure to the apocalyptic virus — that come to foreground in *Twelve Monkeys* but also the problem that the body often poses for the dominant order. In a sense, Cole's body becomes a map for the knowledge and power relationships imagined in the film: the film repeatedly looks at Cole's body in order to demonstrate his lack of power, freedom or choice. Ironically, even this act of looking is also a repetition, another layer of intertextuality against which the film's strategy of returning to look again plays out. The repeated images of Cole's restrained, defeated and dying body are at odds with conventional depictions of the heroic protagonist. Indeed, this contradiction is especially evident given the fact that the body of James Cole is also the body of Bruce Willis.

Twelve Monkeys' initial release followed by mere months Willis' appearance in *Die Hard: With a Vengeance* (1995). In this third installment in the *Die Hard* franchise (which began with *Die Hard* [1988] and continued with *Die Hard 2* [1990]), Willis returns as officer John McClane, an unflappably tough cop with an uncanny knack for fighting his way out of impossible situations. In many ways, McClane embodies the spirit of American exceptionalism and savoir-faire. In *Die Hard*, McClane finds himself outnumbered and outgunned by a group of German terrorists (led with immaculate poise and calculation by Hans Gruber [Alan Rickman]). *Die Hard* is very much a story of its historical moment, hardly out of place among mainstream action films of the late 1980s. What is particularly interesting in *Die Hard*, however, is the careful attention paid in the film to McClane's body. In one scene, McClane — who is literally caught with his pants down (or at least his shirt and shoes off) when Gruber's men storm the building he is in — is forced to run across broken glass to escape Gruber's henchmen. Later, he stands in front of a public bathroom sink gingerly picking shards of glass from his bloodied feet. At the film's conclusion, after being repeatedly beaten, shot at and otherwise physically punished, McClane limps into the office where Gruber is waiting and deftly shoots the man in the head. This last act of violence vindicates the beating that McClane has suffered, and the allegorical message of McClane's broken but unstoppable body seems bloody obvious: no matter the odds, the (American) good guy does it all — saves the day and gets the girl.

Likewise, the representations of the body of Bruce Willis/James Cole in

Twelve Monkeys vibrate with symbolic meaning, but that meaning is quite the opposite from that of *Die Hard*. Cole is as physically imposing as McClane. During his interview with the panel of psychiatrists in 1990, Cole raises his voice at an orderly who is easily larger and stronger than him. Still, the orderly recoils, as if instinctively afraid of Cole. Later in the film, when an assailant threatens Kathryn, Cole brutally beats the man to death with the same violent capacity with which McClane might dispose of a generic baddie. This violence, however, is not depicted as the act of a hero but rather of a desperate man. Despite his physicality, Cole repeatedly appears on screen in positions of submission and containment. Thus, instead of becoming the embodiment of survival or redemption like Connor or McClane, Cole becomes figure of limitation, even incarceration.

In the postapocalyptic future, Cole lives as a prisoner. When he first appears, he is inside his cell, wrapped in the plastic materials of his sleeping hammock. The mise-en-scene of this early sequence is emblematic of the rest of the film: Cole is suspended in space, held tightly and symbolically neither here nor there. Beyond him, the walls of his cell resemble an animal's cage, claustrophobic and framed by wire mesh. Farther into the background, rows upon rows of this same cell repeat, and inside each, the bodies of prisoners hang, fidget and scream. Above the cages, guards patrol endlessly. As D. Brent Laytham points out, "The movie is replete with barriers: cages, bars, fences, manacles, biohazard suits, straightjackets, plastic rain coats, locked doors ... [and] human contact is seldom direct" (79). Moreover, the constant foregrounding of such visual barriers in *Twelve Monkeys* emphasizes the film's interest in making visible the efforts spent to control the bodies of those without power, people like Cole.

Indeed, Cole's lack of political power is made manifest by his concordant lack of control over his own body. This disenfranchisement becomes obvious early in the film, when the scientists select Cole to participate in an experiment. A guard shouts down to Cole, "Volunteer duty!" Cole responds somewhat defiantly, "I didn't volunteer." When the guard grumbles something about Cole causing trouble, Cole's voice softens and he says simply, "No trouble." Soon after, a crane arm descends and lifts Cole out of his prison cell— the visual analog of a scientist reaching into a cage to pick out a lab rat. The scientists control not only Cole's body, but also his voice, his ability to speak, to protest or to refuse commands.

In his first turn of "volunteer duty," the scientists send Cole to the planet's inhospitable surface to collect various specimens for study. In order to leave the underground city, Cole must first don several layers of protective clothing and, finally a biohazard suit. These layers begin immediately against Cole's skin: he wears, for instance, rubber leggings and a skullcap. Atop these, he puts a large, cumbersome, plastic suit. As he dresses, a recorded voice relays a warning: "These are the instructions for the first time probe. Listen carefully. They must be followed exactly. All openings of your garment must be sealed completely. If the integrity of the suit is compromised in any way, if the fabric is torn or a zipper not closed, readmittance will be denied."

In many ways, the biohazard suit is a symbol of the scientists' control over Cole. Even as he leaves the hermetically sealed underground in which he lives, that world goes with him, contains him and prevents him from truly going outside its reach. The world outside the prison, outside the suit, is utterly alien to Cole, and it is open in a way that Cole's world will never be. The suit is a reminder that Cole cannot belong to both worlds at once: even touching the world of the surface, even breathing its air, would irreparably rupture his relationship to the sealed off world to which he quite literally belongs. Furthermore, even as the suit is an emblem of the protection offered by the world of the scientists, its meaning evolves as the film goes on. It is not just the world of the surface — the world that ostensibly belongs to the virus — but it is also any possible way of being in the world outside the regulation and control of the scientists themselves that Cole cannot touch. Thus, Cole's appearance within the biohazard suit speaks to his oppressively tenuous relationship with the power of the scientists, a relationship that thrives on obedience and brutally punishes disobedience.

When Cole returns from the surface — biohazard suit intact — he is reminded of his place in yet another way. After he disrobes, a group of guards roughly scrub Cole's naked body — each guard wearing a biohazard suit of his own. The guards perform their duty with a violent touch; they spray a restrained Cole with water and scour him with long-handled brushes as if to remind him of the power they exert over him. A subsequent scene shows Cole sitting in isolation, drawing his own blood with a garish syringe. Taken together, these scenes emphasize the scientists' attitude toward Cole. He cannot bring any trace of the outside world into the underground — his body, skin and blood must submit to this truth. In this way, the surface and the virus come to mean something other than death and fear — they hint at the existence of imaginative possibilities outside the dominant order.

If the world of 2035 is, in this way, openly dystopian,[9] the world of the 1990s is disquietingly similar. Del Rio suggests, "*Twelve Monkeys* adopts a homogenous visual style that levels out the differences between past, present and future by saturating all of the times/worlds with the same 1990s-vintage gloss and dystopian dreariness" (391). Indeed, the film stages a repetition of Cole's prison cell and biohazard suit when he first arrives in the 90s. When Cole first appears on screen in the "present," he is squatting in a police station holding cell, waiting for psychiatric evaluation. In the cell, Cole is wearing only a woman's raincoat, made of a plastic material that conspicuously recalls the biohazard suit of 2035. Likewise, when Cole is remanded to a mental hospital, the hospital's orderlies bathe and inspect him in a repetition of the earlier scene. In these repetitions, images of containment take on the same symbolic meaning: the body must be controlled, regulated and separated from the outside world, it must be submissive and willing. In drawing this parallel between the postapocalyptic future and the present of the viewer, *Twelve Monkeys* begins to suggest that the same inimical forces that torturously govern the postapocalypse also already hold power in the present.

Importantly, however, it is not only through examples of physical control that *Twelve Monkeys* illustrates an attention to the relationship between power and the body. Rather, it is also through the representation of what Del Rio calls "absolute visibility" (383) that the film demonstrates the power of the dominant order to regulate and contain those within its totalizing gaze. In a way that recalls Foucault's discussion of the relationship between surveillance and control ("The entire [prison] institution ... culminates in the cell, on the walls of which are written in black letters: 'God sees you'") the scientists of 2035 exercise control through both observation and conspicuous visibility (294). In the film, this power is symbolized by the scientists' giant videoglobe — a salvagepunk-styled orb of monitors that hovers in the middle distance between Cole and the scientists whenever Cole is called up for interrogation. The videoglobe shows Cole whatever the scientists wish him to see — often just the faces and places of relevance to his investigation of the virus. However, the monitors also display magnified images of the scientists themselves — images that literally *show* Cole he is being watched. Del Rio writes:

> Besides reminding Cole, in a self-reflexive way, of its own global supervising capacities through the tautological display of a series of disembodied eyes, the gyrating eye also features images of people or objects that act as clues in the investigative mission engaging Cole. By holding in a simultaneous, multiple image events that belong to different spatiotemporal contexts, the rotating eye collapses the irreducible difference of these events under its commanding gaze [391].

By watching Cole, and by reminding him that he is being watched, the scientists exercise a thoroughgoing power over Cole's body, leaving him nowhere in space or time to hide.

The film's emphasis on visibility takes a different form in the present. Here, as in the cages of the future world, the ward's many nurses and orderlies continuously monitor Cole and his fellow inmates. In a different way, however, these inmates are constrained by their own visual consumption of the dominant order and its conspicuous visibility on the television. Jeffrey Goines (Brad Pitt), Cole's appointed tour guide in the mental ward and the future leader of the Army of the Twelve Monkeys, ties the television to the preservation of the status quo. He tells Cole, with all the gusto of a conspiracy nut:

> It's all right there — all right there. Look. Listen. Kneel. Pray. Commercials! We're not productive anymore. No one needs to make things anymore. It's all automated. What are we for, then? We're consumers. Yeah, okay, okay — buy a lot of stuff, you're a good citizen. But if you don't buy a lot of stuff, if you don't — fact, Jim, fact! — what are you then I ask you? You're mentally ill![10]

Indeed, the mental ward patients seem to constantly watch television, and the programs they daily watch become for them a continual reminder of their incarcerated status, as well as their own non-normativity. As Carrol Fry and J. Robert Craig note, advertisements for the Florida Keys continuously play in the foreground of the mental ward, and these advertisements offer foreshadowing for Cole's plan to escape with Kathryn to Key West at the end of the film (6). These commercials figure in another important way as well: the Keys become a symbol for the inmates of a place outside the woes of their present situation. At the same time, however, these advertisements remind the ward's patients of all that might be theirs if they could only adhere to the rule of the dominant order. Thus, the glossy images of the Keys take on a hollow utopian promise of escape; however, like the constant whisperings about parole and pardon among the prisoners in 2035, this promise seems all too good to be true.

Finally, Cole's interactions with the scientists themselves illustrate a parallel between the postapocalyptic future and the present. In each space, Cole appears on screen in positions of disempowerment and restraint. In 2035, when he speaks with the scientists, Cole sits in a chair that restrains him and lifts him off the floor, so that he sits halfway between the floor and ceiling. In the 1990s, he sits in front of the panel, flanked by orderlies who watch his every move suspiciously. The power the scientists have over Cole in these moments is both physical and ideological — they have the authority to name him either criminal or insane. As Elizabeth Rosen puts it, "It is these scientific figures who render judgment in both the present-day and future worlds. They are empowered to decide who is incarcerated and who is pardoned or let free. In the future, they can send people on missions and arbitrarily yank them home" (87). And indeed, this is exactly what the scientists do to Cole. He is their pawn — or perhaps their lab rat — to be used and disposed of as they see fit. Even Kathryn, herself a psychiatrist, says of her profession: "We decide what's right and wrong. We decide who's crazy or not." Thus, as the film's repeated mise-en-scene seems to make clear, the scientists in both the 90s and the postapocalyptic future serve to ground the dystopian aspects of both worlds — they are the law-givers and judges, the bearers of power and the dominant identity.

Finally, *Twelve Monkeys* suggests that the scientists are interested in little more than the preservation of their own power and dominance. If the scientists of the 90s are powerful and obscure figures, in the wake of apocalypse, they only grow stronger, their control more fully realized. Indeed, although the scientists of the future espouse the noble goal of reclaiming the planet for humanity, their real motivation is unavailable in the film. They promise a pardon to Cole for his role in finding the source of the virus, but this promise turns out to be empty — pardoned or not, Cole still cannot choose his way in the world. His pardon does nothing to change his relationship to power. Indeed, when he attempts to disobey, to stay in the 1990s in order to be with Kathryn, the scientists respond by sending agents to the past with orders to kill her if Cole does not again obey. In what is as close to a moment of epiphany and recognition that the film offers, Cole finally understands the scientists' motives in threatening to kill Kathryn: "This part isn't about the virus at all, is it? It's about following orders, about doing what you're told."

Indeed, given the film's careful attention to the dystopian aspects of the future community, it seems clear that Cole's scientists are not interested in orchestrating redemption. Rather they are invested in their own power, in insuring its continuance. In this regard, the virus itself may well be another kind of insurance, a source of power that guarantees their continued dominance. Rosen argues:

> The scientists themselves are morally ambiguous characters, responsible for the humanly engineered virus which decimated the human population and the future cure which will allow humans to return to the earth's surface. The scientists, in their present and future incarnations, are depicted simultaneously as noble figures whose acts of creation can "redeem" the human race, and as creepy, sly, secretive figures whose agendas are unfathomable and who are responsible for getting the human race in trouble in the first place [87].

This ambiguity, together with their disregard for human dignity, solidifies the scientists as the self-invested rulers of a dark future.

Recognizing the scientists in this way adds ominous meaning to the penultimate scene of *Twelve Monkeys*, one that plays out after Cole's death and the initial release of the virus. Fleeing the terminal where Cole has tried to kill him, the man (importantly, a scientist) responsible for releasing the virus boards a plane, carrying with him the very thing Cole has been searching through time for, an original sample of the virus. As the man takes his seat, a woman off camera begins to speak: "It's obscene. All the violence. All the lunacy. Shootings even at airports now. You might say that *we're* the next endangered species. Human beings." To this, the man smiles and replies, "I think you're right, ma'am. I think you've hit the nail on the head." As the camera pans over, the woman speaking comes into the frame — she is none other than a scientist from the future. Turning to the man now seated next to her, she reaches to shake his hand and says simply, "Jones is my name. I'm in insurance." By this point in the film, however, it seems obvious what exactly it is that Jones is there to ensure: the continuation of the dominant order.

It has been suggested that *Twelve Monkeys* is a film that shows a world without hope (Laytham 79). Indeed, the apocalyptic narrative at the heart of the film focuses on a protagonist who seems hopelessly trapped, unable to be free, unable to even have control over his own body. Additionally, the film systematically undermines the liberty, redemption and hope that Cole relentlessly pursues. And, finally, the film goes so far as to show viewers the quiet end of the world, the moment when the virus is released into the air. The film's vision is certainly bleak.

However, *Twelve Monkeys*' is not a narrative about the failure of hope. It is, instead, about the *limits* of hope, about the larger social and political forces that create and enforce those limits. The film's (re)vision of apocalypse is one that refuses to see change as something that belongs to the future, to a world beyond the end of this one. Instead, in its continuous reiteration of Cole's disorientation, limitation and suffering, the film invites its audience to recognize the totality within which Cole — and the audience — is bound. In its unrelenting attention to the limits of change, *Twelve Monkeys* preserves the true value of apocalyptic narrative — its capacity for revelation (Berger 5).

To this end, the revelation at the heart of *Twelve Monkeys* is not that the present situation is hopeless. Rather, what the film recognizes is that any hope for change must be grounded first of all in the recognition of the limitations of the present situation, of those structures and powers that make change seem all but impossible. As Jameson puts it, change begins with "a meditation on the impossible, on the unrealizable in its own right. This is very far from a liberal capitulation to the necessity of capitalism, however; it is quite the opposite, a rattling of the bars and an intense spiritual concentration and preparation for another stage which has not yet arrived" (*Archaeologies* 232–233). Indeed, it is in its recognition of the limitations and contradictions of the present that the quiet hope of *Twelve Monkeys* shines through.

Near the film's ending, once Cole has died, Kathryn — knowing that the young James Cole is somewhere in the crowd — looks frantically about for him. The camera lingers on her face as she finds him and looks tenderly at him. After a breath, she smiles ever so slightly, as if oddly contented about something. Subsequently, *Twelve Monkeys* ends with the young Cole walking out of the airport and returning to his family's car. The camera moves steadily in, until it shows only Cole's blue eyes — the same shot that opened the film. In this final repetition, the estranging strategy of *Twelve Monkeys* comes full circle: Cole has been killed, but he is not dead. He failed, but he gets to try again. Like Kathryn's smile — the hint of something dynamically new — this ending reminds us, the rules don't change, but we do.

Notes

1. I take the theoretical premise for this argument from Phillip Wegner's *Life Between Two Deaths* (Durham: Duke University Press, 2009). Wegner writes, "Walter Benjamin suggests that history be understood as a series of repetitions ... [these repetitions] are the motor of historical movement itself: paradoxically, Benjamin maintains, only in the repetition of what has already occurred do things actually change" (17). See also Walter Benjamin, *The Arcades Project*, 1982, trans. Howard Eiland and Michael W. Jennings (Cambridge: Belknap, 2003).
2. For extended readings of the significance of *Vertigo* in *Twelve Monkeys*, see Laura Rascaroli, "Scopic Drive, Time Travel and Film Spectatorship in Gilliam's *Twelve Monkeys* and Bigelow's *Strange Days*," *Kinema* 15 (2001): 29–35; and Carrol Fry and J. Robert Craig, "A Carnival of Apes: A Bakhtinian Perspective on *Twelve Monkeys*," *Journal of the Fantastic in the Arts* 13.1 (2002): 3–12.
3. For a discussion of the historical relationship between apocalypse and identity, see Norman Cohn, *Cosmos, Chaos and the World to Come: The Ancient Roots of Apocalyptic Faith* (New Haven: Yale University Press, 1993); see also John R. Hall, *Apocalypse: From Antiquity to the Empire of Modernity* (Cambridge: Polity Press, 2009); for a discussion of the troubling relationship between apocalypse and conservative political identity, see James Berger, *After the End* (Minneapolis: University of Minnesota Press, 1999).
4. See also Phillip Wegner's excellent discussion of messianic destiny, conservative identity and apocalypse in the *Terminator* films, "I'll Be Back: Repetitions and Revisions in the *Terminator* Films," *Life Between Two Deaths* (Durham: Duke University Press, 2009).
5. For an extended discussion of the critical capacities of the suffering body in apocalyptic fiction, see also Elana Gomel's insightful essay, "The Plague of Utopias: Pestilence and the Apocalyptic Body," *Twentieth Century Literature* 46 (Winter 2000): 405–433.
6. See, for contemporary examples, Duncan Jones' *Source Code* (2011) and Rian Johnson's *Looper* (2012).
7. To the objection that, in *Terminator 3: Rise of the Machines*, Connor fails to actually stop Judgment day, it is useful to recall that, as cited elsewhere in this essay, the disaster is a signal of the implacable resilience of late capitalism, since John himself becomes the messianic symbol of the continuance of the system and its dominant identity.
8. For an in-depth comparison of Gilliam's *Twelve Monkeys* and Chris Marker's *La Jetée*, see Elena Del Rio, "The Remaking of *La Jetée*'s Time-Travel Narrative: *Twelve Monkeys* and the Rhetoric of Absolute Visibility," *Science Fiction Studies* 28.3 (2001): 383–398.
9. The paradigmatic examples of dystopian literature in this regard are Yevgeny Zamyatin's *We* and George Orwell's *1984*. In each of these texts, state power is fundamentally imbricated in repressive control of the bodies living in the state so that recontaining rebellious citizens happens finally with acts of violence to their bodies.
10. In the spirit of intertextuality, it is amusing to mark the ways in which Brad Pitt's performance as Jeffrey Goines resurfaces in his portrayal of the strident anti-capitalist Tyler Durden in David Fincher's *Fight Club* (1999).

Works Cited

Bartter, Martha. "Nuclear Holocaust as Urban Renewal." *Science Fiction Studies* 13.2 (1986): 148–158. Web. 26 Oct. 2011.
Berger, James. *After the End: Representations of Post-Apocalypse*. Minneapolis: University of Minnesota Press, 1999. Print.
Bloch, Ernst. "'*Entfremdung, Verfremdung*': Alienation, Estrangement." *The Drama Review: TDR* 15 (1970): 120–125. Web. 24 Apr. 2008.

Booker, M. Keith. *Monsters, Mushroom Clouds, and the Cold War: American Science Fiction and the Roots of Postmodernism*. Westport, CT: Greenwood, 2001. Print.
Del Rio, Elena. "The Remaking of *La Jetée*'s Time-Travel Narrative: *Twelve Monkeys* and the Rhetoric of Absolute Visibility." *Science Fiction Studies* 28.3 (2001): 383–398. Web. 20 Dec. 2011.
Die Hard. Dir. John McTiernan. Twentieth Century–Fox, 1988. DVD.
Die Hard 2. Dir. Renny Harlin. Twentieth Century–Fox, 1990. DVD.
Die Hard: With a Vengeance. Dir. John McTiernan. Twentieth Century–Fox, 1995. DVD.
Dr. Strangelove or: How I Learned to Stop Worrying and Love the Bomb. Dir. Stanley Kubrick. Columbia Pictures, 1964. DVD.
Eagleton, Terry. *The Ideology of the Aesthetic*. Cambridge: Basil Blackwell, 1990. Print.
Foucault, Michel. *Discipline and Punish*. Trans. Alan Sheridan. New York: Vintage, 1995. Print.
Fry, Carrol, and J. Robert Craig. "A Carnival of Apes: A Bakhtinian Perspective on *Twelve Monkeys*." *Journal of the Fantastic in the Arts* 13.1 (2002): 3–12. Print.
Gomel, Elana. "The Plague of Utopias: Pestilence and the Apocalyptic Body." *Twentieth Century Literature* 46 (Winter 2000): 405–433. Web. 13 Nov. 2008.
Jameson, Fredric. *Archaeologies of the Future*. New York: Verso, 2005. Print.
_____. *The Seeds of Time*. New York: Columbia University Press, 1994. Print.
La Jetée. Dir. Chris Marker. Argos Films, 1962. Film.
Laytham, D. Brent. "Time for Hope: *The Sixth Sense*, *American Beauty*, *Memento*, and *Twelve Monkeys*." *The Gift of Story: Narrating Hope in a Postmodern World*. Eds. Emily Griesinger and Mark Eaton. Waco: Baylor University Press, 2006. Print.
Quinby, Lee. *Millennial Seduction: A Skeptic Confronts Apocalyptic Culture*. Ithaca: Cornell University Press, 1999. Print.
Rosen, Elizabeth. *Apocalyptic Transformation: Apocalypse and the Postmodern Imagination*. New York: Lexington Books, 2008. Print.
The Terminator. Dir. James Cameron. Orion Pictures, 1984. DVD.
Terminator 2: Judgment Day. Dir. James Cameron. Tristar Pictures, 1992. DVD.
Terminator 3: Rise of the Machines. Dir. Jonathan Mostow. Warner Bros., 2003. DVD.
Twelve Monkeys. Dir. Terry Gilliam. Universal Pictures, 1995. DVD.
Vertigo. Dir. Alfred Hitchcock. Paramount Pictures, 1958. DVD.
Wegner, Phillip. *Life Between Two Deaths*. Durham: Duke University Press, 2009. Print.

Part III: The New Millennium

Tech-Noir and the Critical Dystopia in the 21st Century: Wimmer's Equilibrium

ALEXANDER CHARLES OLIVER HALL

Proposing that Kurt Wimmer's 2002 film *Equilibrium* is exemplary of the critical dystopia in twenty-first century American film moves beyond simply reading the film as such. It is no stretch to suggest that the film is demonstrative of the critical dystopia in twenty-first century American cinema, but it is also exemplary of how the critical dystopia on film is dependent on the conventions of film noir to paint its dark landscapes. Pairing science fiction with these conventions as *Equilibrium* does, however, also locates it within the filmic subgenre of the tech-noir. Taken separately, film noir and science fiction exist within their own respective critical frameworks—film noir contains the critical energy of modernism in its American manifestation, while science fiction contains critical energy in its depiction of what Tom Moylan terms "cognitively substantial yet estranged alternative worlds" (5). Films that pair these critical energies—tech-noirs—then, are inherently critical themselves. Moreover, in the current postmodern critical moment, it might be fair to say that in film the tech-noir has critically picked up where the noir film left off, just as science fiction once seized the critical space of the historical novel. In this sense, science fiction reinvigorates the critical energy of film noir—equaling the tech-noir. Furthermore, combining the critical energy of the tech-noir with the literary form of the dystopia equals a critical dystopia, a conclusion that Wimmer's *Equilibrium* exemplifies. This critically dystopian film can now be viewed as having been somewhat more timely than perhaps Wimmer intended, as fears of the possible results of the Bush administration's new pre-emptive strategies of foreign policy following the World Trade Center attacks on September 11, 2001, play out in an alternative future world where emotion has been identified as that which brings about war, and has thus been all but eradicated. A tech-noir film, *Equilibrium* marries science fiction and film noir themes and stylistics as the means to this critical end, even if it was produced before the 9/11 attacks even took place.

In the title of a recent work by Paul Meehan, the tech-noir is described as "the fusion of science fiction and film noir." The critical energy of this genre is twofold; first, it is an extension of film noir itself, which contained its own brand of critical energy as an American modernist art form, a form which, according to James Naremore, "was quite simply the most respected art among the educated classes — the kind that was regarded as more authentic, more important as a commentary on modern experience, and more relevant to the intellectual concerns of the day" (41). Naremore goes on to point out that "a great many films of the 1940s were clearly indebted to modernist art" (41), which was itself indebted to nineteenth-century artists "whose paradoxical aestheticism was developed in direct response to bourgeois capitalism and the rise of urban mass culture" (42). The noir film, furthermore, became critical of the repressive forces of capitalism insofar as "a political movement or cultural formation within Hollywood struggled against censorship and political repression by using dark thrillers for critical ends" (7). The critical framework of the film noir genre as an American modernist art form, therefore, was made manifest in its generic conventions: "narratives and camera angles were organized among more complex and subjective lines; characters were depicted in shades of gray or in psychoanalytic terms; urban women became increasingly eroticized and dangerous; endings seemed less unproblematically happy; and violence appeared more pathological" (45). Moving beyond the critical moment of modernism, the critical energy of film noir has at least in part become grounded in the postmodern tech-noir, which pairs said energy with science fiction — a genre that reinvigorated the critical energy of the historical novel by allowing for a narrative model of history that positioned the present as the future's past.

The other side of tech-noir's critical energy is its status as a subgenre of science fiction. As Meehan's work indicates, the very definition of the tech-noir says that the subgenre "fuses" film noir with science fiction. The depiction of alternative worlds in works of science fiction allows for multiple types of critique, but of particular interest here is the tendency of the genre to inspire historical thinking by inspiring its readers to consider the present as a depicted alternative future world's past. This historical impulse is an important aspect of the genre's critical framework because it took over the project of inspiring historical thought from the historical novel, which Fredric Jameson —following Georg Lukács— writes was "a narrative form peculiarly restructured to express that new consciousness" ("Progress" 284). According to Jameson, however, the historical novel was "emptied of its vitality" (285) after the "*bourgeois cultural revolution*" (284), and replaced with "the emergence of the new genre of SF as a form which now registers some nascent sense of the future, and does so in the space on which a sense of the past had once been inscribed" (286). Tom Moylan, working from Jameson's conception of the science fiction genre as that which revitalizes historical thinking, writes that "against those who invoke the 'end of history' ... sf enables its readers to cut through the jungle of such arrogant hegemonic claims and find new directions for critical comparisons between what is and what is coming to be, where we are and what we might be doing" (27). Moylan goes on to suggest that "the popular cultural form of sf makes an empowering critical practice available to its readers" (27), which "at its most significant ... can be a part of the larger process of mobilizing the cultural imagination" and "the process of making the world critically 'legible' in a way that not only delivers pleasure and knowledge but also the joys of joining in the collective, historical work of bringing a more just and free society into being" (28). Given the cultural ubiquity of film as perhaps the most popular cultural medium, the science fiction film seems to possess the same critical force that both Jameson and Moylan delineate in the larger science fiction cultural form. Furthermore, if the critical energy of film noir as a modernist form was taken over by the postmodern tech-noir, then a similar development occurred between film noir and tech-noir as between the historical novel and science fiction.

While science fiction in general continues its critical project of reinvigorating historical thought as a kind of utopian "social dreaming" ("Three Faces" 3), to use Lyman Tower Sargent's term, the tech-noir also contains such an impulse. First, as has already been mentioned, the noir film, like the historical novel, was a critical genre in its initial phase. But also like the historical novel, the noir film was stripped of its critical energy; where the historical novel experienced this loss after the bourgeois cultural revolution, so too did the noir film, once grounded in postmodernism. The noir film's critical energy might best be explained by its ability to have achieved "aesthetic representations" of the "current experience" (*The Cultural Turn* 9) of the system under which it was produced. However, postmodern examples of noir films — neo-noir films, which can perhaps be thought of as "post-noir" films, due to their self-conscious attempt to "do" noir — tend to be examples of postmodern nostalgia. Fredric Jameson's example of this phenomenon is Lawrence Kasdan's 1981 film *Body Heat*, which, he writes, can be received "as nostalgia work — as a narrative set in some indefinable nostalgic past" (9). It is in this sense that the noir film seems to have lost much of its critical energy, and its status now as a nostalgic genre, according to Jameson, is "an alarming and pathological symptom of a society that has become incapable of dealing with time and history" (10). But though the film noir genre under postmodernism can bring about such concern, its critical energy survives when paired with science fiction film, equaling the tech-noir. This is evident in the fact that tech-noir films "deliberately borrow both thematic and stylistic elements from the universe of noir," and furthermore that they present a "clouded mirror in which we may perceive the obscure workings of the soul and discern clues to our ultimate fate" (Meehan 2). Beyond this function of the genre, however, the tech-noir also contains the critical energy implicit in science fiction, which Jameson writes exists in its ability to more rightly "defamiliarize and restructure our experience of our own *present*" ("Progress" 286), because "its multiple mock futures serve the quite different function of transforming our own present into the determinate past of something yet to come" (288). Thus, just as science fiction took over the critical historicity of the historical novel, a similar occurrence took place when the tech-noir took up the critical energy of the film noir genre by pairing it with science fiction film. Further, since the tech-noir is an implicitly critical genre, it might be fair to say that tech-noirs that employ dystopian form end up being critical dystopias.

The dystopia ranks among the most critical genres in narrative form. Tom Moylan writes that "dystopian narrative is largely the product of the terrors of the twentieth century," and that its "narrative machine has produced challenging cognitive maps of the historical situation by way of imaginary societies that are even worse than those that lie outside their authors' and readers' doors" (xi). With this in mind, Moylan accepts the definition of dystopia put forth by Sargent: "a non-existent society described in considerable detail and normally located in time and space that the author intended a contemporaneous reader to view as considerably worse than the society in which that reader lived" ("Three Faces" 9). Though the genre "proved adequate to the task of catching not only the extent of the human and ecological devastation brought about by the latest configuration of capitalism and imperialism but also of finding the seeds of opposition within the tendencies and latencies of that existing social system" (Moylan xiv), the 1960s and 1970s gave way to "a myriad of liberation movements" (xiv) that influenced the production of what have since been called "critical utopias," effectively placing dystopian narrative in the proverbial back seat of culture. After the neoconservative turn of the 1980s, however, the dystopia resurfaced as a critical cultural form, equaling what Sargent called the "critical dystopia" ("US Eutopias" 222). Moylan describes that form as "a textual mutation that self-reflexively takes on the present system and offers not only astute critiques of the order of things but also explorations of the oppositional spaces and possibilities from which the next round of political activism can derive imaginative sustenance and inspiration" (xv). This new inherently critical form of the dystopia, which shares much with science fiction (and often manifests as science fiction), often appeared in film, with such examples as *The Terminator*, *Blade Runner*, and *Dark City*— all tech-noir films. Hence, in addition to the ways in which the critical dystopia responds to and criticizes the political temperament of the system under which it is produced, some tech-noir films' tendency to be dystopian makes them critical dystopias thanks to the critical energy of film noir and science fiction used in their narrative form. Wimmer's *Equilibrium* adheres to these characteristics.

Equilibrium's underlying premise is that emotion will lead to devastating war. An opening montage contains a voiceover reporting that humanity only narrowly recovered from a third world war in the early 21st century, which lead to extreme measures for the prevention of a fourth. These measures include the establishment of a totalitarian society called Libria, in which a new type of law enforcement agent, the Grammaton Cleric, seeks out those who attempt to subvert the outlawing of emotion by refusing to take regular "intervals" of a drug called "Prozium." Enclaves of these so-called "sense offenders" keep collections of cultural products— paintings, books, music — much like the harborers of books in Bradbury's *Fahrenheit 451*— which Grammaton Clerics summarily destroy along with the sense offenders. When Cleric John Preston (Christian Bale) accidently misses one of his own intervals, he quickly develops emotions which cause him to question the society he has been fighting to preserve and eventually fight the system from within, with the help of the sense offender resistance (*Equilibrium*).

Appearing a little over a year after September 11, 2001, *Equilibrium* seems to reflect the anxiety in American consciousness about the potential results of the pre-emptive foreign policy of the Bush administration that came about after the attacks on the World Trade Center — revenge is, after all, a product of emotion. The film, however, was shot between October and December of 2000, and is therefore somewhat prescient in its interrogation of pre-emptive foreign policy. Moreover, *Equilibrium* had a quite limited initial release and was not particularly well-received by critics, but in the years since it has gained quite a following, and might now even be considered a cult classic. This is perhaps because the true power of the film's central theme would not be as effective until after the 9/11 attacks and the adoption of the Bush doctrine in United States foreign policy. For this reason, the film is much more timely in post–9/11 American culture. Part of this effect exists in *Equilibrium*'s employment of the stylistics of film noir and the critical framework of science fiction, which are compounded and strengthened by its dystopian narrative form.

The darkness of the film, both figuratively and literally, is established from the outset, when the montage voiceover implicates "our own volatile natures," as that which could cause war to break out; "the true source of man's inhumanity to man," the voice says, is "his ability to feel" (*Equilibrium*). The montage gives way to the depiction of rebel leader Seamus (Dominic Purcell) with his fellow rebels in their hideout, all in saturated color. He sits looking at Adolphe-William Bougueréau's "The Story Book," also in fully saturated color, when one of the rebels frantically arrives to announce the arrival of Libria's agents, who have come to infiltrate their base. Paintings and other cultural artifacts are quickly whisked away as rebels exchange gunfire with the agents outside, most of whom are themselves depicted in desaturated color, and some of whom wear black masks, effectively rendering them faceless. Preston then takes control of the scene in an action sequence wherein he singlehandedly quashes the remaining rebel resistance in the base. There is an exceptionally recognizable noir visual style here, as Preston is almost always lit from the back as he runs toward the door behind which the rebels are holed up. Breaking the door down, Preston becomes a silhouette in the now open doorway before Librian agents shoot out the lights, darkening the screen. At this point, the only light in the scene comes from the guns used in the expertly fought battle on the part of Preston, who uses the gun-kata, a gun-fighting style developed by Wimmer for the film. After killing all of the rebels, Preston is left standing in the foreground lit only by the heat sync of his modified Beretta pistols. Apart from noir photography pastiches in the film, the saturation of the characters becomes a clue as to whether or not certain characters are "feeling." The film's heroine, Mary O'Brien (Emily Watson), for instance, whose wardrobe becomes increasingly saturated itself, is frequently shot in bright, vivid color, suggesting a brightness of her character that becomes the muse for Preston's actions in the film. Meehan writes that in film noir, the "real love" of women characters is "power" (5), which is certainly the case with O'Brien, who brings Preston's initial Grammaton Cleric partner to ruin by sharing an illegal relationship with him. The relationship drives his partner to cease his Prozium intervals, thereby defying the society he has sworn to uphold as a Cleric. Other noir conventions run throughout the film.

Although not a private investigator like the noir protagonists that came before, Preston spends much of the film trying to figure out the allure of emotion he begins to feel, as well as attempting to uncover the corruption underlying Libria's rule. There is a certain amount of what Meehan calls "moral ambiguity" (4) in the character, in that Preston is first presented as an emotionless killer of rebels. But morality soon causes the character's motivations to shift once he has stopped taking his Prozium intervals, and his unrelenting violence is then used against Librian agents. At this point, Preston begins to exist in "a twilight world between that of the cop and the criminal" (Meehan 4), which drives both the plot and the action of the film. Also like the noir protagonists of old, Preston finds himself in traps, and is in these situations also beat up, though he is able to reign supreme against all odds. This conflict is not unlike those of the noir protagonists, who often found themselves "tangled up in desperate situations where they ended up in trouble way over their heads" (Meehan 5). Meanwhile, the villains in *Equilibrium* are also inspired in some ways by their film noir counterparts; they are the hypocritical Dupont (Angus MacFadyen)—the puppet master behind the film's Big Brother character, Father (Sean Pertwee)—and Preston's new partner Brandt (Taye Diggs), both of whom, it is suggested, are themselves feeling throughout the film. It is through their conniving that they are able to convince Preston that his plans to overthrow Libria's totalitarian regime are going smoothly, though late in the film they are revealed to have been privy to these plans all along.

Finally, the city itself, as in the world of noir, acts as one of the film's characters, and forms a central backdrop to the dark plot of the film. Meehan points to the titles of many classic films noir that demonstrate this aspect of the genre, such as *The City That Never Sleeps*, *Dark City*, and *City of Fear* (5). *Equilibrium*'s title is consistent with this aspect of the noir genre in that Libria's name is a derivative of the film's title. Libria itself is also not unlike the cities depicted in film noir, which "held their inhabitants captive like some monstrous rat trap while their grim fates were played out" (5). According to Meehan, "these dark metropoli contained teeming tenements of the poor underclass juxtaposed with the gothic mansions and penthouse suites of the wealthy" (5), to which Libria is no stranger; the Clerics and other upper classes live in the futuristic city of Libria, a city that looks like it must have been inspired by Fritz Lang's *Metropolis* (though Wimmer insists it was inspired by the perspective drawings of buildings by the early 20th century architect Hugh Ferriss), while the underclass (and many of the sense offenders) live outside the overbearing city walls in "The Nethers"—the name given to the areas of ruin still left over from the third world war. The Nethers can be viewed as a direct interpretation of the "mean streets" the film noir city, which "were a maze of blind alleys, fire escapes, rooftops, abandoned warehouses and fog-swept waterfronts" (Meehan 5). But however much *Equilibrium* depends on the conventions of film noir, it is still essentially a science fiction film, which carries with it all the critical elements of that genre.

The basis of *Equilibrium*'s plot depends on the critical impulse brought about by science fiction in its depiction of an alternative future world that could be the result of the present system. The film reflects a contemporary concern about the potential that a third world war could occur, and that such a war would be fought using nuclear weaponry. It also echoes concern about what Wimmer refers to as "numbness," when he says that "this particular film was about numbness. It's about numbness I think as brought on by over saturation potentially from the media. It's about numbness that is brought on by self-medication ... and ... any of the ways that we have made ourselves insensible to the environment around us" (Wimmer). This concern about numbness is especially important, because the film's ability to produce in the viewer a certain sensibility about their empirical world that they had not perhaps had before is essentially the same as producing cognitive estrangement, which Darko Suvin has cited as the critical project of the science fiction genre (24). It seems, then, that on some level what Wimmer is most interested in doing in the film is producing cognitive estrangement in its viewers. Also, since the war that facilitates the dystopian society in the film is said to have been fought "in the first years of the 21st century," according to Father's voiceover early in the film, *Equilibrium* inspires historical thinking by positioning the present as this imagined future's past, and does so with a particular sense of immediacy. This positioning of the present as the future's past is consistent with Jameson's contention that the science fiction genre picked up the critical historicism of the historical novel, thereby putting forth a sense of the future that suggests action in the present can facilitate the kind of change needed to avoid the dark futures of (dystopian) science fiction. The pairing of the critical energy of science fiction with the conventions of film noir in *Equilibrium* makes the film exemplary of the tech-noir film, which can be demonstrated in the ways that the film takes noir themes to a new level using science fiction as its basis for doing so.

Locating *Equilibrium* in the filmic subgenre of the tech-noir is easy enough in the sense that it pairs science fiction with film noir, but it is also useful to look more specifically at how exactly the two genres intersect with one another in the film. Meehan is interested in his work on the tech-noir in the interpretation of the term tech-noir as "black tech," writing that it is "fiction that explores the dark side of technology and how it interfaces with the dark side of human nature" (13). He further writes that "tech-noir casts a jaded eye on the brave new worlds that black tech will be obliged to create and the human dooms that will be their consequence," and that "the evils of technology are merely a reflection of the darkness that lies in the depths of the human psyche" (13). He cites the fears of nuclear proliferation as having facilitated the perceived fear of technology that came about after the atomic bombings of Hiroshima and Nagasaki, Japan in 1945. These fears continue to this day, despite considerable advances in technology outside of military armament, and are central to the premise of *Equilibrium*. As a result of the fears of technology that pervade black tech, the science fictional elements of the tech-noir "mutate" the film noir themes in the genre (14). Examples of this include a certain loss of subtlety in the *femme fatale* characters (à la *Blade Runner*'s snake-dancing Zhora, *Terminator 3*'s robot assassin T-X, and the alien female character Sil in Roger Donaldson's *Species*), gender role reversals (such as *Terminator 2*'s Sarah Connor or *The Matrix*'s Trinity), amnesia, and memory manipulation (14–15). Another mutated noir motif that Meehan points out in the tech-noir is the manipulation of reality, which, he writes, leads "to the formation of a kind of false consciousness" (15). Here is a theme that is an integral part of *Equilibrium*; the citizens of Libria are by law forced to take the drug, Prozium, which takes away their ability to see the evils of the system they live under, producing a false consciousness that seeks to parallel the numbness of the viewer to the evils of his or her empirical world.

Still another noir theme that runs throughout the tech-noir is what Meehan terms a "worm's eye view of psychology" in which protagonists "stand at a crossroads in the garden of good and evil" (16). In *Equilibrium*, Preston must decide after mistakenly missing an interval of Prozium whether to remain off of the drug, which pits him against not only the totalitarian regime of which he is an officer, but even his own family. His wife is revealed early on to have been executed for sense offense, which begins to torment him after he ceases his own Prozium dose, and his own children, especially his son, Robbie (Matthew Harbour), seem to be adamant about upholding the tenets of Libria, which causes Preston to have to lie to them.

The villain in the tech-noir equals yet another theme that is a variation on one from film noir. While *Equilibrium*'s Dupont and Brandt are memorable as noir villains in some ways, so too is the government of Libria itself. According to Meehan, "neo-fascist governments ... provide another source of villainy in many tech-noirs," warning of "the dangers of futuristic police states whose fascist intentions are enabled by high technology" (16). Libria is certainly painted in this light, and technology surely facilitates the administering of the Prozium intervals, both in the development of the drug as well as in the use of pneumatic syringes for dispensing it. In fact, Libria is also demonstrative of the "steel and concrete urban environment[s] saturated with electronic advertising displays" (17) that are so typical of the tech-noir film, and derived from the overbearing cities of film noir. Libria is definitely "sterile looking" (17) as so many of these cities are, though its advertising displays are less a critique of capitalism like those of *Minority Report* or *Total Recall* as much as they are intended to strengthen the totalitarian regime of Libria with their constant government propaganda. With these science fiction-morphed noir themes playing out in the tech-noir comes a substantial amount of critique, leaving the tech-noir an inherently critical genre. *Equilibrium*'s tech-noir sensibility manifests in its dystopian narrative, which locates the critical energy in a dystopian framework, thus producing a critical dystopia.

The critique inherent in *Equilibrium*—a critical dystopia—is surely manifest in the several critical energies already mentioned, including that of both the film noir and science fiction genres melded into the subgenre of tech-noir, as well as fears of nuclear proliferation, the concern about "numbness," and the film's visionary interrogation of pre-emptive foreign policy. But the film also adheres to the form of the critical dystopia on film. For Constance Penley, the genre in film is characterized by its tendency "to suggest causes rather than merely reveal symptoms" (122). Peter Fitting agrees with this idea, writing that "what is important in the critical dystopia and distinguishes it from other dystopias is to be found in the adjective *critical*, which implies an explanation of how the dystopian situation came about as much as what should be done about it" (156). *Equilibrium* contains a dark future world that is the result of nuclear war, which was a fear in American culture beginning with the attacks in Asia in 1945, and continuing still today. Wimmer seems to caution against the realization of nuclear war through the scope of the film, and suggests that it is the cause of *Equilibrium*'s dystopian society, thereby placing the film in the realm of the critical dystopia in cinema. Moylan points to Penley's work on the subject when he writes that the critical dystopia on film gives rise to an examination of "socioeconomic operations that not only produce the present reality but also silence the utopian opposition to it as all serious alternatives are apparently denied or crushed" (193). These "filmic thought experiments," according to Moylan, "help to explore the forms" (193) of what Penley calls "collective political strategies" (122), which Moylan says are "needed to dismantle the present system and lead toward a better, utopian future" (193). The various critical modes in *Equilibrium* are consistent with the concerns of the critical dystopia in their suggestion of causal relationships with the present and the film's imagined future world, in addition to the suggestion of what might be done to counteract such a future world from coming into being in the first place. These causal relationships and promotion of counteractive measures equal more ways in which this tech-noir film ends up a critical dystopia.

As a genre that results from the combination of elements of film noir and science fiction, the tech noir is an especially critical genre. Pulling from film noir's critical energy, which can be considered the manifestation of modernism in its American form, the tech-noir is critical of the capitalist system, just as the film noir had been in its initial phase. Drawing critical energy from science fiction, on the other hand, the tech-noir brings about historical thinking on the part of the viewer by suggesting that the alternative worlds of the films are the result of the present — that is, that the present is the future's past, and, by extension, that what happens in the present has a meaningful impact on what will happen in the future. Furthermore, the tech-noir film's appropriation of the critical energy of film noir is not unlike science fiction's seizure of the critical energy of the historical novel. As a critical film genre, then, the tech-noir becomes a critical dystopia when it employs dystopian narrative form. Kurt Wimmer's *Equilibrium* is one example of a tech-noir film that embodies a critical dystopia, one in which a totalitarian regime outlaws emotion in order to counteract the possibility of war, rendering its citizens numb to the fascistic practices of the system they live under. Such extreme measures are reached because of a third world war that is said to have taken place early in the 21st century, from which society has emerged scared of any potential for a fourth. In this way, historical thinking is encouraged in the film's viewers, as the catalyst for the establishment of such a regime in the future is suggested to have taken place in the present. Also, this aspect of the film can now be linked to the anxiety of Americans about the preemptive foreign policy strategies of the administration of George W. Bush following the World Trade Center attacks in New York City on September 11, 2001, even if the film was made before the attacks and adoption of those strategies even occurred. This, in fact, may explain the popularity of the film in the years since its appearance, especially considering its limited release and overall negative initial critical reception. Another critical angle of the film is the numbness of the people in the film as facilitated by their being forced to drug themselves for the purposes of blocking emotion, which critiques the obliviousness of the subjects of the current system to its evils. *Equilibrium's* protagonist recognizes the truths of the film's repressive society only once he ceases his dose of the emotion inhibiting drug, encouraging the film's viewers to cease their own oblivious attitudes toward the underlying truths of the repressive society of their empirical world. Part of the way these critical energies are realized in the film is through the mutation of film noir themes in the tech-noir genre meld, the critical framework of science fiction, and the dystopian narrative form. Some critics have delineated the specific qualities of the critical dystopia in film in terms of its suggestion of causal relationships for the depicted world of the films, and recommendations for action in the present to avoid such a world. *Equilibrium* contains these attributes as well, equaling yet another way in which the film fits into the mold of the critical dystopia. Whatever the film's generic conventions and narrative form, it contains a utopian impulse in that it keeps alive the possibility of hope for a better system in the subversion of the anti-utopian society by the film's end, which suggests that life can be better (rather than worse) as society moves forward, which is essential for a hopeful concept of the future.

Works Cited

Equilibrium. Dir. Kurt Wimmer. Perf. Christian Bale, Emily Watson, Taye Diggs, and Angus MacFadyen. 2002. DVD. Dimension, 2003.
Fitting, Peter. "Unmasking the Real? Critique and Utopia in Recent SF Films." *Dark*

Horizons: Science Fiction and the Dystopian Imagination. Rafaella Baccolini and Tom Moylan, eds. New York: Routledge, 2003.

Jameson, Fredric. *The Cultural Turn: Selected Writings on the Postmodern, 1983–1998*. London: Verso, 1998.

_____. "Progress versus Utopia, or, Can We Imagine the Future." *Archaeologies of the Future: The Desire Called Utopia and Other Science Fictions*. London: Verso, 2005. 281–295.

Meehan, Paul. *Tech-Noir: The Fusion of Science Fiction and Film Noir*. Jefferson, NC: McFarland, 2008.

Moylan, Tom. *Scraps of the Untainted Sky: Science Fiction, Utopia, Dystopia*. Boulder: Westview Press, 2000.

Naremore, James. *More Than Night: Film Noir in its Contexts*. Updated and expanded edition. Berkeley: University of California Press, 2008.

Penley, Constance. *The Future of an Illusion: Film, Feminism, and Psychoanalysis*. Minneapolis: University of Minneapolis Press, 1989.

Sargent, Lyman Tower. "The Three Faces of Utopianism Revisited." *Utopian Studies* 5.1 (1994): 1–37.

Suvin, Darko. "Estrangement and Cognition." *Speculations on Speculation: Theories of Science Fiction*. James Gunn and Matthew Candelaria, eds. Lanham, MD: Scarecrow Press, 2005. 23–36.

Wimmer, Kurt. Director's commentary. *Equilibrium*. Dir. Kurt Wimmer. Perf. Christian Bale, Emily Watson, Taye Diggs, and Angus MacFadyen. 2002. DVD. Dimension, 2003.

Who's Coming for Dinner? An Examination of *A History of Violence*

LESLIE SEAWRIGHT

A *Betty Crocker* cookbook from 1950 tells readers: "Every morning before breakfast, comb hair, apply makeup and a dash of cologne. Does wonders for your morale and your family's too! Think pleasant thoughts while working and a chore will become a labor of love" (5). Nostalgia for this 1950s family ideology of the United States is still seen in current literature and film, although the picture is becoming more desperate as family dynamics change and women refuse to look only to chores for happiness. Feminists' political and theoretical efforts force examination of a culture that continues to support systems of patriarchy and the bourgeois. The movie, *A History of Violence*, displays the confusion and tragedy experienced by characters as they discover that their own 1950s version of the American dream is a lie. The film demonstrates that this falsified dream never existed for women then or now. As detailed by feminist critics, women continue fight to overcome their own history of violence — a history created and dictated by the patriarchy. Cronenberg's film, *A History of Violence*, exposes the American Dream for a lie and asks the audience to examine the patriarchy, bourgeois, and capitalistic government that created it.

The history of feminist literary and film criticism is complicated by the fact that feminism has no separate individual theory from which to create new meanings and understanding. While the focus is on women, women's issues, the depiction of women and the patriarchy that constricts and confines them, the theory itself relies on several other theoretical platforms from which to analyze. Simone de Beauvoir described feminists in the early 1980s: "feminists are women ... fighting to change women's condition in association with the class struggle, but independently of it as well, without making the changes they strive for totally dependent on changing society as a whole" (qtd. in Moi

91–2). This struggle is evident in feminist film criticism in which critics work to expose stereotypes and promote more realistic visions of female experience.

In feminist film criticism three main influences and reference points appear from which feminist theory develops and diverges. The first, shaped by Lacan's ideas of the Imaginary Order and Kristeva's notion of language as "symbolic," is semiotics (Booker 93). For semioticians constructing film analysis, the work is to be seen as "a systematic network of binary oppositions, organized metaphorically, if not literally like language" (Mayne 85). Of course, this approach has obvious problems. Semiotics was developed to discuss and interpret literary works as opposed to the visual symbolism and methods corresponding to film. The drawbacks of this approach is mainly the difficulty in transferring this very literal approach to that of visual film.

The second major focus of feminist critique and theory has its roots in Freudian and Lacanian psychoanalysis. Specifically with film, Laura Mulvey, the most famous feminist film theorist to use psychoanalysis, focuses on the gaze, scopophilia, fetishism, and the pleasure principle (Mulvey 1975). Surprisingly, her more recent works have dismissed some of her previous study and she now holds several ideas related to socialism and Marxism, with Jameson influences, in particular (Mulvey 2004).[1] Mulvey may have discovered the weakness inherent with psychoanalytical approach to film, which has been discussed by several other critics. Noël Carroll, in regard to the use of the theory notes, "this unquestioning acceptance of the *scientific* authority of psychoanalysis is a continuing feature of epistemologically dubious merit in contemporary feminist film criticism" (351). The questionable science is only one objection offered by critics. Others include the male-biased view of psychoanalysis to begin with, especially in regard to Freud and his description of the female body as that lacking a penis—a lack that must cause horror and castration anxiety in all men who view her.[2] An approach such as this seems far from the feminist ideal of overcoming the problems created by the patriarchy. However, psychoanalysis does offer a vocabulary that can prove useful when describing the representation of women in film, and this fact continues to draw critics to the approach.

The most meaningful theory to use in conjunction with a feminist perspective is the Marxist view. Marx's model suggests that current culture, such as literature, film, and art, represents and reflects the society's political and economic conditions. Thus, by studying culture one can learn information about these other important conditions as well (Booker 73). This approach stresses that film conveys information, messages, and ideologies to the spectators (Mayne 85). The ideology functions as a type of representation of society and the culture that it creates. In this way, one can look at a film, identify the ideology displayed and then speak to that ideology as somewhat representative of current culture. This approach seems especially beneficial for feminists who seek not only to expose the patriarchy but limit its power. If the ideology can be identified and acknowledged as representing current culture then new ideologies can be implemented and implanted in feminist films in order to change society. Judith Mayne described that Marxist-feminist thought, "seem[s] to offer a way not only to understand the cinema but to change it" (85). This approach also allows for the identification of the commodification that occurs so often in women's lives, both on film and off. Wives are constantly commodified as housekeepers, babysitters, cooks, drivers, and prostitutes. The economic value of their role in society is immense and ultimately frightening to the patriarchy. This idea and others will be investigated in regard to *A History of Violence*.

The American Dream and its family ideology have ties to the 1950s time period; although, their roots go much further back into history. During the '50s the creation of the family ideology was ramped up in a desperate effort to secure the nuclear family in a time of nuclear threat. The cold war was terrifying, and the capitalist democracy of the U.S. drove to incite fear of communism into the hearts of every American. The American Dream became more ingrained during this time because it was important to the government for people to believe the dream so that they would not start to entertain new ideas of political structure or socialism. The dream told them that America was the only country in the world where a family could succeed and be happy. Poor men turned to rich men, and families were always healthier and wealthier than their parent's generation. This ideology created a very hierarchical structure (which was not original but served the American Dream well) of a father-centered family. He ruled the family while mother cooked, cleaned, raised the children, and made father happy. Father's responsibility was to bring money home, which of course was easy because they all lived in America. According to this model, all in the family are happy if such a structure can be followed. Any deviation from the ideology will result in unhappiness and possible collapse of the entire family structure. The ideology is important because by giving the father power, it grants power to the government to rule over the people in the same way a father rules over his house. This idea could also be found in 17th century Europe. There, the monarchy derived its power from the common belief that just as God granted the father power over his house, so should the monarchy rule the people (McDonald 260). Thus, the benefits of patriarchal power serve both the father and the government.

The creation of the American Dream was also critical in the 1950s because this followed a time during World War II when women were found working in factories and building planes. After the soldiers returned home, the working women posed a real threat to the ability of men to resume their status as providers. The economic system demanded that women return home so that men could again fill the factories and offices; otherwise, a surplus of workers would result in rampant unemployment. The idea that women ever worked and could identify with the working class was masked by the allusion of the happy housewife. She was ahistorical and had always existed only to serve her family in the home. The idea that women could work in a production other than their already commodified lives at home was lost. They were denied the camaraderie of a potentially powerful proletariat. Thus, desperation for a nostalgic time when women were protected and provided for following the insanity of a world at war and during a time of nuclear anxiety created the lie of the "American Dream."

Cronenberg's film, *A History of Violence*, explores this ideology and the patriarchy that shaped it. Viewers are mentally and emotionally unprepared for the opening scene of this movie. Two bored and tired looking men are killing and maiming their way across the country. This is a shocking surprise to an audience watching their slow and almost comic departure from a motel in the opening scene. The cruel and incomprehensible killing of a little girl holding a doll forces the audience to remember the title of the movie. The little girl whimpers upon entering the room and finds her mother lying dead. She holds her doll, a now meaningless symbol of security, and looks at the man.

The scene suggests that children are often left to look upon the violence done to their mothers and other women. Their legacy is one of pain and cruelty as expressed by the bloody body of her mother and worthless female doll the girl clutches. Neither can protect the girl now and the suggestion continues that neither could have protected her before. She looks to the man, innocently believing there is hope or help in his arrival. Of course, he destroys all these ideas by drawing his gun up to her head. What becomes interesting in this scene and in their next appearance in the film is specifically who the mass murderers kill and threaten. While the audience assumes these two men have killed many men and women, the camera only shows the bodies of one woman and the shooting of a little girl. At the coffee shop, Tom, the main character, is threatened with a gun, but it is ultimately the waitress they prepare to rape, injure, and kill.

The reality of women as victims of violence, even as children, is clearly expressed through the selections and actions of the crazed mass murders. The deeper underlying patriarchal thought could be the wish to rid the world of all females—to execute even the children and be freed from the threat of rebellious women. The murderers demonstrate their ultimate power over females through their violent acts upon them. The act of killing the girl seems meaningless, and the audience is left to wonder at the incalculable cruelty of the shooting. It is symbolic that this is a small motel and not a corporate owned super-hotel. The appearance of the little girl wandering out from the living quarters of this place suggests that the motel is family owned and operated. The owner was probably one of those killed along with the little girl. Their idea of the American Dream is destroyed in one very quick and meaningless act. There is the sense that not even money seemed to motivate these two crazed killers, a thought that is baffling to a capitalist sensibility. However, one imagines these two leave a scene of carnage as easily as they created it. The ideology of the family and its structure is left behind. The "American Dream" for this family is gone, its mere existence a lie. This scene foreshadows the destruction of the Stall's American Dream and the violence to be committed upon the family's women.

As the sound of the gun rings in the audience's ears from the murder of the girl at the motel, another little girl, Sarah, screams from a nightmare in her bed. Her mother and father rush in to comfort her as she too holds a stuffed doll. She tells them she fears monsters in her closet, and Tom reassures her, "There are no such things as monsters." This line is ironic after viewing the murder of another innocent girl only seconds earlier. It reaffirms the deception that accompanies violence upon women. This is the segment of society that is often suppressed, beaten, and raped, yet society tells itself it isn't so. No, there are no monsters. No, there is no patriarchy to hold women down. No, women are not in danger physically, mentally, or emotionally in this society. All women in the film suffer this denial of violence. Tom's lie is only one of many during the course of the movie. Ultimately, his deception endangers his wife and daughter as they become legacies of his violence, as the false consciousness of the U.S. population works to deny the lies told to women.

The ideology of the family supports the deception of its members. Women cannot know that their jobs as housekeepers, child watchers, cooks, and sexual partners are commodified in the capitalist system. The oppression of their lives with the implementation of their daily duties is, instead, held up to be celebrated. Their tasks become further commodified through instruction books, TV shows, and honorary awards and competitions, such as Mother's Day and cooking contests. From a Marxist perspective, people distance or alienate themselves from real conditions of life because the material alienation of real conditions forces them to create representations that deceive them. The reality of capitalist production are so alienating that people make up stories or representations that distance them from the reality of the system (Klages). A woman's true condition of basic slavery to her husband and children at every level must be masked with an ideology that promotes the slavery in endearing terms. The pictures shown must be one of a happy family at the dinner table, all praising mother for her efforts. In this way, the realization of her alienation from her husband, children, and society can be avoided. Terry Eagleton notes, "If people do not actively combat a political regime which oppresses them, it may not be because they meekly imbibed its governing values. It may be because they are too exhausted after a hard day's work to have much energy left to engage in political activity, or because they are too fatalistic or apathetic to see the point of such activity" (34). This seems the case with women and the ideology of the American Dream. Women are so exhausted performing the duties for which they are praised, it is difficult to realize the reality of the situation. Today, with working women often expected to function as mother/wife and provide the same support of the non-working housewife, such a situation becomes desperate as women seek the new dream of the "American Working Mother," who can do it all and have all. In the end, the ideology is the same, and it is capitalism that seeks to promote its patriarchal power at the expense of the working class and women.

The film depicts Edie, the mother and wife, in a fascinating way. She is a lawyer, yet as an audience we never see her go to the office, work from home, defend a client, or even talk about her day in terms of her work. She provides a very domesticated model of a 1950s era mother. She is constantly seen with the children, in the home, or trying to secure safety for herself and her husband with the aid of the local cop. In her first scene, she acts as driver, picking up Tom as he walks home. Edie has planned an exciting night for the two, as she next exits the bathroom wearing a cheerleader outfit. Here is the small restaurant owners wife, the American Dream girl, a cheerleader, ready to take control sexually or submit to his commands, whichever he prefer. The scene presents both options sexually, so there is no allusion that she is seeking to pleasure herself in any way or gratify her own nature by taking charge. Her short-lived sexual aggression is dismissed as Tom rolls on top of her and gains dominance. Toril Moi notes, "Women are denied the right to create their own images of femaleness, and instead must seek to conform to the patriarchal standards imposed on them" (57). Despite Edie's job as a lawyer, her representation of mother and American dream girl seem all she can play in this movie. All other avenues of expression are refused her. The family ideology ignores her importance as a member of working society and emphasizes her role as wife/mother or wife/whore.

Edie functions only to serve others as her division of labor dictates. The irrationality and delusion of the selfless wife is made clear in this film after the betrayal of Tom's past is divulged. Gilbert and Gubar describe this selflessness of women: "To be selfless is not only to be noble, is it to be dead. A life that has no story ... is really a life of death, a death-in-life" (25). Edie has no story. She has adopted the story of her husband and is destroyed when this story is found to be a lie since she has no knowable past or history of her own. The audience learns about Tom's real past and even Tom's pretend past, "You mean you're not an orphan" (*A History of Violence*), but Edie is only known as related to Tom and his lies. She has no separate history or reference point. She is ahistorical in this family. The ideology does not permit her a separateness from her family members. She is an individual only as related to Tom.

This reminds us of her status as oppressed, or rather, her function in the economic system in regards to her division of labor. Tom uses Edie as a wife, mother, and cover for his past. He embodies the Western world's capitalist attitude where things are bought and used without consideration to the conditions of the third world workers that made them. There is no thought for Edie and how she may react and feel once his past is discovered. Marxist theory argues, "the labor of individuals as a source of commodities, eventually leads to the treatment of human beings as abstract economic quantities" (Booker 74). Through this alienation and commodification of women, stereotypes are formed and become part of the family ideology.

Mary Ellmann in her book, *Thinking About Women*, lists common stereotypes of women in literature. I argue these stereotypes are also easily identifiable in film. She attests that the assignment of stereotypes since World War II has been done in a more demoralizing fashion than before this time. This demoralization is most prevalent in regard to the assignment of power. Men retain a powerful protector position, as women became more and more helpless (Ellmann 71). She argues this is due to the atomic bombing and concentration camps of World War II, in which millions were killed regardless of gender or age. The feeling of helplessness experienced by society was projected onto women and manifested by frantically emphasizing the stereotypes of weak women and strong men (Ellmann 71–74). The desire for nostalgia and a return to a safe and predictable life (that was always really a lie) forced the cultural shift to a more unbalanced power structure for men versus women.

Of the eleven stereotypes outlined in Ellmann's book, Edie fits several categories. The categorization of women in film, and specifically, of Edie in *A History of Violence*, serves to further alienate her and define her role in the patriarchal society. In the family ideology, she becomes as definable as she is formless. She becomes as understandable as she is illogical. The ideology defines the stereotypes and in turn, women acting within the ideology demonstrate the stereotypes. Edie exhibits formlessness, instability, materiality, and confinement in the film. I have discussed her existence as formless in regards to her lack of a personal history before meeting Tom. She is only known as an extension of Tom, and despite her job as a lawyer, the audience only sees her function as a mother and wife.

Edie often exhibits instability in the face of dealing with the reality of the mob men who seek to hurt her husband and in realizing of her husband's betrayal. In the first instance, Edie and Tom meet with the sheriff after the mob men first visit the café. After the sheriff leaves, Edie turns to Tom and starts to sob on his shoulder. At this point in the film, it is unknown the real threat the mob men possess. Her instability seems reactionary and weak. Tom, exemplifying the powerful male, stands strong and shows no fear. Later in the film when they are in the hospital, Tom tells Edie the truth about his past. Edie reacts illogically and asks laughable questions such as "You mean you never lived in Portland" (*A History of Violence*). She is so distraught and confused as he sits calmly in bed that she goes to the bathroom and vomits. In this scene, her American Dream is exposed as a fraud. Edie realizes that her life has been a lie and the man she trusts, an imposter. The ideology ingrained in her dictates the instability she expresses in this moment. In regards to the stereotype of instability, Ellmann claims, "Heroines now shriek or mope or pass out or go black in the face—they lose control. Meanwhile the men, their sensibilities activated by experience, *go* or *run* mad" (86). Edie mopes about the house, loses control of her body through vomiting, and retreats emotionally and physically throughout the rest of the movie. She is regarded as unstable. However, the audience does not consider Tom's instability as he kills his brother and many others. The calm demeanor with which he manages his madness separates him from his powerless and unstable wife. She, unlike Tom, does nothing.

Edie's exemplification of materiality in the film is especially disturbing in regard to the Marxist-feminist approach used to evaluate the film as a whole. Ellmann remarks, "Grown women ... are supposed to act like brain-damaged children, entirely absorbed in indiscriminate sensory impressions. This is understood to account for their persuasion by candy, perfume, and flowers, their later occupation with clothing, appliances, furnishings" (98). During Edie and Sarah's trip to the mall, Edie becomes so involved in buying shoes that she allows Sarah to wonder off and into the arms of Fogarty and his mob men. Her neglectfulness has been precipitated by a consumer drive to purchase shoes for herself and her daughter. This activity so consumes her that her daughter was put in danger. Edie's materiality has produced negative effects for her family in this instance. The deeper meaning suggests that consumerism, as a part of the American Dream, always leads to danger and disaster. It also suggests that the two are inseparably paired. There is no dream without consumerism and vice versa. The two work together to build an ideology of constant "want." One wants new shoes, just as one wants to move from Philadelphia, open a restaurant and start a family. Both endeavors are based in lies. The myth of the American Dream is revealed as easily as a failed shoe purchase.

The American Dream also results in confinement for women, which is the last stereotype clearly exhibited in the film. As Ellmann notes, "Range is masculine and confinement is feminine" (87). Edie is confined by her role as wife/mother. She is confined to the house in the face of violence despite the fact that violence happens within the house as much as it happens outside of it. She is also confined by the masculine last name she traditionally adopts in marriage. As previously addressed, Edie is trapped by ideology into the confining role of wife/mother with the stereotypes that those roles possess. Despite her disgust at finding out her husband is a fraud (making her American dream a fraud as well), Edie lies to the sheriff the last time he questions Tom about his past and the mob men. She tells him, "Tom is who he says he is," convincing the sheriff to leave. She defends her husband even when an opportunity to tell the truth and be rid of him presents itself. Edie is confined by the "stand by your man" ideology of the family structure.

The house in the film also serves to physically confine Edie and Sarah. They are rarely seen outside the house and are forced to return to it by the men during times of possible violence. Fogarty and his men show up at the house and reveal they have Jack, Edie's son. She again exhibits instability and goes screaming towards him as Tom grabs her. He tells her to go back into the house to be with Sarah. Although Edie is terrified about her son and wishes to take him from Fogarty, she obeys and goes back into the house. Now, Tom can perform his masculine duty of protecting the family without the aide of any women. They remain inside the house, powerless victims of the violence outside. In the graphic novel, Edie overcomes the confinement of the house and rescues Tom by shooting Fogarty with the shotgun (Wagner 91). In the movie, however, she is denied this victory and Jack, the male son, comes to rescue his father. The confinement of the house aids in the alienation Edie feels as a result of the family ideology and the American Dream. The movie allows no room for a powerful woman savior. Only Jack, another male, is capable and has the opportunity to save Tom.

Edie cannot escape the violence of the outside world by merely being confined inside the home. The demented sex scene that she and Tom share emphasizes the isolation and alienation that results from the stereotyping and ideology Edie endures. After lying to the sheriff, she slaps Tom and he begins to choke her. The house that confines her contains as much violence as the outside world. She is disgusted by the lies that have destroyed her life and the fraud she has lived with for fifteen years. Edie tries to escape from

Tom up the stairs, but he grabs her and forces himself on her. She soon acquiesces and the two violently writhe on the hardwood steps. The scene presents Edie's own attempt to hurt and violate Tom. The anger racing through her body at the deception of this man and the endangerment of her children, forces her to react and hit him. She becomes disgusted with her own attempt at violence, and ultimately, the sex leaves both frustrated and Edie abused. She throws Tom off of her and retreats to the bedroom. The dream of success for the family is destroyed. The home is not a safe haven, for within it remains the patriarchal dictatorship that rules Edie and the family. The perceived safety of home thus destroyed leaves only emptiness for the audience. Sex has not saved the couple nor has the small calm town been able to prevent violence. The audience has no resolution for either of these problems.

Edie's last name serves to confine her in a different way. When Tom reveals his past in the hospital, Edie seems especially concerned that her last name and that of her children is a lie. She has given up her identity literally and figuratively for Tom. She has accepted his lies and way of life. Amy Taubin, in writing about the film, notes that the name "Stall" has an institutional quality. Tom is stalled between his life of crime and the small business owner life he wants. The name's prison-like quality, with the "t" and double "l" creating the bars of the family's future, signify the confinement of Edie (Taubin par. 11). She suffers the loss of her identity, name, future, and the American Dream fantasy. Ellmann argues that "women come to seem deciduous, men evergreen. Things fall from women, repeatedly, cyclically. With marriage, they drop even their last names.... Eventually they lose the capacity itself for experiencing these former loses" (184). We see this in the film as Edie becomes numb. The confusion and frustration resulting from the sex with her husband leaves her cold. She will not speak again in the film. The scene following their violent sex reveals her naked body to Tom and the audience as she walks out of the shower. She is exposed and left open to the cruelty of the patriarchy and the lie of the American Dream. Her stripped body suggests the naked and empty soul. Her fantasy world is as exposed as her body. There is no safety at home, in her town, or with her family. She is stripped of all the delusions of comfort and peace.

Cronenburg described the small-town atmosphere of Millbrook, Illinois, where the film supposedly takes place, as the "Garden of Eden, a fantasy of the past when things were better. It's that yearning, that aching for the reality to be true" (qtd. in Taubin par. 4). But the reality isn't true, and the perceptibility of people to fall for it remains high because there is a longing for Utopia.[3] There is nostalgia for a past that never existed when things were better, easier. If Utopia exists, however, the audience realizes it is not with the fantasy of the American Dream. Cronenberg is really dealing with the reality of American life in which nothing happens. Capitalism has stalled daily life just as Tom is stalled tying to change his past and Edie is stalled in the ideology of the American Dream.

Frederic Jameson describes this phenomena:

> [T]his very triviality of daily life in late capitalism is itself the desperate situation against which all the formal solutions, the strategies and subterfuges, of high culture as well as mass culture emerge: how to project the illusion that things still happen, that events exist, that there are still stories to tell [87].

Thus, in the "All-American" town of Millbrook a family seeking the American Dream is terrorized by the father's past. A story unfolds and many events happen, yet in the end we are left with a sense of loss — a realization that life is not as it seems, that life does not happen, and this family has no story, no future.

It is difficult for an audience to not feel the same way at the conclusion of the film. We feel stripped of all former allusions of the American Dream and the safety it implies. The American Dream and its capitalist mechanisms have been exposed and their fraudulent nature examined. When Tom returns from his killing spree to join the family for dinner, there is no spark of energy or hope left in this family. Despite the appearance of a Betty Crocker homecoming with tidy children sitting in front of a laboriously cooked dinner, the family is silent and alienated from one another. Even the camera cannot bring the family members together, as each member remains locked in separate frames (Taubin par. 14).

The film analyzes the fictitious nature of the American Dream and the damage this dream produces in families and women. The ideology of the dream creates and perpetuates stereotypes that trap women in traditional roles while telling them these roles will make them happy and productive. The subversive nature of the sex scene suggests that women can resist but ultimately they become cold and numb living a life of lies. Mayne argues that "a given film may "seem" to function as a simple vehicle for sexist ideology, but when read in a critical way is shown to undermine the very values it presumably conveys" (87). While Edie seems the stereotypical wife and mother in the film, one comes to understand that the true villain is not the mob, or Tom. The villain is the family ideology supplied through the American Dream and reinforced by capitalism.

Notes

1. Mulvey has published numerous articles on psychoanalysis and film criticism. Her most famous article, "Visual Pleasure and Narrative Cinema," has sparked discussion and controversy since its publication in 1975. A leading figure in feminist film theory, Mulvey and her viewpoints and ideas are still important to the field.

2. Several critics address Mulvey's use of psychoanalysis specifically. Stephen Prince's "The Pornographic Image and the Practice of Film Theory" challenges the approach in regard to pornography films. Noël Carroll, in "The Image of Women in Film: A Defense of a Paradigm," argues that psychoanalysis is not methodologically sound.

3. My references and ideas in regard to Utopia are formed from Fredric Jameson's writings on the topic. They are informed primarily by his books *Signatures of the Visible* and *The Political Unconscious*.

Works Cited

A History of Violence. Dir. David Cronenberg. Perf. Viggo Mortensen, Maria Bello, and Ed Harris. New Line Cinema, 2005.

Booker, M. Keith. *A Practical Introduction to Literary Theory and Criticism*. White Plains, NY: Longman, 1996.

Carroll, Noël. "The Image of Women in Film: A Defense of a Paradigm." *The Journal of Aesthetics and Art Criticism* 48.4 (1990): 349–360.

Eagleton, Terry. *Ideology: An Introduction*. London: Verso, 1991.

Ellmann, Mary. *Thinking About Women*. New York: Harcourt Brace Jovanovich, 1968.

Jameson, Fredric. *Signatures of the Visible*. New York: Routledge, 1990.

Klages, Mary. "Louis Althusser's 'Ideology and Ideological State Apparatuses.'" 21 April 2007. http://www.tamilnation.org/ideology/klages.htm.

Mayne, Judith. "Feminist Film Theory and Criticism." *Signs* 11.1 (1985): 81–100.

McDonald, Russ. *The Bedford Companion to Shakespeare*. Boston: Bedford/St. Martin's, 2001.

Moi, Toril. *Sexual/Textual Politics: Feminist Literary Theory*. London: Methuen, 1985.

Mulvey, Laura. "Looking at the Past from the Present: Rethinking Feminist Film Theory of the 1970s." *Signs* 30.1 (2004): 1286–1292.

_____. "Visual Pleasure and Narrative Cinema." *Visual and Other Pleasures*. Indianapolis: Indiana University Press, 1989, 14–26.

Prince, Stephen. "The Pornographic Image and the Practice of Film Theory." *Cinema Journal* 27.2 (1988): 27–39.

Taubin, Amy. "Model Citizens." *Film Comment* 41.5 (2005): 24–28. *ProQuest*. 20 April 2007. http://www.ProQuest.org/search.

Wagner, John. *A History of Violence*. New York: Vertigo, 1997.

A *Marxist Look at* Avatar
TIM DELANEY and ELLEN REED

A Marxist perspective is quite applicable to a number of films but it seems particularly appropriate to the movie *Avatar* because of its many socio-economic aspects. Economically-speaking, *Avatar* has been a huge commercial success. On January 26, 2010, *Avatar* officially topped *Titanic* as the top-grossing film of all-time at the box office. It may be worth noting that using calculations such as the Consumer Price Index (CPI), a formula that calculates for adjusted inflation dollars, *Gone With the Wind* has actually grossed more than any other film when the value of the box office receipts are adjusted (Pomerantz, 2010). In real dollars, *Avatar* earned over $1 billion in just 19 days and was the first film to make more than $2 billion in U.S. box office receipts and more than $3 billion worldwide.

If Karl Marx was somehow introduced to the futuristic concept of movies and movie theatres and people spending the wages of their labor on such pleasurable, non-productive leisure pursuits as movie-going, he would still be overwhelmed by the notion of a film earning millions of dollars, let alone billions. Furthermore, if Marx was to learn that nations such as the United States were struggling with huge national debts he would have to surmise, that the profits of the film *Avatar* would surely be sufficient to pay off such a debt. We know differently, as the national debt of the United States on August 30, 2012, was over $15.9 trillion (U.S. Treasury Department, 2012). According to the U.S. National Debt Clock (2012), the estimated U.S. population on that date was over 313 million and if each American paid his or her share of the debt, that figure would be over $51,000. A number of people, including wage-earners, will have a hard time paying off "their share" of debt. The National Debt has increased an average of $3.88 billion per day since September 28, 2007. If you are looking for any signs of progress in the nation's attempt to halt the growing debt consider that in May 2010 the national debt was increasing at an average of $4.12 billion per day. Most of us will take little solace in this knowledge.

The economics of the national debt is incomprehensible for those of us living in the twenty-first century let alone a citizen of the nineteenth. Marx would also be baffled, if not alarmed, to learn about how many people live in the world today. The estimated world population of over 7 billion people casts a huge shadow over the estimated 1.5 billion people that were on the planet at the time of Marx's death in 1883. Marx would surely wonder why scholars and social makers had not heeded his many warnings about the ever-expanding population growth. In his "Economic and Philosophic Manuscripts of 1844," for example, Marx stated, "There are too many people. Even the existence of men is a pure luxury; and if the worker is 'ethical,' he will be sparing in procreation" (Tucker, 1978: 97). Marx and his best friend and oft-co-author Friedrich Engels' concern for population control was directed at those who could not afford (based on the worker's ability to provide adequate food and shelter for his children) to economically support children. The implication that it was unethical for poor people to have children is not only elitist but hypocritical on Marx's part considering he was nearly completely reliant on Engels for handouts to provide for his own children. As a working-class agitator, Marx rarely earned enough money to take care of his own children. Four of his seven children died in childhood largely due to their impoverished living conditions. On the other hand, Engels could have easily afford to raise children, economically-speaking.

Marx's concern for overpopulation echoed the feelings of other early alarmist social theorists including Thomas Malthus and Herbert Spencer. Malthus had claimed that overpopulation would lead to conditions favorable to apocalyptical doomsday in the form of the Four Horsemen — war, famine, pestilence, and disease. Spencer argued that overpopulation would lead to the *survival of the fittest*. Social thinkers beyond the nineteenth century also warned about the negative consequences of overpopulation.

Clearly, the warning has not been heeded. Marx explained to us that there is a limit to the natural and social resources available to the masses (a very relevant topic when we examine the socio-economic factors that led to humans colonizing Pandora in the film *Avatar*). If the masses continue to swell in number, the consequences can only be negative for humanity, Marx decried. Among the many negative consequences of overpopulation that are very evident today is world hunger and malnutrition. Currently, there are approximately 925 million people world-wide suffering from hunger and malnutrition, a figure that comes close to the total world's population at the time of Marx's birth (World Food Programme 2012; World Hunger Education Services 2012). Beyond the obvious problems associated with hunger and malnutrition (e.g., 5 million deaths of children under age five occurs each year in developing countries) is the realization that hunger could trigger global social unrest.

About Avatar

As stated earlier, the national debt increases by nearly $3.88 billion a day. Hollywood would have to crank out two movies a day that grossed as much as *Avatar* in order to try and balance the budget. Balancing the budget, however, is not the job of movie makers. Instead, their primary responsibilities rest with providing entertainment, knowledge, and/or a focal point by which discussion of critical issues is established.

Pandora and the Na'vi

Despite the huge box office figures, there are some who have never seen the movie *Avatar*; thus, a little background on the film is warranted. In this 2009 blockbuster film, virtual realities come face-to-face with "real" characters. This epic science fiction film written and directed by James Cameron is set in the future (2154) on Pandora, a moon in the Alpha Centauri star system, where humans are mining a precious mineral called unobtanium (meaning, unobtainable precious metal). Unobtanium is so rare on Earth that it sells for $20 million a kilo. The value of this commodity drives the RDA Corporation. However, the expansion of the imperialist mining industry threatens the existence of the indigenous Na'vi. One clan, the Omaticaya ("The People"), is especially vulnerable. The Omaticaya live communally in a skyscraper tall tree called Hometree. The Na'vi are a sentimental humanoid species. They are blue-skinned, very tall (generally around 10 feet in height in adulthood), lean with no body fat, and highly athletic. The Na'vi also have long tails. The physical characteristics and home dwelling of the Omaticaya lead the humans to negatively label them as "blue monkeys."

The RDA Corporation has established a base on Pandora. There are three specific subsets of RDA operating on Pandora. One operation is responsible for mining unobtanium; a second division conducts research; and the third entity is a private security force, heavily armed and technologically advanced, designed to assure the continued mining and safety of human personnel. Parker Selfridge (played by Giovanni Ribisi) is the Administrator and heads the RDA colony on Pandora. Colonel Miles Quaritch (Stephen Lang) is in charge of the military and exerts a great deal of influence over Selfridge's decision-making. The research division is headed by Dr. Grace Augustine (Sigourney Weaver). She interacts with the natives of Pandora in an attempt to better understand their culture and the natural environment of Pandora.

Pandora is a wonderfully spectacular world with a wide array of animal species (dinosaur-like) such as blue lemurs, a hammerhead type of primitive elephants, flying dragons, illuminating butterflies (the seeds of the "Sacred Tree") and so on. Like their humanoid counterparts, each of these animal species are oversized. The physical environment of Pandora also includes floating mountains (the Hallelujah Mountains) with waterfalls, floating rocks, and a Sacred Tree that is interconnected with past and present Na'vi people. Eywa, the great spirit of Na'vi, serves as a deity, or goddess, of all life. The Na'vi believe that all life forms on Pandora are connected through a network of energy that flows through all living things and that all energy is only borrowed, then one day you have to give it back. Near the conclusion of the film, Dr. Augustine explains that the forest has an electro-chemical communication capacity via the interconnectedness of all the trees' roots. She claims that the Pandora forest is like the syntax between neurons inside human brains.

Although all forms of life are interconnected on Pandora, elements of both Charles Darwin's *natural selection* and Herbert Spencer's *survival of the fittest* are clearly intact. Violent confrontations between the species of Pandora are necessary as each needs a food source. The Na'vi have adopted a philosophy that involves honoring the death of some life form (e.g., an animal) that had to give its life for the sake of the survival of the people. This philosophy is akin to Native Americans and their honoring of the buffalo. They respected the buffalo, but still needed to kill the animal to survive. Native Americans received no pleasure from killing buffalo, but nonetheless, it was necessary. They certainly did not kill buffalo for sport. The Na'vi have the same type of relationship with many creatures on Pandora. They would not kill for sport, but instead, for survival.

At their very core, humans are not "fit" for Pandora. They are not strong or fast enough to survive the challenges of the natural environment. More importantly, they cannot breathe the air on Pandora. Because of their intellect, however, humans have learned to survive many hostile environments. The humans on Pandora wear oxygen masks and rely on the heavily armed and technologically-advanced military. The Na'vi are no match for the weaponry possessed by the humans. The scientific researchers have found another way to adapt to their new environment. They have created Avatars. Avatars are hybrid Na'vi. The researchers lie down in a chamber, similar to a tanning booth, and have their minds transferred to specifically-designed Avatars. Through the use of Avatars, the researchers are able to survive the Pandoran air. Over the course of time that the humans have been on Pandora, the scientists have learned quite a bit about the Na'vi. They can speak the language of the Na'vi and, in turn, have taught them English. The researchers have attempted to gain the trust of the Na'vi. They are trying to explain the human need for precious minerals. At the same time, the researchers are trying to broker a peace between the two species in order to avoid a possible RDA military assault on the Na'vi if they attempt to interfere with the mining.

The Narrative Approach

The film incorporates a narrative approach to story-telling. It is Corporal Jake Sully (Sam Worthington), a paraplegic marine, who provides the description of events. The film begins with Sully expressing his dissatisfaction with being a paraplegic, "When I was lying there, in the V.A. hospital with a big hole blown through the middle of my life, I started having these dreams of flying. I was free. Sooner or later though, you always have to wake up. " This foreshadowing statement will prove to become quite prophetic once Jake immerses himself in the Avatar program of RDA.

Jake explains that he is on his way to Pandora to take over the contract responsibilities of his recently deceased twin brother, Tommy. Tommy was a scientist who had learned the ways of the Na'vi. The RDA research division had created an Avatar specially designed to match his DNA. And although Jake was not trained in the Na'vi way, it was determined by the RDA Corp that the researchers needed security when their Avatars explored Pandora. Jake was excited about getting a new start in life. It was now up to him to learn how to be a "driver" of an Avatar. Jake quickly learns how to operate, or drive, his Avatar. He is excited about running and jumping, even if it is only in a virtual context. For Jake, it feels real. He feels as though he has tapped into his full human potential. It will only be a matter of time, however, before he begins to confuse one world for the other.

Although Jake is taking over for his brother in the research division, he is a Marine, and as he narrates, "There's no such thing as an ex-Marine. I may be out, but you never lose the attitude." Col. Quaritch asks Jake to serve as a spy for him and gather "intel" on the Na'vi. In return, the Colonel promises Jake an operation that will give him the use of his legs. Jake agrees. On his first assignment with a research team, Jake is separated from the group, chased by a wild beast, and falls over the edge of a cliff. The research team attempts to find him but they are forced to leave the area before nightfall because the Colonel has ruled that it is too dangerous for humans to be out of the compound at nighttime. Jake is on his own. Confronted by other beasts, Jake appears close to death when suddenly he is saved by Neytiri (Zoe Saldana), a Na'vi princess and huntress. Neytiri fights off a pack of attacking wild dogs. So ferocious are the dogs, that Neytiri is forced to injure and kill some of them. When Jake offers thanks for Neytiri's assistance, she screams at him, "Don't say thanks for this. This is sad." She offers a prayer over the dead body of one of the wild dogs. Neytiri explains to him the interconnectedness of all living things on Pandora. She is upset with Jake that he acted so foolishly and yelled at him for being there in the first place. Surprised by this, Jake asked why she decided to help him if she valued the lives of the dogs so much. Neytiri informs Jake that she believes there is something special about him.

Neytiri leads Jake to her tribe. In classic conflict theory form, the tribe immediately distrusts him. He learns that humans are considered "demons" among the Na'vi. They also realize that he is an Avatar, or a "Dream Walker" as the Na'vi call them. Neytiri's parents are the leaders of the Omaticaya tribe. Neytiri's mother, Mo'at, a psychic, looks Jake over ever so closely. She senses something special in him and instructs Neytiri to train Jake in the ways of the Na'vi. Jake learns of Eywa, the Great Spirit. He learns the Na'vi language, customs, values and norms. But Jake is leading a double life and is becoming alienated from his sense of self. He is embracing the Na'vi culture and romantically falling for Neytiri, but he is also still providing logistical information to Col. Quaritch. Jake learns from the RDA Corporation that the largest deposit of unobtanium lies directly beneath Hometree, the home of Omaticaya. Administrator Selfridge orders Jake to convince the tribe to move, or else... Jake is given three months to gain the trust of the Omaticaya. During the next three months, Jake accomplishes his goals. Predictably, he has lost his detachment and has gained empathy toward the Na'vi. He has mated with Neytiri; and the Na'vi mate for life. All is good for Avatar Jake. But, he fears what is about to come.

As one might see coming, an ultimate conflict and showdown is pending between the RDA's military and the Na'vi. The Omaticaya, understandably, do not want to leave their home. The military decides to employ a "shock and awe" campaign and blow Hometree to bits. A great sadness and sense of despair descends upon the Na'vi. When the Na'vi attempt to fight back, Colonel Miles Quaritch responds, "We will fight terror with terror." The Colonel realizes that Jake and the Avatar researchers are assisting the Na'vi, so he has the program shut down. Through the use of a remote station, the researchers are able to escape the RDA compound and reactivate the Avatars just in time for Jake to help the Na'vi win the day. At the movie's conclusion, the Na'vi have sent the remaining RDA colony back home to Earth; a planet that is "no longer green." And Jake? He is taken to the Tree of Souls where his human essence enters his Avatar and, presumably, he lives out his life as a Na'vi.

Social commentary and 3-D special effects go hand-in-hand in this marvelously written and directed film. What would Karl Marx think about *Avatar*?

Marxist Critical Analysis

There are numerous aspects of *Avatar* that fall within the Marxist paradigm. From a sociological perspective it seems most appropriate to begin with the relevancy of conflict theory to the critical analysis of *Avatar*.

Conflict Theory

Although Marx did not formulate conflict theory, one of the most popular and enduring sociological theories of the past fifty years, the works and ideas of this great thinker paved the way for its creation. Conflict theory emphasizes the role of power and the inequality found systematically throughout society. Conflict theorists argue that society's norms and values are those of the dominant group and that the privileged group imposes its will on subordinate groups in order to maintain its power position (Delaney, 2005). Jonathan Turner (1975) explains that conflict theory examines such phenomena as power, force, coercion, constraint, and change in social systems. The conflict perspective views society as a system of social structures and relationships that are shaped mainly by economic forces. Those who are economically wealthy control the means of production and thus dominate society because of their advantageous power position (Delaney, 2005).

> Conflict theorists assume that social life revolves around the economic interests of the wealthy and that these people use their economic power to coerce and manipulate others to accept their view of the society — and the world. Because there is a clear power differential among individuals and social classes, resentment and hostility are constant elements of society. The obvious implication of this social reality is that conflict is inevitable [Delaney, 2005: 70].

Marx argued that the imbalance of power is the seed of conflict in any society, and this would be true even in Pandora. The arrival of humans on Pandora was similar to the arrival of European explorers (or, as some might suggest, imperialists) in the Americas. Consider, initially indigenous people would be amazed by people arriving by ship to their home land. Where did they come from? How did they travel so far? Surely, these must be superior beings, one might summarize. Face-to-face meetings would be cordial at first as the true intentions of the strangers would not be revealed. Marx worked his entire adult life trying to empower the proletariat in their class struggle against the ruling bourgeoisie class.

Avatar begins with the RDA Corporation already firmly entrenched with its mining operations on Pandora. Consequently, we are not privy to all the steps involved in setting up the human colony. (As of this writing, Cameron has promised a prequel to *Avatar* wherein these details will be explained.) What we do know is that there exist pockets of resistance among the Na'vi against the powerful RDA Corp. Vehicles return to the compound with Na'vi arrows stuck in their giant tires so surely some natives are upset over the mining of unobtanium. The use of primitive weapons such as bow and arrows might seem pointless against the technologically-advanced weaponry of the RDA's military but Marx himself was involved in many workers' rebellions that seemed hopeless and yet each of these failed uprisings were perceived as important steps toward the desired world-wide proletariat revolution. Such was the case in Pandora where smaller protests by individual rebel groups had no real effect against the RDA Corporation. The cumulative by-product however would lead to the unity of the five clans of Pandora against the RDA Corporation and this represents a type of proletariat revolution. The depiction of the five clans of Pandora reminds this author of a poster of Sitting Bull, a famous Native American Sioux chief and warrior that adorned the bedroom wall of my older brother when I was a child. Sitting Bull, trying to unite Sioux tribes against the American military, is quoted as having said, "They can cut off our fingers one at a time, but if we join together, we make a mighty fist." Comparisons abound between the struggles of the Na'vi against the RDA Corporation to that of Native Americans against the U.S. military. In fact, much of the film is a critical analysis against the power elites of society today, especially mega corporations and U.S. military policies and tactics.

Economic Determinism and Power

Long before successful 1992 presidential candidate Bill Clinton uttered the famous phrase "It's the economy, stupid," when asked what the most important issue among voters was, Karl Marx had claimed that economics influences nearly all human decisions. Marx's reliance on economics as the prime explanation for much of the struggle between the different social classes helps to explain why he is often referred to as an *economic determinist*. Marx believed that those who control the means of production have the power. Further, those with power have the economic means to keep their advantageous position. Thus, as far as Marx was concerned, money equals power. Luckily for Marx, he had a friend like Friedrich Engels who was willing to help fund Marx in his attempt to lead a proletariat revolution.

The basic tenet of conflict theory rests with the possession of power. Power is attained, Marx insists, by those who control the means of production. As we saw in *Avatar*, conflict can exist at multiple levels, including the organizational and societal. Conflict exists at the organizational level between the different branches of the RDA Corporation. Dr. Grace Augustine, RDA's leading researcher, wants to study the unique natural environment of Pandora. She also wants to learn about the culture of Na'vi. She believes that such scientific pursuits should take on a higher priority than mining a mineral. Furthermore, Augustine argues that the best way to quell the growing conflict between the Na'vi and RDA involves a long-term study of the cultural differences between the two groups in hopes of gaining some resolve that benefits both parties.

As we know, however, the primary purpose of RDA is to extract the precious commodity of unobtanium. RDA has discovered that the largest deposit of unobtanium rests directly below the home of the Omaticaya clan. In his economic determinist mind, Administrator Selfridge believes that the most efficient way to mine unobtanium would involve the Omaticaya "simply moving to another tree" so that the RDA military can destroy Hometree and begin mining. The RDA scientists are appalled at such an idea. Spellman further disparages the Omaticaya by referring to them as "fly-bitten creatures." In other words, he is equating the Na'vi to savages and certainly not of the value of humans. This thought process follows the "logic" of most imperialists; that is, the best way to justify destroying a native population is to think of them as non-equals, or inferior creatures.

As an aggressor, Colonel Quaritch encourages Spellman to send in the military to destroy Hometree. Augustine argues that ecosystem of Pandora and countless lives will be destroyed if the military is allowed to attack Hometree. Using one last grasp of "rationality," Spellman wonders aloud, we gave them medicine, taught them English in schools we built, we offered them roads ... what else do they want from us? Using a research video log provided by Jake Sully that states the Na'vi want nothing and need nothing from RDA, Colonel Quaritch convinces Spellman to order an attack on Hometree.

In one of, if not the most, dramatic scenes of *Avatar*, the RDA military attacks Hometree. The fire power is overwhelming and relentless. In a relatively short period of time, the enormous tree falls. The Omaticaya, who have a true connection to Hometree, are horrified and saddened beyond belief. For many movie viewers the scene is reminiscent of the collapse of the World Trade Center Towers. When the film was first released many viewers experienced depression after watching this particular scene. According to Jo Piazza (2010), "James Cameron's completely immersive spectacle 'Avatar' may have been a little too real for some fans who say they have experiences depression and suicidal thoughts after seeing the film because they long to enjoy the beauty of the alien world Pandora" (p. 1).

Conflict at the societal level occurs after Jake Sully's avatar convinces the Omaticaya to unite with the other four clans. Much like Sitting Bull, Sully believes that the united five clans of the Na'vi will form a powerful, revolutionary force that surpasses that of the RDA. The military's radar notices the formation of the five clans. In an attempt to put down the rebellion as quickly as possible, Colonel Quaritch orders a pre-emptive strike on the Na'vi. In a clear attempt to draw comparisons between this conflict and the Iraq War, Quaritch rallies the troops by saying, "We will fight terror with terror." His primary target is the "Tree of Souls." This sacred tree is like the master computer of the moon. All creatures on Pandora, past and present, are interconnected at this location. If the Tree of Souls is destroyed, the Colonel reasons, the Na'vi will remember this day forever and never dare interfere with RDA again. He then proclaims, we will use a "shock and awe" campaign against the "hostiles."

Avatar concludes with an epic battle between the capitalists with their mighty military and the "underdog" Na'vi along with all the other creatures of Pandora. From a Marxist perspective this massive combined effort of rebellion exemplified his dream that "Workers of all lands unite." (Note: This quote appears on Marx's gravestone.)

Class Theory and Class Struggle

Marx frequently uses the term *class* in his writings, but he does not have a consistent application on its usage (So, 1990). Various meanings of the term appear in his works, but it does seem clear, at the minimum, that he viewed social classes as structures that are external to, and coercive of, people (Ritzer, 2000). Suffice it to say, most reviewers of Marx's class theory cite his quote in the "Manifesto of the Communist Party" (co-authored with Friedrich Engels), "The history of all hitherto existing society is the history of class struggles" (Marx and Engels, 1978: 473). In other words, history is nothing but the existence of a power struggle between social classes. Marx and Engels believed that most of history was a two-class system that consisted of the "haves" and "have-nots." Marx and Engels acknowledged that there were subsets of social classes within the general scheme of "haves" and "have-nots." As Collins and Makowsky (2010) explain:

> Within these classes there could be further divisions. For example, in feudal society the nobility was divided into ranks from king down to knight and included the landowning clergy of the powerful medieval Church. There were also minor classes not based directly on the central economy, such as servants, guild masters, journeymen, apprentices, and free peasants. For Marx the property divisions were crucial because they marked the breaking lines in the social structure. When conflicts became intense, classes would have to group themselves along these divisions [31].

Because the dividing line between people ultimately came down to property, those who owned the means of production would make up the "haves" and those who do not would constitute the "have-nots." Marx and Engels used the terms bourgeoisie, capitalists and owners of the means of production to describe the "haves" and the terms proletariat, workers and the masses to describe the "have-nots"—the social classes of his era. The bourgeoisie, Marx argued would use any means at their disposal to maintain their power advantage over the proletariat. The masses will become envious of the goods and services (e.g., food, shelter, political power) available to the select few. Under capitalism, factory owners and bankers grew wealthy by exploiting the workers. The workers, however, had no finished products to profit from; they had to work for a wage. As a result, the workers become alienated and resent the owners. Such conditions perpetuate class struggle and conflict. Class struggle necessitates the control of the proletariat. Because conflict is variable, the intensity of the authority and control over the workers, by the ruling, or power, class is also variable.

The RDA Corporation are clearly the capitalists of on Pandora. Their sole purpose for traveling years from Earth to this distant moon was to mine unobtanium. The value of unobtanium is so high that the capitalists justify any means, including genocide, in order to attain the mineral. As the imperialists with the ability to travel across galaxies, RDA represents a technologically evolved social class. The Na'vi represent the proletariat and the Omaticaya clan literally translates to "the people." As mentioned earlier, RDA is willing to mine unobtanium at any cost. They have justified class conflict in the name of economic riches. On Pandora, the conflict led to all-out war.

Marx would be pleased that the proletariat revolution was successful. Furthermore, as a gun runner himself, Marx would be supportive of Jake Sully's and Dr. Augustine's avatars provision of weapons and technological knowledge to the Na'vi in their class struggle against their capitalist oppressors.

Utopia and Communism

When Jake Sully first arrived to Pandora with fresh military recruits, they were warned by Colonel Quaritch that Pandora was worse than hell. In fact, hell would be a nice vacation from Pandora, the Colonel insisted. The new recruits were told that the Na'vi were dangerous killers and that the natural environment of Pandora was deadly to humans. Conversely, the Na'vi considered Pandora a type of utopia. The clans lived in commune-like settings and shared what the natural environment provided. Although the clans had chiefs and psychics that served as leaders, it appears that the Na'vi were all treated equally. In essence, the Na'vi had established a communist society.

Marx is best known for his ideas on communism. As a humanist, Marx wanted all humans to reach their full potential. He hoped to eliminate alienation, the division of labor, private property, and other obstacles that he believed hindered this goal (Delaney, 2004). Marx believed that capitalism was a major barrier in individuals' pursuit of reaching their full human potential; consequently, he hoped to overthrow capitalistic systems. As Pampel (2000) explains, Marx devoted a great deal of his life to understanding capitalism through scientific study, and to ending capitalism through revolution.

Marx and Engels worked tirelessly to stimulate a worldwide working-class revolution against the capitalists. When the capitalists were defeated, Marx and Engels had hoped to replace capitalistic socio-economics systems with communism, a class-less society. In class-less societies the struggle between the haves and the have-nots would also be eliminated. Thus, class conflict would disappear. Under Marxist communism, government was deemed unnecessary as rule would be established by the collectivity. Thus, the communist system, Marx and Engels presumed, would eliminate the abuse of capitalists against the workers *and* eliminate the governmental abuse of citizens. They truly believed that the world would be a better place under communism. The main tenets of communism were detailed in the *Manifesto*.

In *Avatar*, the story begins with the capitalists already on Pandora. The viewing audience is provided glimpses into the way of life of the Na'vi. There is no sign of government, although there is a leadership role performed by certain members of each clan. Otherwise, the natives seem to be treated as equals. Such a society would seem to fit the parameters of Marxist communism. But the Na'vi have, arguably, a social system that extends beyond what Marx and Engels envisioned as they were connected to the environment as well. As a product of their times, Marx and Engels did not concern themselves with the rights of the natural environment as an integral aspect of communism; certainly not in comparison to the role of the environment in *Avatar*. The *Manifesto* has four sections. The first section describes all of human history as highlighted by class struggle; the second section describes the position of communists as sympathizers to the proletariat class and rejects bourgeois objections to communism; the third contains criticism of other types of socialism; and the fourth section provides a short description of communist tactics toward proletariat unity.

Humanism and Human Potential

Although some analysts of Marxist theory may downplay the importance of his humanistic tendencies, Karl Marx may certainly be viewed as a humanist. It should be noted that humanism, as a concept, has different meanings to different people but as it is interpreted here humanism involves a commitment to making the lives of all humans better. Marx's dedication to assisting the proletariat in their quest to crush the shackles of oppression perpetrated against the workers in an attempt to help each of them reach their full human potential that makes him a humanist. Marx became especially concerned about the workers when Engels showed him his father's factories in England. Marx learned first-hand about the horrendous working conditions faced by factory workers in the early stages of industrialization and was deeply saddened and hurt by the suffering and exploitation that the working class suffered under capitalism. The working conditions of factory workers was one more critical explanation as to why Marx and Engels promoted communism.

Toward his later years, Marx came to see the value of capitalism. He recognized that the technological advancements of the capitalistic system freed many humans from hard labor and that a surplus of material goods was now available to the masses. As Ritzer (2011) explains, Marx acknowledged the truly revolutionary force that capitalism had become and he was pleased that it overthrew the traditional, feudal world. Nonetheless, Marx simply labeled capitalism as a necessary evil toward communism. Capitalism was evil because it created an oppressive environment that hindered most individuals' pursuit of reaching their full potential. Marx argued that a society that allows all individuals an equal opportunity to develop fully not only helps the individual, but the collectivity as well (Acton, 1967).

Today, there are those who promote the socio-economic system of capitalism and those who scorn it (e.g., the "Occupy" movement) as Marx once did. Most middle-class persons have benefited from the capitalistic system and in turn, those benefits have assisted many of the masses in their pursuit of reaching their full human potential. Still, the philosophical question remains, "Ho do people know when they have reached their full human potential?" Each of us has unique desires and needs. Marx, a philosopher himself, found the comfort of economic-determinism as a means to measure whether one has attained their full potential. For people who have met the basic needs (food, clothing and shelter), reaching fulfillment and finding happiness— modern elements of reaching one's full potential—implies more than economic stability. In *Avatar*, Jake Sully found fulfillment in his avatar body. Throughout the film it was quite clear that Jake, as a paraplegic, was not happy with his life's circumstances. However, as an avatar, he could run and jump and accomplish things he could not do with his human body. And a proponent of technologically-driven production would point out that such a rationalistic system is what helped to create avatars. Furthermore, it was the technological capitalistic avatars that helped the proletariat Na'vi win the revolution against the evil RDA Corporation. Thus, capitalism cannot be purely evil. There are college students across the United States and around many parts of the world that have benefited from the capitalistic system as more and more people become the first in their families to graduate from college. In contrast, during Marx's era, most of the proletariat were uneducated and had little chance of ever hoping to attain a basic education let alone a college education. Marx would counter, however, by pointing out that people in developing nations have not benefited from the spread of capitalism. Further, he would remind us that people in developing nations are oppressed and alienated under capitalism and would never reach their full potential because of capitalism.

Alienation

Reaching one's full human potential is a difficult challenge under a capitalist system, Marx argued. Among the negative by-products of the capitalist system is alienation. As articulated by Marx, alienation is a condition in which humans become dominated by the forces of their own creation, which confront them as alien powers (Coser, 1977; Cooper, 1991). The capitalist society, by the very design of its structure, was responsible for four general types of alienation on the worker, all of which can be found in the domain of work.

The first type of alienation involves workers being alienated from the object(s) they produce. Workers receive a wage for their labor. The final product is far-removed from the workers; it is in the hands of the capitalists to make as much profit as possible. In addition, workers often lack detailed knowledge of aspects of the production process in which they are personally involved. On Pandora, the RDA miners fit the parameters of this type of alienation. They would work all day mining for unobtanium and get paid a wage, but it is the RDA Corporation benefited tremendously from the labor of the workers. The rank and file military members were treated the same way. They too work for the RDA Corporation for a wage while the heads of security profit the most.

The scientists, especially Grace Augustine, are also alienated from the primary object they produce. Dr. Augustine and the other members of the research team spend most of their time trying to learn about the biosphere and the Na'vi way of life. While spending time in their avatars, the scientists learn the language and culture of the Na'vi. The scientists back in the lab translate the data produced by the avatars into workable bits of knowledge. This knowledge commodity is invaluable to the RDA Corporation. The researchers have become alienated because the product they produced, knowledge, has been misused by the military and the mining divisions of RDA in their attempt to maximize mining production, and thus, maximize their profits.

In the capitalist system, workers are also alienated from the process of production. This represents the second type of alienation described by Marx. The labor of the workers is not directed toward satisfying their own needs; instead they labor for the capitalist. Workers may value the paycheck, but eventually they come to see industrial work as boring and tedious. On Pandora, most of the workers do not seem alienated from the process of their labor. The scientists absolutely love their jobs; especially those who are transformed into Avatar bodies and get to explore the natural and social environments of Pandora. The researchers in the lab have so much exciting and breakthrough data to analyze they must feel like kids in a candy store. The military personnel may complain that Pandora is worse than hell, but they seem to love playing technological, rock 'em sock 'em robot soldier; especially when the enemy is nonhuman as that eases their consciences. The most content of all on Pandora are the Na'vi. They seem very happy to be a part of the process that links all natural things on Pandora. As Marx would point out, it was because the Na'vi had adopted a communal lifestyle.

Marx's third category of alienation involves the worker feeling alienated from self. Because the process of specialization dominates the capitalist system, the worker performs a limited function(s), or task, repeatedly. As a result, the worker can never reach his or her full human potential. Eventually, the number of individuals feeling alienated will expand into a mass of disenchanted workers. Jake Sully has experienced a great deal of self-alienation. Before arriving on Pandora, Jake was a Marine who, during battle, became injured and lost the use of his legs. He did not feel like a complete person. He was a Marine, and Marines do things that require the full use of all limbs. Jake was so depressed about himself that he readily accepted an invitation to go to Pandora and fulfill the requirements of his twin brother's RDA research contract. Jake narrated that he had no clue about the job his brother did, but feeling wanted lessened his self-loathing. This was just the beginning for Jake. Although Jake was supposed to act in the best interest of the Research Division, he eagerly accepted Colonel Quaritch's request to provide "intel" on Pandora for the military. Jake did this because it made him feel like a Marine. Further, the Colonel promised him an operation that would give him the use of his legs. Both of these things would help Jake eliminate his sense of self-alienation. As the film progresses, Jake becomes attached to his Avatar persona. He reaches a point where he is longer sure which world is "real"—his human world, or his Avatar world among the Na'vi. As the transition in sense of self shifts to that of identifying himself as a Na'vi, Jake becomes alienated from his human self.

The fourth type of alienation involves the worker becoming alienated from his or her follow workers. Jake Sully, while experiencing various form of self-alienation, was also becoming alienated from his follow military comrades. At one point, he was alienated from the research team (when they first learned that he was providing sensitive information to the military). Jake felt alienated from his follow clan brothers and sisters after he informed them of his betrayal. He would be accepted back into the Omaticaya clan when he helped lead the Na'vi revolution against the humans.

Marx felt that it was important for fellow workers to bond with one another: "Marx's assumption was that man [humans] basically wants and needs to work with others cooperatively in order to appropriate from nature what they require to survive" (Delaney, 2004: 76). As portrayed in *Avatar*, humans are not the only species that want and need to work cooperatively in order to secure from nature what they need to survive. The Na'vi were connected to all forms of life on Pandora. And, as mentioned earlier, during the dramatic scene in which Hometree is destroyed by the RDA military, the Na'vi experienced a great deal of alienation from the greater environment. They were quite literally disconnected. As reported in Jo Piazza's article "Audiences Experience 'Avatar' Blues," a number of movie goers reported on various fan online sites that "fans have expressed feelings of disgust with the human race and disengagement with reality" (par. 1).

Among the sources of alienation that seemed to particularly disturb Marx was religion. Marx felt that religion served as a major obstacle in people's attempt to reach their full human potential.

Religion

Marx argued that the masses remained docile and accepted their position as second-class citizens on Earth because their religion had taught them that they would be rewarded in the afterlife. The workers relied on prayer for positive changes in their earthly lives rather than participating in collective action for the good of the masses. The promises made to the masses from religious leaders and holy books of an "eternal salvation" and "eternal happiness" seemed like a fair trade-off to most. (Note: This is an example of what Marx called *false consciousness*— the inability to see what constitutes one's own best interest.) After all, what's 45 to 50 years of misery — the approximate life expectancy of people during Marx's era — on Earth when you have eternal salvation to look forward to (*Encyclopedia of Death and Dying*, 2010)? Marx argued that the capitalists encouraged the weak-minded masses to embrace afterlife consideration because such support of the status quo kept them in power. Marx went so far as to suggest that "Religion is the opiate of the masses" (McLellan, 1987; Hadden, 1997).

Opiates are drugs that dull the senses, rendering people powerless against those who control the means of production. Marx argued that religion had the same affect on people. When people are high on drugs or religion, as Marx argued, they experience a false sense of happiness. They also become lethargic and less likely to challenge the status quo and thus are incapable of producing a social system that strives for equality within a society.

Marx's disdain for religion follows this pattern: First, he believed that religion was a distraction for man from his essence; second, he felt that while man was in this distracted state he allowed himself to become shamefully exploited and controlled; third, because man is being distracted, exploited, and controlled, he loses sight of his human essence (Delaney, 2004). Put another way, a religious person is no longer in control of his or her own destiny (Carlebach, 1978).

Religion and God were projections based upon the human imagination, Marx argued. Over time, man's imagination has elaborated to form stories which have become historic events passed on from one generation to the next. This reification process is what helped to solidify human belief in religious ideals, principles, and values, including a belief in God.

The Na'vi are quite spiritual. They worship the Great Spirit Eywa, respect all forms on life on their moon, pray at the Tree of Voices, and interconnect with ancestors from the past at the Tree of Souls. The spiritual interconnectedness shared among all life forms on Pandora would appear to be a unifying force rather than an alienating one. Jake Sully learned about the spirituality of Pandora shortly after his first avatar research mission. He met Neytiri who taught him that killing an animal, even one who attacks and means deadly harm, is not a joyful moment but rather a sad one. After she said a prayer over the dead body of the wild dog, Neytiri explained to Jake that her people respect all the creatures of Pandora. Neytiri then introduced Jake to her clan where he first learned about Eywa. Soon, he would learn about other spiritual places such as the Tree of Voices, "a place for prayers to be heard and sometimes answered."

For thousands of years, religious people have often turned to prayer in time of need. People will pray for a variety of things for themselves and their loved ones. Generally, these prayers go "unanswered." People with faith maintain that prayers left unanswered is not a sign that there is no God; rather, they rationalize their belief in a "higher power" by saying such things as "God works in mysterious ways" or "Not all of God's prayers are answered." The role of prayer was displayed in *Avatar* as well. Near the end of the film, Dr. Augustine faces the death of her natural body. The Na'vi gathers together and pray for her human essence to be transformed into her avatar. Mo'at, the spiritual leader of the Omaticaya, explains that in order for Augustine to permanently transfer from human to avatar, she must "pass through the eye of Eywa and return" [to the natural world of Pandora]. Eywa is equated to God and thus, all-powerful. And yet, the transformation was unsuccessful. The prayers of the collective believers are left unanswered. Do the Na'vi lose their faith when faced with the realization that their prayers have not been answered? No, they do not. Instead, the Na'vi rationalize that Augustine was "too far gone" and that "it was too late" for her to be saved. In this regard, the Na'vi rationalize their spiritual beliefs the same way religious adherents do. As the film concludes, however, Jake Sully's essence is successfully transformed to his avatar. Thus, Eywa, like God, works in mysterious ways.

The spirituality of the Na'vi seems to work positively for them in most regards. Marx would reiterate that the Na'vi people do not live under a capitalistic system of economics and politics. Instead, their society was akin to agrarian societies that predated capitalism in Europe. There was such an ample supply of natural resources available to provide subsistence for the small population of the Na'vi that conflict among the clans was nonexistent. (Note: At least in the information provided to us in the film.) Marx tried to convince us that under communism all the people would share equally in the scarce resources and because of this conflict would be eliminated. That's the beauty of a classless society, Marx would proclaim, from each according to his ability, to each according to his needs.

Final Thoughts

The beauty of Marxist theory, whether one believes in all, some or none of his ideas, is the relevancy of so much of his work to so many aspects of contemporary society, including films. It would be possible to write an entire book just on Marx's analysis of *Avatar*. We could have, for example discussed other topics such as class consciousness, false consciousness, commodification and private property, concepts that are all applicable to *Avatar*. We did, however, cover an essential portion of this theoretical perspective. It is our belief that if Marx could some how join us in the present-day among the things that would marvel him would be the world of film and the phenomena of movie-going.

Works Cited

Acton, Harry Burrows. 1967. *What Marx Really Said.* New York: Schocken.
Carlebach, Julius. 1978. *Karl Marx and the Radical Critique of Judaism.* Boston: Routledge & Kegan Paul.
Collins, Randall, and Michael Makowsky. 2010. *The Discovery of Society,* 8th ed. Boston: McGraw Hill.
Cooper, Derick. 1991. "On the Concept of Alienation." *International Journal of Contemporary Sociology* 28: 7–26.
Coser, Lewis. 1977. *Masters of Sociological Thought,* 2d ed. New York: Harcourt, Brace & Jovanovich.
Delaney, Tim. 2004. *Classical Social Theory: Investigation and Application.* Upper Saddle River, NJ: Prentice Hall/Pearson.

_____. 2005. *Contemporary Social Theory: Investigation and Application.* Upper Saddle River, NJ: Prentice Hall/Pearson.
Encyclopedia of Death and Dying. 2010. "Life Expectancy." http://www.deathreference.com/Ke-Ma/Life-Expectancy.html.
Hadden, Richard W. 1997. *Sociological Theory.* Orchard Park, NY: Broadview.
Marx, Karl, and Friedrich Engels. 1978. "The Manifesto of the Communist Party," pp. 473–500 in *The Marx-Engels Reader*, 2d ed., edited by Robert C. Tucker. New York: Norton.
McLellan, David. 1987. *The Young Hegelians and Karl Marx.* New York: Macmillian.
Pampel, Fred. 2000. *Sociological Lines and Ideas.* New York: Worth.
Piazza, Jo. 2010. "Audiences Experience 'Avatar' Blues." CNN.com, January 11. http://www.cnn.com/2010/SHOWBIZ/Movies/01/11/avatar.movie.blues/index.html.
Pomerantz, Dorothy. 2010. "Is Avatar Really King of the Box Office?" *Forbes.com*, January 27. http://www.forbes.com/2010/01/27/avatar-box-office-business-entertainment-avatar.html.
Ritzer, George. 2000. *The McDonaldization of Society.* Thousand Oaks, CA: Pine Forge Press.
_____. 2011. *Sociological Theory*, 8th ed. Boston: McGraw Hill.
So, Alvin. 1990. "Class Theory or Class Analysis? A Re-examination of Marx's Unfinished Chapter on Class." *Critical Sociology* 17: 35–55.
Tucker, Robert C., ed. 1978. *The Marx-Engels Reader*, 2d ed. New York: Norton.
Turner, Jonathan. 1975. "A Strategy for Reformulating the Dialectical and Functional Theories of Conflict." *Social Forces* 53 (3): 433–444.
U.S. National Debt Clock. 2012. "The Outstanding Public Debt." http://www.brillig.com/debt_clock/.
U.S. Treasury Department. 2012. "The Debt to the Penny and Who Holds It." http://www.treasurydirect.gov/NP/BPDLogin?application=np.
World Food Programme. 2012. "Hunger Stats." http://www.wfp.org/hunger/stats.
World Hunger Education Service. 2012. "2012 World Hunger and Poverty Facts and Statistics." http://www.worldhunger.org/articles/Learn/world%20hunger%20facts%202002.htm.

A Myth (Not So) Betrayed: Ridley Scott's Robin Hood and the Political Evolution of the Greenwood

JACOB LEWIS

Of all the stories we still tell from the European middle ages, few seem have as much modern social and political relevance as Robin Hood. While he is as chivalrous as any knight of Camelot, Robin Hood speaks to our liberal, even anarchic, tendencies; in the greenwood there is no once and future feudal order, only a community of equals who fight for justice against a corrupt system. The core of the myth as we now have it even seems to echo one of the tenets of socialism: that one can create a better society by "spreading the wealth around." All our modern versions of the legend, filmed or otherwise, agree on the fact that Robin Hood makes his corner of the world better by doing so. Thus, it would seem that if Marxism is going to praise anything in particular about the European middle ages, it could do worse than pick Robin Hood.[1]

However, we should be careful of praising the politics of Robin Hood without first determining which, if any, of those politics are truly there in the legend. Most of us know these stories through film; indeed, modern visions of Robin Hood depend entirely on Errol Flynn, or at least an animated fox. Our Robin Hood is mediated, and, as Kevin J. Harty points out, medievalized: "Any film about a medieval figure is an example, first and foremost, of medievalism, the attempt as old as the birth of the early modern or Renaissance period to revisit or reinvent the medieval world for contemporary purposes" (Harty 87–100).

All films about Robin Hood do this to some degree, in part because of audience expectation — modern viewers would hardly stand for a two-hour ballad or a village pantomime — but also because he is, as Douglas Gray remarks, "everybody's Robin Hood," infinitely adaptable.[2] Indeed, the character of Robin Hood is accessible to everyone, offering a variety of political uses: sometimes politically neutral, more often a figure of one social revolution or another. But for most of us, the modern Robin Hood story should dress up its politics in a hearty dose of nostalgia: spectacular tournaments, robbery turned to charity, and swashbuckling heroics in the castle and the greenwood.

This is not the case in Ridley Scott's *Robin Hood* (2010), the most recent cinematic version of the legend. Scott's film is in many the culmination of a cinematic evolution many of us may not have noticed: the gradual shift away from the leftist Robin Hood of the Thirties and Sixties toward a more "realistic" portrait that, like the legend itself, is far more conservative. Scott's version of the legend changes the message of both community and justice, shifting them toward more libertarian ideals of unregulated commerce and strictly local autonomous authority. While Ridley Scott's revival of a more medieval Robin Hood is not a surprising response to early 21st-century economic and political realities, its message of rebellion against tyranny is hampered by muddled politics and impractical solutions.

Robin Hood: The Legend

In order to understand the politics of Scott's *Robin Hood* (2010), we must have a sense of the conversation surrounding the legends of Robin Hood. As Robin Hood is a popular folk hero, the origins of his stories and his original role in them is harder to pin down than, say, England's other national hero, Arthur Pendragon. Like Arthur, however, the meaning of Robin Hood in popular culture has varied a good deal over the centuries, and it can be difficult to say that there is any one "true" social value for Robin Hood; indeed, as Stephen Knight has noted, "what Robin does not stand for is anything static" (Knight 5).

It is unlikely that these stories are based on any particular historical personage; while many a larcenous "Robert," "Robin," and "Hob" has been found in the historical record, as R. B. Dobson notes, we should be wary of assuming they are the origin of the legend: "all attempts to discover the birth of the Robin Hood legend must now at least contemplate the paradoxical possibility that names can come before things and that the original genesis of the outlaw hero may be not so much the appeal of his adventures as the coining of his name" (Dobson 76). Thus, pinning Robin Hood to a specific historical moment—the late 12th century, the reign of Richard I or of John, or both—ignores the actual, far later, historical circumstances under which his legend was born and through which it developed.

The literary history of Robin Hood is equally nebulous, born as it is out of popular, orally-transmitted culture. Most of the literary material — the bulk of it being ballads, gestes, and songs — dates from the 14th and 15th centuries, suggesting, as R. H. Hilton says, that the legends are "a by-product of the agrarian social struggle" of the late 14th century (Hilton 42). Dobson describes it best as "primarily the outcome of a process of slow and largely improvised evolution and accretion (and later of deliberate parody and buffoonery) by innumerable and now completely forgotten tellers of tales" (Dobson 66). The name of Robin Hood appears a bit earlier in the manuscript record than his tales; he is mentioned briefly in various historical accounts and the works of Langland, Chaucer, and Gower as a shorthand for "popular culture" and something to be ridiculed or disdained. This attitude is not present, of course, in the Robin Hood ballads, *gestes* and plays that survive. However, the ballads as we have them now are no longer popular items; they were printed early on and seem, if B. H. Bronson is to be believed, to have fallen out of popular memory (Bronson 13–14). But as Stephen Knight points out, the heart of the tradition is live performance of the material, especially the plays, and the written record is only a small window into the full cultural role of Robin Hood (Knight 50). The Robin we see in the early narratives is hard to characterize, though a few themes stand out. In the earliest ballad, "Robin Hood and the Monk" (c. 1450), he quarrels with Little John, leaves his band, and is nearly killed by a larcenous monk, the message being that there is "security in solidarity from the danger of the abbots and organized religion, and also from the perils of town law" (Knight 53) Other ballads add to the legend tales of cleverness, a disdain for money, and a strong devotion to the Blessed Virgin Mary.

Later 15th and early 16th century works build upon these themes, often through one specific adventure — Robin and his men burlesque the judiciary system, actively and violently resist a variety of bullies, and rescue men from the gallows. These stories in turn grew up alongside a tradition of plays — the earliest at Exeter in 1426 (Knight 264) — that often, as far as we can tell, enacted scenes from the ballads, and may well have inspired new ballads in turn. Moreover, as Douglas Gray points out, the occasions for these plays, the "church-ales" and parish games, "provided 'a structure for charitable giving in a convivial atmosphere' (into which Robin Hood and the Greenwood could easily be inserted)" (Gray 27). These festivals celebrated and forged the community, but this was a community writ small, the size of a village or a manor. The earliest Robin Hood is the champion of the shire; he is not yet the virtue of a nation.

That scope developed in the early modern period. Indeed, Robin Hood becomes nationalized and romanticized in the later 16th and early 17th centuries. This is also the age in which the legend is first assumed to be historical or semi-historical, and writers attempt to pin Robin Hood to a particular time and place. Both trends are best expressed in two plays by Anthony Munday, *The Downfall of Robert Earle of Huntington* (1598) and *The Death of Robert Earle of Huntington* (1599). These plays, both commissioned for an elite audience, are the first to depict Robin Hood as a dispossessed aristocrat. Scott Nolen writes that Munday's changes "strengthened the conservative depiction of the outlaw as a friend of the legitimate crown, further eroding the enemy of authority depicted in the early ballads" (Nolen 57). In other words, these plays are the first works to suggest that Robin Hood is a rebel *with* a cause, namely to restore the "rightful king" and so himself be restored to power. These plays, and the contemporary works of William Shakespeare, Michael Drayton, Ben Jonson, and Martin Parker, shift Robin away from the Puckish prankster and anarchic outlaw to something more socially and politically motivated. As England began to see itself as a nation in the modern sense, its heroes began to espouse not local but *national* community — the newly united kingdom and its regents, barons, and church.

The Robin Hood inherited by the 18th and 19th centuries was a noble, proto-Protestant do-gooder, someone whose loyalty is to the entire realm of England and whose rebelliousness is quaintly tamed. This is, for example, the Robin Hood of Sir Walter Scott's *Ivanhoe* (1820). Scott's chief contributions to the legend are the Saxon/Norman conflict and the famous archery contest; otherwise, his Robin is still the tame lieutenant, acting, in Stephen Knight's words, "as military support and security officer to the forces of good" (Knight 176) The success of *Ivanhoe* spawned numerous imitators and, as part of the Victorian focus on mass education, a host of novels for adolescents. Of these, the most influential is Howard Pyle's *The Merry Adventures of Robin Hood of Great Sherwood in Nottinghamshire* (1883). This is the work that created the modern legend by presenting an organized and regularized narrative from the first combative between Robin and Little John all the way to King Richard's pardon of the outlaw band. This is also the work that firmly establishes Robin Hood as part of that particularly English brand of medievalism and nationalism known as "English heritage." Stephen Knight describes it this way:

> [H]ere [in the past] was a setting to generate a sense that the country had once been great and powerful in simpler and more admirable ways than the modern world permitted, and that this force could be communed with through the landscape, ancient monuments, noble buildings, and literary realizations of that past world.... Englishness was constructed as an instrument of eliding conflicts at home and abroad, just as chivalry or bourgeois morality had in other times and genres — romance and the novel especially — been ways of resolving social and ideological conflicts [Knight 206].

The legends of Robin Hood, especially those from Scott, Pyle, and their successors and imitators, were assimilated into the civilizing project of Victorian and Edwardian England. For the English Victorians, Robin Hood was identified with Simon de Montfort, a 13th-century baron who had rebelled against Henry III and who, in the 19th century, was seen as a champion of parliamentary liberty and the rights of the common man. Robin Hood was seen as one of his lieutenants who never gave up; in the words of one of the attendees of the 1841 Sherwood Forest Festival, Robin Hood was "one of those noble patriots who rose with the Barons under Simon de Montfort in defence of that deathless germ of English liberty, Magna Charta" (Barczewski 75). By the close of the 19th century, Robin, once an anarchic imp who cared only for his band of men, himself, and the Blessed Virgin, had become the standard-bearer of Englishness and a model for truth, justice, and the British Way.

The pre-filmic political history of Robin Hood is vital to our understanding of Ridley Scott's *Robin Hood* for two important reasons. First, despite what the film repeatedly suggests, the idea of a historical Robin Hood is impossible; any attempt by modern storytellers to ground Robin Hood in history must be read as a deliberate and possibly politically motivate method for discarding key elements of the legend as it stands now. Second, that legend arose from a 13th- and 14th-century sense of injustice, but at its heart, it celebrated the community as a whole—everyone in the parish cared for, all the people happy and well. Even into the 19th century, this is the fragment of myth that endures, a sense that someone will respond to the needs of the people and make things right. What had changed by the invention of film was the expansion of that community to the whole of England and her people—indeed, to anyone who wanted the "true light" of "English civilization."

The Politics of Robin Hood Films

Much of our modern sense of the Robin Hood myth is indebted to three films: Allan Dwan's *Douglas Fairbanks in Robin Hood* (1922), Michael Curitz's *The Adventures of Robin Hood* (1938), and Richard Lester's *Robin and Marian* (1976). These three works shape the tone and content of the modern legend. The earlier films establish a visual style and lighthearted do-gooder mentality that persists through Disney's *Robin Hood* (1973); they are largely boys' own adventures with some political or social messages depending on the time. Starting with *Robin and Marian*, however, the later films begin to strip away the "capering elf of the greenwood" and replace him with characters who have "depth" and "maturity"—codes for modern mores in medieval garb.

Although seven film versions of Robin Hood had appeared before it (Knight 218–220), the cinematic legend can only be said to have truly started with *Douglas Fairbanks in Robin Hood* (1922). This film, created at lavish expense and largely out of Fairbanks' own pocket and ego, established several ideas that would persist well into the late 20th century: the emphasis on spectacle and tournament; an overabundance of incredible archery; and, most importantly, the motif of robbing from the rich to relieve the poor. One feature that is not picked up with any consistency is its sense of historicity. The film's opening title card features an interesting claim: "History — in its ideal state — is a compound of legend and chronicle and from out of both we offer you an impression of the Middle Ages" (Dwan). Despite its early date, *Douglas Fairbanks in Robin Hood* freely admits that it is, in Scott Nolen's words, "a product of its time, an uneasy combination of impressions about past epochs and popular attitudes from the period of its making" (Nolen 96). Unlike many other film depictions of Robin Hood, Fairbanks' movie tells us to let go of our demand for real history and enjoy pure spectacle.

This is perhaps best reflected in the film's utter lack of politics, save, as Kevin J. Harty has noted, in one respect: "*Robin Hood* is subversive in its portrayal of the medieval; it offers a uniquely American view of the medieval, and it lays claim for America to a history not its own" (Harty 91). As much as these early Robin Hood films try to be "English," we must remember that they are products of the Hollywood system and the increasing demand for a highly profitable blockbuster. Moreover, American audiences have little stake in the historical or cultural accuracy of the English past; American films are therefore more free to pick and choose the facts and politics they wish to emphasize.

If Fairbanks' Robin Hood established the legend as an American adventure, the Michael Curitz's and William Keighley's *The Adventures of Robin Hood* (1938) established the quasi-historical pattern that much of the later films would embrace. It opens not with the careful hedging of history and romance found in *Douglas Fairbanks in Robin Hood*, but rather with the simple facts that

> in the year of our Lord 1191, when Richard, the Lion-Heart, set forth to drive the infidels from the Holy Land, he gave the regency of his kingdom to his trusted friend, Longchamp, instead of to his treacherous brother, Prince John. Bitterly resentful, John hoped for some disaster to befall Richard, so that he with the help of the Norman barons, might seize the throne for himself. And then on a luckless day for the Saxons ...

This title card then dissolves into the news that Richard is being held prisoner by Leopold of Austria, a move that apparently precipitates the entire round of heavy taxation that leads to Robin Hood. While the cards themselves are mostly right,[3] they do introduce an ahistorical sense of Norman-versus-Saxon derived from that that paragon of historical accuracy, Sir Walter Scott. Moreover, while it did not invent the notion that Prince John is a bloodthirsty tyrant, it does make clear that, in Kevin J. Harty's words, "Prince John's misuses of power justifies taking the law into one's own hands. Robin even complains about the fact that Richard's absence forces him to take such extraordinary measures, and his complaint at one point includes a condemnation of Richard for his absence. The good ruler is the ruler who first tends to problems at home" (Harty 93). Yet as Knight points out, the best historical echo of this film's Normans is probably *Triumph of the Will*; both films resonate with "both linear form and street violence," and Robin, in Knight's estimation, is "an image of European resistance [that is] the height of liberalism set in a framework which is nationalist and so, with some irony, itself fully racist in basis" (Knight 230). Whether one reads it as a commentary on racist nationalism, a paean to the New Deal, or a demand for intervention in an increasingly tumultuous Europe, it is clear that *The Adventures of Robin Hood* speaks directly to the politics of its time, and lays the groundwork for the explicitly political Robin Hood story, a thread to which many directors and show runners would return in the subsequent decades.

The intervening decades saw a number of parodies, homages, and knock-offs of both the earlier films. Robin Hood was parodied numerous times; Bugs Bunny (1949), Daffy Duck (1958), Tom and Jerry (1958), Huckleberry Hound (1959), and even Yogi Bear (1959) have all had a go, as have the Rat Pack (*Robin and the 7 Hoods*, 1964). Several television versions appeared, including the BBC's *Robin Hood* (1953) starring Patrick Troughton, and ATV's *Robin Hood*, (1955–1958) starring Richard Greene; and the CBC even sent Robin Hood to space in *Rocket Robin Hood* (1966–1969). All these works, in addition to keeping the myth alive, continue to play up the social and political versions of Robin Hood established in the earlier films: that he is a champion of justice, a robber of the rich and savior of the poor, who is, in the words of the ATV show's theme song, "Feared by the bad / Loved by the good." This is the liberal Robin Hood we have come to believe in; indeed, it is probably the one that most of us grew up on, whether in the cartoons from Warner, Hanna-Barbara and Disney, syndicated reruns of the Richard Greene *Robin Hood*, or even a late-night viewing of Errol Flynn himself. When we hear the name "Robin Hood," we have come to expect derring-do, caring for one's neighbors, and a firm fist-shaking at the rich and privileged—and nothing more.

This is precisely the attitude against which directors and screenwriters have been working since the 1970s. In 1976, Richard Lester, best known for the Beatles' first feature film, *A Hard Day's Night* (1964), made the first "realist" Robin Hood film, *Robin and Marian*. Robin (Sean Connery), no longer an eternal twenty something, returns from the crusades to find Marian

(Audrey Hepburn) has become not only a nun but an Abbess as well. They reconcile, wrestle with the time they've lost, and ultimately die together — not, admittedly, the usual topics for a Robin Hood film. However, this is a film that strives not only for realism, but a grim, almost pessimistic sense of realism at that: Robin and Little John are amused yet perturbed by the ballads circulating about them, while Robin himself is aghast at the horrors he committed during the Third Crusade and is entirely disillusioned about the mission of Richard and his army. Although Stephen Knight argues that the film has fallen out of the Robin Hood "repertoire" and that no one else has adopted its premise, I would argue that it, along with the lesser-known Hammer film *Wolfshead: The Legend of Robin Hood* (1969/1973), heralds a great change in the Robin Hood repertoire: the shift from swashbuckling romanticism to unrelenting "realism" that usually strips away both the nostalgic and the hopeful tones of the earlier films.[4]

This is the case in both of the 1991 films: the better-known Kevin Costner vehicle *Robin Hood: Prince of Thieves* and the lesser-known *Robin Hood* with Patrick Bergin and Uma Thurman. Both films attempt to lend historical weight to the legend with varying degrees of success. Costner's Robin, caught returning from the Crusades, is freed from prison by a black Muslim, Azeem (Morgan Freeman); together they arrive in England to pick up the pieces and rebel against the system. *Prince of Thieves* straddles the fence between the "real middle ages" and the late 1980s pretty strongly, combining authentic-looking costuming, props, and "medieval squalor" with modern feminism, racial politics, and some of what has been universally acknowledged as the worst acting in history from both Costner himself and Alan Rickman as the Sheriff.[5] *Robin Hood: Prince of Thieves* represents one end of the "historical" pole — a film in which "authenticity" becomes a set-dressing for clearly modern values and ideas. The other end of that pole would be John Irvin's *Robin Hood*, which only saw a wide release on the fledgling Fox network. This film is much closer to its source material and to the historical middle ages — it is set around Barnsdale, sees Robin encounter and adopt the Welsh longbow,[6] and shows a genuine concern for medieval estate and ecclesiastical politics. However, this attention to historical detail comes at the expense of some of the more important elements of the legend, most notably the "rob from the rich to give to the poor" motif. In Irvin's film, giving to the poor is an afterthought; Robin and his men steal from the Normans out of revenge, not noble charity. When we take these two films together, it becomes apparent that one may either present modernity in historical drag, as in *Prince of Thieves*, or history without the modern connections, as in *Robin Hood*. Neither film inspires confidence in the legendary message that a band of people can look out for one another and work for social fairness and economic justice.

In the last century, Robin Hood has become a mostly liberal myth, so much so that Kevin J. Harty can claim that "Traditionally, Robin Hood has been an anti-authoritarian figure. His deeds fly in the face of the political and ecclesiastical establishment. His popularity among the flower children of the 1960s is, therefore, understandable" (Harty 97). While Harty's assessment is generally correct, his connection between the radicals of the 1960s—derided as "flower children"—and the anarchic, even borderline chaotic Robin of the ballads and popular plays is questionable. The Robin Hood that 60s radicals and activists grew up on was largely a creature of his time; his politics were their politics: postwar liberalism, quasi-communism, equality and brotherhood for everyone. The myth changed with the times, and the one we have now is starkly different than anything Fairbanks or Flynn might have endorsed.

Ridley Scott's Robin Hood *(2010)*

So where does the *Robin Hood* of Ridley Scott fit within the mythos? The answer is complex, but certainly medievalist; indeed, the closest cousin to the film's Robin is probably Twain's Connecticut Yankee, Hank Morgan, who "attempts to destroy medieval social structures and systems and replace them with their more modern — and in his view — better counterparts" (Harty 92). *Robin Hood* features a protagonist who is the heir of a revolutionary legacy; Robin Longstride's father, we learn, was a stonemason who was beheaded for writing Magna Charta. The film seems to imply that revolution was his destiny all along, and does so through a traditional hero's journey: Robin is called on a quest by Robert Loxley, faces and overcomes adversity, learns who he is at the hands of a wise mentor — Robert's father — and returns to his people with the knowledge necessary to overcome their foe. It is hard to miss the message here. Like Robin, we are being called to discover the "true" roots of our present adversities, to justify our actions in the present by rediscovering a buried past.

Indeed, *Robin Hood* is a movie deeply concerned with historicity. This is apparent even before the film starts; its tagline, "the untold story behind the legend," appeals to a modern view of history, wherein the "what actually happened" is more important than the legend that we tell — is indeed inextricable from it. Since the legend of Robin Hood is just that, a legend with little to no basis in verifiable historical fact, Scott's movie in fact has no duty to *be* as true to history as it claims. Instead, it makes its own history, playing fast and loose with historical fact and social norms to suit its greater purpose: the fabrication of a more clearly conservative myth.

Robin Hood establishes this first through its title cards. These evoke, and have the same function as, the cards from *Douglas Fairbanks in Robin Hood*: they establish place, time, and the director's understanding of the events to follow. They are the clearest argument for the politics of this movie, and as such are worthy of study.

The first card reads: "In times of tyranny and injustice when law oppresses the people, the outlaw takes his place in history."[7] This bold statement makes a number of claims worth investigating. Its first part casts law itself as the villain of the movie, ignoring the men, institutions, and even circumstances that created those laws. Moreover, it does not specify *which* law is oppressing the people. Laws, after all, come in a variety of forms and uses; sumptuary laws, for example, freeze class representation, while murder laws ensure that everyone is treated fairly in the event of a terrible, man-made death. How, then, are we to determine which of these laws is oppressive? The film seems to suggest that all laws are themselves repressive; should we therefore have no laws? This statement is all the more worrisome when one realizes that the traditional problem that Robin Hood legends address is not "the law" but *taxes*— and 12th-century England's taxation was not enshrined in law the way a modern tax code is. Indeed, the entire point of clauses 12 and 14 of the 1215 Magna Charta exist in part to create the laws by which English citizens may be taxed. The "law" to which this statement would refer has no historical basis at the beginning of the film; its target is thus modern. The second part of the syllogism, "the outlaw takes his place in history," is equally problematic; what does "tak[ing] his place in history" mean? The intended message, of course, is one that resonates most with an American mythology full of outlaw gangs and vigilante heroes: to "take one's place in history" in this sense implies rising to the challenge, being tried and found fit for the times. But history is a fickle judge; and as we have already seen, the actual history of Robin Hood is less a clear-cut chronicle of the actions of a Great Man and more a gradual development of an easily re-contextualized mythology. Thus, even within its first two cards, the film undercuts its claim to historicity by imposing modern notions of law, economics, and justice onto the past.

This card is followed by a second pronouncement, reassuring us that "England at the turn of the 12th century was such a time." As proof of this, the film shows us a scene in which the feral children of the Greenwood raid Pepper Harrow, the Loxleys' estate. Since we have not been properly introduced to Marian or her situation at this point, it is easy for the viewer to misidentify Marian and her men as "typical" English citizens. The scene implies that such thefts happen frequently and to anyone, when in fact what we are witnessing is a specific, targeted raid by feral children on their nearest and largest hoard of grain. If this is indeed the "tyranny" to which the opening cards refer, then it is a perfect example of the way that *Robin Hood* muddles its message. These children — referred to here as "little bastards" by Marian (Cate Blanchett) and "maggots" by her servants — are in fact the *very children of Sherwood*, who have taken to the forest in desperation. Marian's disdain for them is understandable, but to imply that they are tyrannical, as opening cards do, is to blame two victims for the circumstances of their crimes. Neither the citizens of Pepper Harrow nor the feral children are the cause of these laws, nor do they have — as the movie later makes crystal clear — any hand in shaping the oppressive tax system. This is the apparent "historical" example with which Scott opens *Robin Hood*: not the rob-the-rich-give-to-the-poor class warfare we expect, but rather inter-class conflict between two disenfranchised groups.

We should not be surprised that Ridley Scott's *Robin Hood* makes scant few nods toward known facts; after all, the Robin Hood legend itself has no basis in history and therefore no real historical facts to abandon. But the *cloak* of historicity achieves another purpose, one that has eluded filmmakers since the 1990s: it finally allows modern ideology to transcend the Medieval/Modern barrier, and gives avant-garde American politics a veneer of tradition and historical "truth." To some extent, *all* medieval movies ask us to draw connections between past and present.[8] Scott's *Robin Hood* encourages us to apply the lessons of the past to the present — and suggests that we should "take our place in history" by operating outside the rule of law.

At first glance, this does not appear much removed from the lessons of *The Adventures of Robin Hood* (1938), *Robin and Marian* (1976), or even John Irvin's *Robin Hood* (1991). As in the earlier films, misuse of power by men of high status forces less noble figures to confront and defeat their tyranny. Unlike its ancestors, however, Ridley Scott's *Robin Hood* does not provide us with a comfortable out: there is no Richard to save the people from John.

Instead, the people themselves must provide a revolutionary solution. While this would seem to be a democratic message easily embraced by progressives, a closer examination of the ideology driving this movie reveals its conservative and surprisingly anti-progressive biases. Indeed, Ridley Scott's *Robin Hood*, following in the precarious footsteps of "realist" Robin Hood films before it, returns the myth to its more brutal and closed-society roots while preserving the nationalist outlook of the 19th-century legend. This creates a Robin Hood who is wildly divorced from the modern, progressive legend, and while that may fit in current political situations in both Europe and the United States, it is perhaps not the best move we could make with the Robin Hood legend today. Scott's film, establishing its politics in its opening narration, has two simple lessons for its audience: "All non-local authority is corrupt" and "The 'common man' can work justice through carefully planned violence."

"All non-local authority is corrupt"

Like their cinematic predecessors since *The Adventures of Robin Hood*, the elite figures of Scott's film are motivated almost entirely by selfish greed. When we first meet Richard (Danny Huston), for example, we are told by a title card that "bankrupt and of wealth and glory, [Richard] is plundering his way back to England after ten years on Crusade." Plunder is an odd choice of words, as if the king had been reduced to a pirate captain. This card conflates two moments in history: Richard's ignoble return to England in 1194, and his siege of the minor stronghold of Chalus-Chabrol in 1199. Little explanation is given *for* Richard's penury, or his decision to besiege this particular castle. Instead, the movie treats the siege like a protracted ATM transaction: Richard needs money to pay his soldiers, so he hits the nearest castle. Richard's attitude toward money is understandable, given he is also the mouthpiece of class prejudice that will haunt the film. Having asked Robin Longstride whether God will forgive him for his actions on Crusade, Robin responds by reminding the king of an episode in which innocent women and children were slaughtered for the crime of being Muslim. In Robin's eyes this was a merciless act that rendered all Richard's men "godless." To Richard, Robin's response is irritating in its honesty: he turns to his aide, Robert Loxley (Douglas Hodge), and says, "Honest, noble, and naïve: there is your Englishman. Right there," before imprisoning the whole party in stocks for insubordination. Richard's contempt for both "the Englishman" and the idea that the slaughter of innocents is wrong shows us the empty heart of his character. In a stark reversal of the traditional characterization of Richard in Robin Hood stories since the Renaissance; this man is uncaring, unsympathetic, and unloved by his men; Robin's only comment on hearing of Richard's death being "if you thought it was hard getting wages while he was alive, try getting paid by a dead king." Richard is little more than a greedy, lazy thug, and this characterization sets the stage for all the elite figures that follow.

John, for example, is from his very first scene an insolent whoremonger: he rejects his mother's scolding in front of his "French" mistress, declaring that as putative king of England he can do whatever he likes. "Whatever he likes," as it turns out, is largely to bother everyone about taxes. It is his first point when meeting Robin, who has disguised himself as Sir Robert Loxley in order to return the crown. John proposes a reward, only to take it back because "your father owes taxes ... I think we'll start with this." Indeed, throughout the film, John's foregoing concern is taxation; he claims that Richard's wars have drained England's budget. In a pivotal scene, John holds court to discuss an increase in taxes as a way to pay off Richard's returning army. William Marshall (William Hurt) suggests loans as a temporary relief for the cash-strapped barons: "These are difficult times. You can buy time. There are money chests from Sicily to Normandy yet if you know where to look." While this "Marshall Plan" would indeed help the barons recover by giving them time to harvest their crops and sell their wool, it is rejected by both Godfrey, who ahistorically dismisses it out of hand as unbecoming of a king, and John himself, who points out that "the crown is owed money at home. The northern barons plead poverty? Well, that has always been the song of rich men." John's claim resonates especially with Americans who are familiar with the debate over the Bush-era tax cuts[9] and the Obama administration's continued policy of encouraging higher taxes for those making $250,000 or more. As they have placed the talking points of an American tax debate in the mouths of the film's *villains*, it would be easy to assume that the filmmakers are advocating a conservative or even libertarian approach to politics. Moreover, the only response to John's suggestion is Godfrey's plea to take men to the countryside and extract the taxes from "merchants and landowners" by force. When Marshall objects to the idea of "English men killing English men," Godfrey responds by saying, "No man loyal to the crown has anything to fear. Loyalty means paying your share in the defense of the realm." By tying taxation, loyalty, and brutality together, Godfrey echoes the language of the left in order to evoke the worst fears of the right: taxes are "paying one's fair share," but only a brutal, power-hungry despot can determine what "your fair share" is. Naturally, this plan receives John's full approval, and cements both their roles as avaricious, power-hungry men.

This scene is also the point at which John ceases to be the main villain; those duties are instead fulfilled by Godfrey, who has already shown that he acts entirely in his own self-interest. Earlier in the film, Godfrey murdered Robert Loxley's party because he believed that Richard was among them. Having learned that Richard is dead, he allowed his men to loot the caravan, and tortured the dying Loxley to find out Richard's fate. These actions, seemingly done at the command of Philip of France, are clearly in Godfrey's own interest; ruthless in his murder of the English, he abandoned his own men once Robin's party attacks, and escaped as quickly as he could. Later, Godfrey, having gotten license from John, uses French soldiers to extract taxes from the northern barons by force. These soldiers care little for the English they are ordered to kill, and seem to take perverse delight in slaughtering, torturing, and raping the citizens of England in general and Pepper Harrow in particular. Godfrey, like John, is ambitious, and will use whatever means available to achieve his own ends. *Robin Hood* is unrelenting in its depiction of the English state's leaders — and, by extension, the entire English state — as morally bankrupt. The film denies the possibility that the state could be ameliorated or restructured; the one peaceful solution, Magna Charta, is literally destroyed at the end of the film. While it is true that the first few drafts of Magna Charta were rejected by John, who at times enlisted the Pope to annul the compact, the document *did* eventually exist and grant certain freedoms to the various estates of England. The film denies this history, however, and instead presents endless rebellion as the only viable solution.

Just as the state is corrupt in Scott's film, so too is the church. Although historically a strong force for charity and a community far stronger than any medieval state, the church has long been dangerous in Robin Hood legends. In the 2010 film, the church's major representative is Father Tancred, a reedy, bureaucratic-looking man who denies Marian the grain she needs to feed her family and her estate. As it happens, this denial leads to a small but interesting issue of characterization in the movie. Robin's first (and *only*), robbery is against the convoy of grain bound for the Archbishopric at York. By itself, this scene is straightforward, and could easily have come out of the ballads. But Ridley Scott chose to follow this scene with one in which Godfrey's men slaughter everyone in York Minster, including a particularly gruesome death for Father Tancred. While this scene seems to be played for revenge against Tancred, it also creates an unsettling parallel between Godfrey and Robin: both care little for the Church. This is a stark departure from the Robin of the ballads, a devout Marian who will die for his right to pray; it is also a stain on Robin's character, since his *only* robbery is against the church rather than any of Godfrey's or John's taxmen. While the church may seem unsympathetic, this film's attacks on it have far greater repercussions for the morals of its primary characters.

Whether episcopal or royal, the elites in Ridley Scott's *Robin Hood* are untrustworthy, needlessly violent, and rapacious beyond belief—with one exception. The Loxleys are held up as a model of virtuous noblemen; however, in order to maintain this view, the film carefully mis-identifies their class position. Although Robert Loxley is clearly the right-hand man of the king, a man so noble he can be entrusted with returning the crown to England, his estate is consistently underplayed. His manor house has only three visible rooms: the kitchen, the main hall, and Marian's bedroom. The village below, which as it houses the Loxley's tenants and serfs, should fall under the jurisdiction of the manor, is separated from the main itself by acres of fields and the remnants of a large stone arch. The shots of the Loxley estate diligently separate Nottingham, the fields, and the manor house of Pepper Harrow, obscuring the size of the estate and consequently the social and economic power the Loxleys wield. Moreover, while Marian speaks of "her people" repeatedly to Father Tancred, Robin, Godfrey, and the Sheriff, we are never quite certain of her relationship with those people, other than a few house servants whom she clearly has mastery over. The film goes to great lengths to elide the fact that the Loxleys are, by the standards of the time, quite wealthy, and are people of uncommon privilege and power. The best example of this elision is the continuous suggestion that Marian is indistinguishable from a peasant. When Robin first meets her, she is grubbing in the barnyard; later, when Godfrey invades the estate looking for Robin, Marian is swept up with the rest of the peasants and is only identified when she reaches the head of the tax line. Contrary to medieval notions that nobility is always easily identified no matter the disguise,[10] the film implies that Marian is no different from the people she controls, and by extension, no better than any of them. Ultimately the film resolves this class tension by erasing it completely: the final scene, of Robin, Marian, and the boys in the greenwood closes with Marian's voice assuring us that here there is "no tax, no tithe, no rich, no poor, [only] fair shares for all at nature's table." The Loxleys, whose class position should be much higher and who, by the logic of the movie, should therefore be corrupt, are clumsily exempt from the film's portrayal of class; ultimately, in order to resolve this tension, the movie simply gives up and removes it completely—hardly a viable solution to any class dilemma.

The "Common Man" Can Work Justice Through Carefully Planned Violence

But viable solutions are not what this movie is about. Instead, it offers a combination of questionable utopianism and stale violence as a way to overcome what it places in the nebulous category of "injustice." It does this through three motifs: the motto "Rise and Rise Again / Until Lambs Become Lions"; the establishment of Robin as a man of inward nobility; and, most daringly, the mythic of the origin of Magna Charta.

As it is a call for constant rebellion, the motto "Rise and Rise Again / Until Lambs Become Lions" is clearly the central point of Ridley Scott's *Robin Hood*. Movie audiences may be forgiven for thinking that the phrase is biblical, though it is likely very modern; the best source for it would probably be the poem "Rise and Rise Again" by New-Age prophet Matreya Friend of All Souls.[11] Within the movie, Robin first encounters it buried under the wire wrapping of Robert Loxley's sword; later, it is revealed to be the motto of Robin's father, a rebellious stonemason, who hid it underneath the paving of the cross at Barnsdale. The repeated hiding and discovery of the motto is directly tied to Robin's discovery of his past and his father's role in an earlier rebellion; indeed, the first scene plays that discovery rather effectively, as Robin is pricked in the hand by the loose wire, which in turn pricks his memories of his father's execution. This is echoed by its second reveal at Barnsdale, which leads in turn to Robin's discovery of the buried Magna Charta. The motto drives the action of the plot, and sets the stage for the film's denouement.

Its meaning in the film is equally muddy. For Robin, it means the return of his past, and the realization that his father was, in Walter Loxley's words, a "great man" and "ahead of his time." When Will Scarlet (Scott Grimes) asks Robin what the phrase means, Robin replies, "It means never give up. " This is clear from the first half of the phrase, but the second part reveals a more clearly revolutionary message. When interpreted through conventional imagery of the masses (the lambs) and the English royalty (lions), we realize that message is not equality — that would be "until lambs become (one with) the lions" — but replacement: those who are now just "one of the herd" will rise and replace the power elites of England. This is, in other words, precisely the trajectory taken by Robin Longstride, who starts out as just one of Richard's bowmen and becomes the lord of a manor by the height of the movie. Ironically, the film undercuts the power of this message through Robin himself. In what turns out to be a very medieval attitude toward social climbing, the film shows us that just as Robin ends up once more landless and unencumbered by title, so to may potential revolutionaries find themselves at the bottom of fortune's wheel. Moreover, the film suggests that the phrase is easily co-opted by any disenfranchised group, including other lords; when Baron Baldwin confronts King John in the fields outside Barnsdale, he cries that he and the other lords "are not sheep, to be made mutton of by your butchers!" Given that the barons themselves can identify themselves as lambs, this particular uprising is not as uplifting as its motto would have us believe. Nevertheless, the motto does justify the film's violence; indeed, it promises endless violence in the pursuit of a better position in life. It is therefore a perfect model for the film's blend of utopianism and violence.

The vehicle for this bloody campaign is Robin Longstride, a man whom the film would like us to see as a prime example of natural nobility. Robin is indeed a man of conviction; we see him care for his fellow archers during the siege of Chalus, and condemn the king for slaughtering innocent Muslims. He is also a pragmatist: he knows when it's time to leave a fight; he allows his men to loot the corpses of the English soldiers killed by Godfrey, and believes that pretending to be a knight will get him safest passage to England. Like the Robin of the ballads, we see him care and fight for anyone who falls under his charge: his own men, Little John, the peasants of Pepper Harrow and Nottingham. Indeed, his one robbery of the rich is for his own community: he steals the Nottingham grain bound for York, and has it planted in the dead of night so that Friar Tuck can claim it is a "miracle." He is also shown to have an innate sense of natural law. When Marian tells him that killing the deer of Sherwood Forest is treasonous and punishable by death, he replies that "these things are God's gifts first before [they are] the king's possessions. If it's illegal for a man to fend for himself, how then can he be a man in his own right?" In a move that would make any American libertarian proud, Robin ties masculinity to "fending for himself," and so demonstrates that he knows right and wrong far better than his social superiors. Thus, Robin acts charitably and nobly toward his immediate circle of allies, and some of his attitudes would be at home in any Robin Hood story or ballad.

But just as the film's rebellious motto is undercut by the actions of its rebellious protagonists, so too is Robin's apparent "peasant virtue" undercut by the circumstances by which he becomes Robin Hood. This is achieved through a theme of payment, first introduced with the meeting between Robin and Little John and carried throughout several key events in the film. Traditionally, Robin and Little John meet by fighting with poles over a river ford. In Scott's film, however, they meet at the gambling tables, where Robin is playing a shell game for food and coin. When Little John accuses Robin of cheating, they fight it out, and are comrades afterward. Depicting Robin as a con man is not unusual — the ballads do it, as do later tales — but using it as the meeting between Robin and Little John starts a repeated association between payment and pivotal moments in Robin's life that implies he is always for sale. This is reinforced both by Robin's final comments on Richard's death — "try getting paid by a dead man" — and, most notably, at the end of the scene in which Robert Loxley asks Robin to return his sword to Nottinghamshire. As Loxley dies, the camera frames his face in the upper right side of the screen; behind his head, and spread all around him, are a pool of small silver coins, suggesting the slow transfer of Loxley's wealth and prestige to Robin. Likewise, when Loxley's father Walter (Max von Sydow) asks Robin to continue pretending he is Loxley, he expresses the deal in terms of payment: "The sword for your time, Longstride." Despite his apparent inward nobility, at critical moments, Robin appears to be for sale to the aristocracy, even as he "buys" his way up the social ladder.

As a man of inward nobility who has successfully bought his way into legal nobility, Robin is thus able to bring his unusual opinions about freedom and justice to the assembled aristocrats at Barnsdale. He interjects on a debate between Richard and the rebellious barons to deliver a stirring bit of folksy wisdom:

> If you're trying to build for the future, you must set your foundations strong. The laws of this land enslave the people to its king. A king who demands loyalty but offers nothing in return. I have marched from France to Palestine and back. And I know that in tyranny lies only failure. You build a country like you build a cathedral: from the ground up. Empower every man and you will gain strength.... If your majesty were to offer justice, justice in the form of a charter

of liberties allowing every man to forage for his heart; to be safe from conviction without cause or prison without charge; to work, eat, and live on the sweat of his own brow, and be as merry as he can — then that king would be great. Not only would he receive the loyalty of his people, but their love as well.... What we would ask, your majesty, is liberty — liberty by law!

Here the movie enters its most daring territory: it rewrites the history of Magna Charta. What John does not know is that Robin's father had a hand in drafting just such a "charter of liberties," and secretly buried it at the Barnsdale cross. In his plea for "liberty by law," Robin reverses the movie's earlier claim that "in times of tyranny and injustice when law oppresses the people, the outlaw takes his place in history." Robin's place in history, the place to which the "rise and rise again motto" and Walter Loxley have both pointed him, is to uphold the law. However, his liberties sound more like the American Bill of Rights than anything found in Magna Charta: the right to fair trial, the right to work, the right to "forage for his heart" and "be as merry as he can." In short, life, liberty, and the pursuit of happiness. The real Magna Charta guarantees few of these rights; the document Robin seeks sounds more like the mythical, tyrant-killing charter it rose to in later centuries. Perhaps we should not be surprised that a legendary figure asks for a legendary form of a document; but doing so deeply muddies the film's already clouded politics.

Ridley Scott's *Robin Hood* falls somewhere in the middle of the political Robin Hood films. It is certainly a film that resonates deeply with the events of its time, as were *The Adventures of Robin Hood* (1938) and *Robin Hood: Prince of Thieves* (1991), though Scott's film is closer to the former inasmuch as it has any politics at all. As a film that lays heavy claim to historical truth, it falls a little flat — but then, most Robin Hood films do — indeed, so do all films based on legend rather than history. But it does get a few things about the legend right. Most notably, this *Robin Hood* film *does* actually praise communitarianism, especially for communities based on mutual trust and voluntary membership. It uses the metaphor of family quite well, and goes beyond the semi-clannish attitude toward community found in both the original ballads and in early film versions of the legend. That said, it does so on some very shaky grounds, most notably in its staunch anti-taxation policy and its somewhat naïve praise of nature as an endless bounty capable of supporting everyone. The film is also not clear as to the "wrongs to be righted in the country of King John."

While Scott's movie might be praised for being true to the original texts of the legend, it is nevertheless the wrong time to "revive" the individualist Robin Hood. *Robin Hood* is a film that asks us to resist "tyranny," but flatly states that a tyrannical system cannot be changed from within. Robin

Longstride is given the chance to fight alongside the rebellious barons, to have a hand, as his father did, in creating Parliament and the beginnings of a democratic state — but the movie forbids this, forcing him instead into the role of outlaw. *Robin Hood* thus implies that corrupt systems must be abandoned, not rehabilitated; this reflects an anti-state pessimism that runs through the heart of modern Western democracies.

But this is not entirely the fault of anyone involved in Ridley Scott's *Robin Hood*. The legend itself praises local communitarianism only — look out for one's friends and family and to hell with the rest. It has been worked over numerous times in the support of conservative ventures — the Protestant church, English heritage, American exceptionalism — and its liberal, progressive heritage is recent, found only in the "rob the rich to give to the poor" motif of Howard Pyle's *The Merry Adventures of Robin Hood*, Errol Flynn's *The Adventures of Robin Hood*, and ITV's *Robin of Sherwood* (1984–1986). The legend of Robin Hood is thus a prime example of the pitfalls of using medieval texts and their Romantic offspring as metaphors for social change. While it can be a legend that stresses community and social justice, it can also stress mindless violence and the need for a great man of history. If we are to find any progressive uses for stories from the past, we must be very aware of the ideologies at the heart of those stories and the various uses to which they have already been put.

Notes

1. The author would like to thank the editors for their support, as well as both Grant Bain and Krista Cody for their insightful comments.

2. Douglas Gray, "Everybody's Robin Hood," *Robin Hood: Medieval and Post-Medieval*, Helen Phillips, ed. (Dublin: Four Courts Press, 2005), 21–41, 21. His discussion of the seemingly infinite adaptability of the legend is 22–23.

3. The only problem is that Longchamp was co-regent with the Bishop of Durham, and then only after the Earl of Essex died.

4. See Nolen, *Robin Hood*, 157; Knight, *Robin Hood*, 238. Knight gives very little credit to these films' effect on the legends they portrayed, but he is wrong to do so: attempting to make fantasy films seem more genuinely historical has been a wellspring for big-budget films since the mid-seventies, hitting not only Robin Hood but also King Arthur and even Sherlock Holmes.

5. See Nolen, *Robin Hood*, 176–178 for a roundup of the critical reviews. Nolen himself pulls no punches in his description of Costner: "only in Hollywood could a man be paid $7 million for such inferior work" (p. 178).

6. The longbow would have been a curiosity in the 12th century; see Kelley DeVries, "Longbow Archery and the Earliest Robin Hood Legends," *Robin Hood in Popular Culture: Violence, Transgression, and Justice*, Thomas Hahn, ed. (Cambridge: D. S. Brewer, 2000), 41–60.

7. This and all subsequent quotations from the film are taken from Ridley Scott, *Robin Hood* (Hollywood: Universal, 2010).

8. See, for example, Bettina Bildhauer and Anke Bernau, "The A-chronology of Medieval Film," *Medieval Film* (Manchester: Manchester University Press, 2011), 1–19, esp. pp. 2–3.

9. Specifically, these are two pieces of legislation the Economic Growth and Tax Relief Reconciliation Act of 2001 and the Jobs and Growth Tax Relief Reconciliation Act of 2003. Both pieces of legislation were set to expire in 2010, and the debate over whether to extend them (ultimately

resolved with the Tax Relief, Unemployment Insurance Reauthorization, and Job Creation Act of 2010) was still playing out while *Robin Hood* was filming.

    10. See, for example, Geraldine Barnes' discussion of the various failures of medieval romance heroes to disguise themselves in *Counsel and Strategy in Medieval Romance* (Cambridge: D. S. Brewer, 1993), 95.

    11. Maitreya the Friend of All Souls, "Rise and Rise Again," *The Holy Book of Destiny* (Seattle: Amazon CreateSpace, 2011), 4. Although the publication date is later than the film, the quotation appears to be older, and Maitreya the Friend of All Souls has been teaching in Southern California since 1977.

Works Cited

Barnes, Geraldine. *Counsel and Strategy in Medieval Romance.* Cambridge: D. S. Brewer, 1993.

Bildhauer, Bettina, and Anke Bernau. "The A-chronology of Medieval Film." *Medieval Film.* Manchester: Manchester University Press, 2011.

Bronson, B. H. *The Traditional Tunes of the Child Ballads, Vol. 3.* Princeton: Princeton University Press, 1966.

Curtiz, Michael. *The Adventures of Robin Hood.* Warner Bros., 1938.

DeVries, Kelley. "Longbow Archery and the Earliest Robin Hood Legends." *Robin Hood in Popular Culture: Violence, Transgression, and Justice.* Thomas Hahn, ed. Cambridge: D. S. Brewer, 2000.

Dwan, Allen. *Douglas Fairbanks in Robin Hood.* United Artists, 1922.

Gray, Douglas. "Everybody's Robin Hood." *Robin Hood: Medieval and Post-Medieval.* Helen Phillips, ed., Dublin: Four Courts Press, 2005.

Harty, Kevin J. "Robin Hood on Film: Moving Beyond a Swashbuckling Stereotype." *Robin Hood in Popular Culture: Violence, Transgression, and Justice.* Thomas Hahn, ed. Cambridge: D. S. Brewer, 2000.

Hilton, R. H. "The Origins of Robin Hood." *Past and Present* 14, Nov. 1958.

Knight, Stephen. *Robin Hood: A Complete Study of the English Outlaw.* Oxford: Blackwell, 1995.

Lester, Richard. *Robin and Marian.* Columbia Pictures Corporation, 1976.

Maitreya the Friend of All Souls. "Rise and Rise Again." *The Holy Book of Destiny.* Seattle: Amazon CreateSpace, 2011.

Nolen, Scott Allen. *Robin Hood: A Cinematic History of the English Outlaw and His Scottish Counterparts.* Jefferson: McFarland, 1999.

About the Contributors

Brooke Beloso is an assistant professor of gender studies at Butler University. Her work has focused on issues of cyberprostitution in the American legal system.

Gregory Borse is an assistant professor of English at the University of Arkansas at Monticello, teaching world literature, modern poetry, literary theory and criticism, film and literature, and philosophy.

Jeremy Burns is a doctoral candidate at the University of Arkansas. His interests are American popular culture, American literature, and science-fiction film and literature.

Traci J. Cohen is a graduate of the graduate program at CSU–Sacramento and has worked as an academic coach. She has contributed widely and presented her work at Comic-Con.

Tim Delaney is chair of the Department of Sociology at SUNY–Oswego. His interests include popular culture, particularly film and television, and deviant and criminal behavior.

Kevin K. Durand is the dean of academics at LISA Academy College Prep School and a professor of mathematics and physics. He is co-editor, with Mary K. Leigh, of *Riddle Me This, Batman!* (McFarland, 2011) and *The Universe of Oz* (McFarland, 2010).

Alexander Charles Oliver Hall is a teaching fellow at Kent State University. His work focuses on literary and cultural studies.

J. Eric Lambert is a visiting assistant professor at Kalamazoo College. His interests include naturalism and the human condition.

Mary K. Leigh is a doctoral candidate and doctoral fellow at the University of Arkansas. Recent work with Kevin K. Durand includes *Riddle Me This, Batman!* (McFarland, 2011) and *The Universe of Oz* (McFarland, 2010).

Jacob Lewis is an instructor at the University of Arkansas. He specializes in utopian trends in late Medieval English texts, particularly the ways by which allegory and dream-visions can open up utopic spaces.

Ellen Reed is a sociology graduate student at SUNY–Oswego.

Leslie Seawright is an assistant professor of English at Texas A&M University at Qatar. Her areas of study include rhetoric and composition.

Alan Williams is a graduate student at Illinois State University. He studies digital humanities, composition and rhetoric, and comic studies.

Index

Acton, Harry Burrows 157, 162
Affleck, Casey 14
Alfred 39, 53, 57, 76, 120
alienation 13, 14, 20, 21, 83, 84, 85, 86, 89, 91, 93, 94, 95, 137, 139, 141, 155, 158, 159, 160
Aristotle 14
autonomy 68, 86, 88
Avatar 145, 146, 147, 149, 150, 151, 152, 153, 154, 156, 157, 159, 160, 161, 162, 163

Barnes, Geraldine 184
Bartter, Martha 106, 119
Benjamin, Walter 6, 8, 40, 43, 44, 47, 48, 52, 103, 119
Berger, James 106, 108, 109, 118, 119
Bergson, Henri 40, 43, 44, 45, 46, 47, 48, 49, 50, 51, 52
Berlant, Lauren 36, 38
Blade Runner 29, 77, 79, 80, 82, 83, 84, 89, 90, 94, 95, 125, 128
Bloch, Ernst 104, 105, 119
Booker, M. Keith 17, 20, 21, 27, 109, 120, 134, 139, 144
bourgeoisie 5, 8, 9, 10, 11, 12, 15, 16, 19, 20, 60, 67, 101, 151, 154
Bronson, B.H. 166
Brown, Julia Prewitt 99, 103
Burton, Tim 5, 9, 16

Caan, Scott 14
capitalism 4, 23, 40, 41, 42, 43, 44, 45, 46, 48, 51, 52, 70, 74, 109, 118, 119, 122, 124, 129, 138, 143, 155, 157, 158, 162
Carlebach, Julius 161, 162
Carroll, Noël 134
Carter, Helena Bonham 16
Chaplin, Charlie 40, 41, 42, 43, 45, 51, 52
Chesley, Lloyd 34, 38
Christianity 21, 24, 25, 27
class consciousness 11, 14, 15, 22, 162
Clooney, George 16
Collins, Randall 154, 162
communism 22, 135, 155, 156, 157, 162

Conan Doyle, Sir Arthur 10
Cooper, Derick 158, 162
Coser, Lewis 158, 162

Deleuze, Gilles 47, 52
Del Rio, Elena 110, 111, 114, 115, 119, 120
Depp, Johnny 16
Desser, David 34, 39
DeVries, Kelley 182
Dick, Philip K. 77, 81, 82, 89
Dickens, Charles 4, 10
Die Hard 112, 113, 120
Do Androids Dream of Electric Sheep 77, 79
Doane, Mary Ann 51, 52
Dr. Strangelove, or How I Learned to Stop Worrying and Love the Bomb 29, 106, 107, 120
Dwan, Allen 168
dystopia 17, 18, 19, 22, 23, 27, 77, 105, 110, 114, 116, 117, 119, 121, 124, 125, 128, 129, 131

Eagleton, Terry 111, 120, 138, 144
Ellmann, Mary 139, 140, 141, 142, 144
Engles, Friedrich 18, 19, 20, 22, 27, 32, 35, 39, 41, 42, 52, 146, 152, 154, 156, 163

Faraci, Devin 39
feminism 57, 133, 171
Fitting, Peter 130, 131
Ford, Tennessee Ernie 4, 12
Foucault, Michel 115, 120
Frear, Stephen 53, 55, 56, 69, 73, 74

Gilliam, Terry 16, 104, 109, 119, 120
Glasser, Richard 47, 52
Gomel, Elana 107, 119, 120
Gomery, Douglas 97, 103
Gone with the Wind 145
The Grifters 53, 55, 56, 57, 58, 68, 69, 70, 71, 73, 74, 75, 76

Habib, M.A.R. 75, 76
Hadden, Richard W. 160, 163

187

Index

Hanks, Tom 4, 16
Harty, Kevin J. 164, 169, 170, 172
Heimpel, Rod S. 56, 59, 76
Heldreth, Leonard 34, 39
Hilton, R.H. 166
A History of Violence 133, 135, 136, 139, 140, 141, 144
Hitchcock, Alfred 53, 55, 56, 57, 61, 63, 65, 68, 69, 71, 74, 76, 105, 120
Huntington, John 18, 27, 167

Industrial Revolution 4

Jameson, Fredric 18, 27, 109, 118, 120, 122, 123, 128, 132, 134, 143, 144
Jay, Martin 50
Jesus 21
Joe Versus the Volcano 4, 5, 11, 14, 16

Knight, Stephen 165, 166, 167, 170, 171, 182
Kracauer, Siegfried 30, 32, 33, 34, 37, 39
Kristeva, Julia 134
Kubrick, Stanley 106, 107, 120

Lacan, Jacques 134
Lang, Fritz 17, 28, 29, 31, 38, 39, 127
Laytham, D. Brent 113, 118, 120

Market Theory of Value 13
Marx, Karl 3, 4, 5, 6, 7, 8, 9, 10, 11, 13, 14, 15, 16, 17, 18, 19, 20, 22, 23, 27, 32, 34, 35, 37, 39, 41, 42, 52, 77, 78, 79, 83, 84, 85, 86, 87, 89, 90, 91, 92, 94, 95, 96, 98, 103, 134, 145, 146, 150, 151, 152, 154, 155, 156, 157, 158, 159, 160, 161, 162, 163
Marxism 4, 5, 7, 8, 10, 11, 12, 13, 15, 16, 17, 18, 20, 22, 23, 24, 25, 26, 30, 37, 38, 40, 41, 53, 57, 58, 60, 61, 67, 77, 83, 84, 90, 98, 134, 135, 137, 139, 140, 145, 150, 154, 156, 162
The Matrix 29, 129
Mayne, Judith 134, 143, 144
McCarthy, Joseph 16
McDonald, Russ 135, 144
McLaughlin, Neal 32, 39
McLellan, David 160, 163
Meehan, Paul 34, 39, 122, 124, 126, 127, 128, 129, 132
Metropolis 17, 18, 19, 20, 21, 22, 23, 24, 25, 26, 28, 29, 31, 32, 33, 34, 35, 36, 37, 38, 39, 127
Meza, Ed 29, 39
Les Miserables 11
Moi, Toril 138
Monty Python 3, 6, 8, 16
Moylan, Tom 121, 123, 124, 130, 132

Mulvey, Laura 134, 143, 144

Naremore, James 122, 132

The Office 11
Oz, Frank 97, 98, 103

Pampel, Fred 155, 163
panopticon 42
patriarchy 40, 42, 48, 50, 51, 52, 60, 133, 134, 135, 136, 137, 142
Paycheck, Johnny 5, 11, 12
Penguin 96
Penley, Constance 130, 132
Piazza, Jo 153, 160, 163
Pitt, Brad 15, 16, 115, 119
Plato 91
Pomerantz, Dorothy 145, 163
poverty 10, 49, 51, 176
Prince, Stephen 144, 169, 170, 171, 181
proletariat 5, 8, 9, 10, 11, 12, 15, 16, 17, 19, 20, 21, 22, 27, 32, 33, 34, 35, 36, 37, 38, 60, 62, 67, 75, 136, 151, 152, 154, 155, 156, 157
property 7, 12, 15, 16, 18, 51, 85, 87, 154, 155, 162
Psycho 53, 55, 56, 57, 58, 61, 62, 64, 67, 68, 70, 71, 72, 73, 74, 75, 76

Quinby, Lee 105, 111, 120

religion 14, 17, 21, 22, 23, 24, 25, 26, 35, 87, 94, 160, 161, 166
Rickman, Alan 16, 112, 171
Ritzer, George 154, 157, 163
Rosen, Elizabeth 116, 117, 120
Rubin, Gayle 41, 42, 48, 51, 52
Ryan, Meg 4, 15, 16

Sandis, C. 56, 76
Sargent, Lyman Tower 123, 124, 132
Scarecrow 132
Schuehly, Thomas 29, 39
Scott, Ridley 79, 164, 165, 168, 172, 174, 177, 178, 181, 182
Sinclair, Upton 4
Sleepless in Seattle 4
socialism 18, 134, 135, 156, 164
Sondheim, Stephen 5, 9
Strozykowski, Michelle 32, 39
Suvin, Darko 128, 132
Sweeney Todd 5, 8, 9, 11, 16

Taubin, Amy 142, 143, 144
Terminator 3: Rise of the Machines 106, 119, 120, 128
transgenderism 62

Twelve Monkeys 104, 105, 106, 107, 108, 109, 110, 111, 112, 113, 114, 115, 116, 117, 118, 119, 120

Vertigo 105, 119, 120, 144
virtue 78, 85, 87, 88, 166, 180
Von Harbou, Thea 31, 39

Wagner, John 141, 144

Wegner, Phillip 106, 109, 119, 120
Whale, James 29
Willis, Bruce 104, 112
Wimmer, Kurt 121, 125, 126, 127, 130, 131, 132

Žižek, Slavoj 87, 92

www.ingramcontent.com/pod-product-compliance
Ingram Content Group UK Ltd.
Pitfield, Milton Keynes, MK11 3LW, UK
UKHW042013140426
5217IPUK00015B/1139